FUNNY B

FUNNY BONES

My Life in Comedy

Freddie Davies

Scratching Shed Publishing Ltd

First published by Scratching Shed Publishing Ltd in 2014
Registered in England & Wales No. 6588772.
Registered office:
47 Street Lane, Leeds, West Yorkshire. LS8 1AP
www.scratchingshedpublishing.co.uk
Hardback ISBN 978-0992703677
Paperback ISBN 978-0992703660

A catalogue record for this book is available from the British Library.

Typeset in Warnock Pro Semi Bold and Palatino
Printed and bound by CPI Group (UK) Ltd, Croydon, CR0 4YY

For my darling Vanessa,
my son Kent, daughter-in-law Nikki,
and my grandchildren Ella and Farren

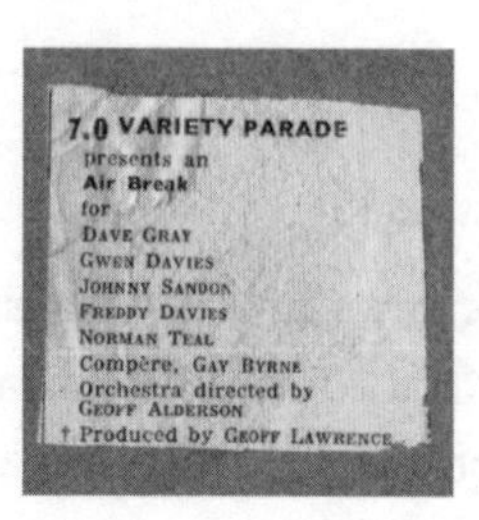

7.0 VARIETY PARADE
presents an
Air Break
for
DAVE GRAY
GWEN DAVIES
JOHNNY SANDON
FREDDY DAVIES
NORMAN TEAL
Compère, GAY BYRNE
Orchestra directed by
GEOFF ALDERSON
† Produced by GEOFF LAWRENCE

First ever broadcast - 8th February, 1964

Contents

Foreword

By Ken Dodd, OBE

A FAMOUS name – Freddie Davies. That is probably why you picked up this book.

You are picturing a sun-tanned, athletic Adonis. He's nothing like that – he's a funny man, a comical chap, unique, a one-off, a multi-tasking entertainer.

Have you ever hit your elbow in just the right spot and felt a tingling or prickly sensation? That's your funny bone. Every comedian needs a highly developed funny bone.

It also helps to have a humorous physio, physinog – fissiog – a funny face! Freddie ticks all the boxes – a well developed, honed over the years, funny bone *and* he has the perfect face for comedy and radio.

A performer to his fingertips, nothing beats standing up on stage in front of a live audience. Who can forget him bursting on to our TV screens sporting his trademark homburg hat pulled down over his ears and intoning his catchphrase – 'I'm thick, thick, thick up to here!' And of course his feathered friends, the 'boojies' – Freddie 'Parrot Face' Davies became a shining star.

But this wasn't an overnight success. Freddie served his time on the working men's club treadmill. Dressing rooms with a star plastered on the door to hide the word 'Gentlemen.' Grim conditions that were eased by a saucer of Trill, a piece of cuttlefish and a mirror and a bell to keep him amused.

Funny Bones is about the making of a comic, explaining how Freddie's love for theatre and comedy grew – the cheers and tears on the journey to much deserved fame.

As an added bonus, it's also the story of his grandad, the comedian Jack Herbert, who let the young lad watch his act from the wings at theatres like the Salford Hippodrome.

Freddie has many talents: comedian, centrefold model for the 'Bird Fanciers' Gazette', actor, film star, singer, producer and now author. How can one man be so energetic and have so many jobs and yet enjoy every one? And of course Mr Davies is also a pioneer in the field of social networking, being the first person in the persona of Samuel Tweet to begin tweeting!

What you get in this book is the full story, from soup to nuts (he's big in Brazil) and it's an indispensable memoir of different showbiz worlds from someone who has been there, done that, and got the T(weet) Shirt.

But what makes this autobiography such a good read is that he's never afraid to share the lows as well as the highs of his subsequent careers. An invaluable record of the world of showbiz from someone who was there, who saw it all and is still here – a COMEDY SUPERSTAR!

Ken Dodd,
May 2014

Prologue

'YOU'VE definitely had a heart attack, Mr Davies.'

It sounds odd, I know, but the doctor's words were reassuring. I'd been in a kind of limbo ever since the strange sensation had passed, not knowing what to make of what had just happened.

A few hours earlier I had been watching my neighbour, John, merrily ploughing away at my lawn when an overwhelming feeling of losing all power had travelled from my head down through my shoulders, leaving me helpless as I slumped on a garden chair. Weakly apologising for leaving him to it, I fumbled in my pocket and managed to get out the angina spray which my GP had given me that day. I squirted it under my tongue as instructed, but it wasn't long before I passed out.

I'd gone to my doctor because of a tightness in my chest; he'd given me an ECG, which had been clear, but now the hospital doctor was explaining that they'd done a blood test which confirmed that it had indeed been a heart attack. I felt pleased for a moment, glad the mystery had been solved, before it hit me: a *heart attack*?

'But you're alright,' she continued, looking straight at me, 'you're not going to die, we're going to sort you out. You're in the right place.'

I KNOW your life is meant to flash before you when you're facing death. I can't say it did in my case – but then I'd already had a bit of a head start that summer. I'd been on a variety tour, reprising Samuel Tweet, my lisping 'Parrotface' character, almost fifty years on from his first appearance on *Opportunity Knocks*. The moment I pulled the familiar homburg back down over my – now whitened – locks, the memories had come flooding back: not just of my years at the top but the long struggle to get there, and the small matter of what happened in the decades after fame ebbed away.

One way or another I have managed to survive in this business – thank God – even if I've had to reinvent myself a few times along the way. And that, if anything, is the theme of this book: survival. It applies to my life as well as my variegated career, if this recent health scare is anything to go by: whatever the odds, it seems that Samuel will live to splutter another day.

But what made me, and that strange alter ego which I've never quite been able to shake off? A bit like the hospital, you could say I was in the right place at the right time: a Northern comic in the early 'sixties when everything in the North was fashionable, from the Beatles to Uncle Tom Courtenay and all.

The opportunity which came knocking via the original TV talent show was peculiarly well timed, too: I'd already undergone a baptism of fire in the working men's clubs of the North East and a hefty dose of desperation had forced Samuel Tweet into being only a few months earlier.

But the origins of Tweet, and the urge to perform which has never left me, go back a lot further than that. Back, in fact, to the man whose sparkling example first made it all seem possible.

JACK HERBERT

1: Early Days

MY life in comedy began with Jack. He was my grandad and I idolised him. Other kids at school talked of becoming bus drivers or train drivers, but from just about as far back as I can remember I knew there was only one thing I wanted to be: a comedian, a funnyman, like Jack Herbert.

Jack was known throughout the business as a very good front cloth comic – a stand-up, as we'd say today. His career spanned the entire variety era, from its glory days to the tatty nude shows which helped kill off the family audience. In the 'fifties he even played a few of the clubs springing up around Manchester which were to provide a tough new training ground for my generation.

And Jack was there, one day in 1947, when I was hoisted onto a chair in the back room of the Crooked Billet, near Slough, to tell jokes in public for the first time.

It was my cousin Pauline's pub, so I can only assume that the regulars were happy to indulge a cheeky, precocious ten year old. Evidently they hadn't seen Jack on stage, because I did his entire act – which may be a unique example of one comic beaming his encouragement as another steals his livelihood.

That's where it all started for me. Afterwards they passed the hat round and I felt like a comic from that moment on. I didn't know how I was going to do it, how I was going to get there; that was all to come out later. But my path was set – as far as I was concerned, anyway.

I SAY that Jack was my grandad, and I thought of him that way, though he was actually a later partner of my grandmother, Ruth Beaumont. I was born into a showbiz family as Gran had been a soubrette, which seems a very old-fashioned word now – a comedienne and singer, basically – and my mother Joan had been a dancer in touring revues. She was twenty when I was born, on the 21st of July, 1937, in a terraced house in Brixton, London, which later received a direct hit in the blitz. I always believed my father had died in the war; it wasn't till many years later that I was to learn differently.

In 1940, like most children from the big cities, and London in particular, I was evacuated, first to Seend in Wiltshire and then to Babbacombe near Torquay, Devon. My great grandmother, Ruth Orr, looked after us while my mother Joan worked; by this time I had a baby brother, Michael, two years younger.

It was in Babbacombe that a tragic accident occured which overshadowed the rest of my mother's life. Michael sadly died, aged two. He drowned in a garden pond. The war effort had taken all the iron it could find for munitions, and park and street railings which would normally have been round private gardens had been requisitioned; Michael had simply climbed over a park bench and, without too much effort, crawled into a private garden with a pond.

I remember, even at four years of age, my mother's screams in the police car. Bless her, she suffered for the rest of her short life, and after three further offspring she died, sadly, a very depressed woman aged just fifty-four.

After the tragedy of my brother's drowning my mother said she just had to go: 'I can't stay here anymore.' So my great grandmother took us to Salford, Greater Manchester.

It wasn't the safest of places to relocate: Metropolitan-Vickers were manufacturing Lancaster Bombers in nearby Trafford Park and at the end of the previous year Salford had been blitzed over two nights, with hundreds of lives lost. But it was a matter of necessity.

We were accommodated in a two room flat in a dilapidated old mansion house at 9 Leaf Square, Pendleton, in a line of fine Georgian houses, by then semi-derelict. Great Grandmother Ruth came from Salford and her brother Sam was the park keeper in Peel Park; they had kindly arranged the flat for us to live in and it was to be my home until my National Service in 1956.

No. 9 Leaf Square had ten imposing steps leading up to the front door. Inside there was a large hallway – very *Upstairs Downstairs* – with two former reception rooms to the left which had been partitioned into two rooms each and let as self-contained flats. The ground floor front flat was occupied by Great Grandmother's brother Sam and his harridan of a wife, Maggie. Auntie Maggie did not see eye to eye with my mother and, being a strict teetotaller, resented the fact that my mum went to the pub and even dared to enjoy herself on the odd occasion. I recall her having some kind of barney with my mother then yelling up the stairs, determined to have the last word: 'Aye, but *we* don't sup ale!'

This dreadful flat cost the princely sum of ten bob (50p) a week. We had just two rooms and a shared kitchen and toilet on the first floor back. Up another flight of stairs lived the Ruddys, Tommy and Betty; Betty Ruddy gave birth to two children in their tiny, partitioned-off flat. Another room was occupied by a man who worked for Metropolitan-Vickers. We all of us shared that same toilet.

Our living room had a big iron double bed, two old armchairs and an old fashioned grate which provided the only heat in the flat. My mother and Great Gran slept in the big iron bed and I had the back bedroom. When Gran and Jack came to stay we would all have to sleep head to toe. Mother was a very smart woman in her younger days and easily obtained a job at British Home Stores on Regent Road in Salford, so we were able to pay the rent – just.

I was ashamed of the flat and never invited any of my friends round. It was just too shabby, I felt, even though most families just after the war were in a state of shock, with men not returning from battle, and many kids who went to John Street School probably lived in worse surroundings than us. A friend from that time remembers me as always being smartly turned out, always trying to better myself; maybe it was because this was something I had some control over, unlike where I lived.

My mother called herself Mrs Davies, though this was in fact her maiden name. Before Jack came on the scene, Gran had apparently married a Dutchman called Devus then anglicised the name because it sounded too much like 'Devious'.

The absence of a husband did not excite much curiosity in those days, however, as lots of kids didn't have dads because of the war. As I'd never had a dad around and didn't know what it was like to have one, I couldn't say I was aware that it mattered to me. But it probably explains the importance of Jack in my life: even though he wasn't my blood grandfather I always felt a very close bond with him, particularly a comedy bond.

I would walk to school every day, which would take about ten minutes. This involved my crossing the road, a source of considerable anxiety to my mother after what had happened to my little brother, Michael. We lived quite close to a very big main road, the A6. There were no traffic lights in those days, so you would ask someone to help you – 'Would you show me across the road, please?' – and an adult would take you over. There were tramlines in the middle and it was huge – the actual street was called Broad Street and it really was a broad street. Mother was totally neurotic about that.

As I grew a little older I became aware that Broad Street also seemed to mark a class divide. On the right of this very wide road facing north was a more genteel kind of living: the occupants of these houses were better off, their children were dressed better and went to the grammar school, while the other side of the street had many slum dwellings. Leaf Square was situated on the genteel side of the street, although I had a guilty sense of being an imposter when I thought of our home's secret shabbiness inside. But it must be said that I had many chums from the poorer side who always welcomed me into their homes, even though I did not feel able to invite them to mine.

I made a conscious effort to join the cubs at the Pendleton Congregational Church – which was on the right hand side of Broad Street – because they put on an annual pantomime. The natural progression was to go to Sunday School, which is what I did, though I don't recall feeling particularly religious about it.

Funny Bones

The house at 9 Leaf Square was owned by a man called Hepworth who also owned number 7, next door. He had a wholesale confectionery business and kept hundreds and thousands of wonderful sweets and toffees on the premises. I would often steal the odd box of Mars bars from his van as he was loading up and hide them in the cellar of our house. Unfortunately this was damp and a haven for mice so when I eventually sneaked down to gorge myself on the chocolate it was usually well nibbled.

When darkness fell the sirens would go and we could hear the bombs dropping on Manchester. London got the biggest hits but the North West also suffered and Liverpool saw its fair share. We would stand on the top doorstep at number 9 Leaf Square to see the sky ablaze, in particular when a doodle bug made a direct hit on Salford Docks, three quarters of a mile away.

It all seemed like a big adventure to us and we were without fear, invincible – or so it seemed to me at the time. Now I can only guess at what my mother was feeling. But I suppose that, for her, the worst had already happened.

2: Watching and Learning

THERE was one positive benefit to living in Leaf Square. It was just around the corner from the Salford Hippodrome and, as soon as we moved, I would be taken there regularly, or we'd go to visit Jack and Gran somewhere and watch them and the other acts from the wings. I remember they always had to ask the stage manager whether I could stand there because it was in his way really, but usually it was okay.

From this privileged position I saw the various permutations of Jack's act – Jack on his own, Jack Herbert and Partner (Grandma Ruth), Herbert and Hatton (Jack's brother Cyril) – many times over the years, along with many other acts.

Jack had funny bones. He looked comedic for a start, with a big, lugubrious face that moved a lot, of the Les Dawson type – though with apologies to Les, I must point out that he was known as Handsome Jack. He had an entirely different persona on the stage: when he went on he was no longer my grandad and simply became this ... well, funny man. He'd put a little bit of red on his mouth and eyes and it looked as if he was a loveable uncle as he walked on: 'Mr Herbert has a style which ensures a friendly feeling,' as one review put it, and the word 'joyous' was used more than once over the years to describe his act.

He was quite tall and fairly well built: a gentle giant, to my young eyes. That's what worked so well in the double with Ruth, who seemed dwarfed by comparison, but with a feistiness in her stage persona which more than compensated.

He'd come on, and she'd say: 'Where've you been?'

And he'd say: 'I've been to the Post Office to collect a wire.'

'You mean a telegram.'

'No,' he'd say, 'a wire.'

Getting riled, she'd say: 'A wire's a telegram and a telegram's a wire!'

To which he would ill-advisedly reply: 'Well, what's a postcard – a parcel?' And she'd hit him with a rolled-up newspaper.

He'd make to strangle her, holding out his hands and saying: 'Put your head in there!' so she'd hit him again with the paper, making a huge loud crack which he'd react to, saying: 'Do you mind? Take the iron bar out of it!'

A young actor called Peter Chelsom heard me describing Jack's act one night in the bar in Ipswich and, twenty years later, the paper slap routine was revived for his film *Funny Bones*. It's extremely effective in the film, which I'll discuss in more detail later, but as so little of Jack has survived it's ironic that one of his funniest bits of business has been immortalised for its dramatic, rather than comedic, effect.

Ruth was a bit older than Jack, and when she retired

in the late 'forties he carried on doing the single act. The single act was different from the double, though they were both quite silly – it was differently silly, let's put it that way. He wore a little trilby, he'd have the red in, as I said, and he'd come on to the strains of *Faraway in Honolu-lu-lu*, which he'd sing at the end of the act.

It's difficult to describe his delivery. He wasn't like anyone else. No Max Miller-type attack: very gentle, very understated, but he wasn't slow, and he definitely wasn't playing a gormless character. He was, to use that word again, silly.

But despite the zaniness, he was essentially an Everyman, one of his audience, and he spoke and sang of their concerns. He transformed the well-known slushy ballad *We Make Mistakes* ('and feel sorry ...') into a lament for ill-luck with the football pools ('We make mistakes every Saturday ...').

His closing gag was the one about the feller ringing the hospital and saying: 'How's my wife doing? She's pregnant.' And they said, 'Well nothing's happened yet, ring us back in ten minutes.'

So he rang back in ten minutes and they said, 'Oh, you're the father of a bouncing baby boy' – he said, 'Marvellous, marvellous, marvellous!' – they said, 'Ring us back again in half an hour.'

So he rang back in half an hour and said, 'Any news?' They said, 'Yes, you're the father of a bouncing baby girl.' He said, 'That's two.' 'Yes,' they said, 'ring us back in half an hour.' 'Good God,' he said.

So he rang back in half an hour and the voice said, 'You're the father of another baby girl.' He said, 'That's three.' They said, 'Ring us back in half an hour.'

He went in the pub and got absolutely ... leathered.

He dialled the wrong number and somebody at Lord's Cricket Ground answered. And he said, 'How are they doing?' And they said, 'They're all out now and the last two were ducks.'

And then it would be into *Faraway in Honolu-lu-lu*, which may have been another parody:

Faraway in Honolu - lu – lu,
Lives a girl called Ragtime Cowboy Joe
Her father was an Irishman and his name was
Hung Fu,
Her brother was a dirty dog and so they hung him
too,
In Honolu! (*dundundun, dun dun dun*)
In Honolu! (*dundundun, dun dun dun*)

She's not a real Hawaiian as you might think
She's a cross between a whippet and a Chink,
But I know that she, awaits for me,
Beneath the pickled onion tree,
If I could ride a bike that's where I'd be...

Where some of them are thin, some of them are fat –
That was their mother's fault, they can't help that!
Oh, that's a place you really ought to go –

The girls out there, dress rather bare,
And oh, the dances they do!
They will sing their songs so gaily,
Dressed in nothing else but a ukulele,
Faraway in Hono –
exiting...
Faraway in Hono –
Faraway in Hono – luuu!!!

WHEN Jack and Ruth toured they would often visit and I would be allowed backstage at the various theatres they were playing in the area: Queens Park Hippodrome, Accrington Palace, the Palace, Preston, Leeds City Varieties, the Palace, Hull and Hulme Hippodrome (Manchester) to name but a few.

Shows were classified during this period as either Number 1, Number 2 or Number 3 circuits, the Number 3s being somewhat down the scale. The Number 1 shows usually played the Moss Empire or Howard and Wyndham circuits which were allegedly a cut above the rest of them.

THE connection with Jack gave me privileged status at my 'local.' Salford Hippodrome was part of the Broadhead theatre circuit (Number 2-3) and Percy Broadhead, a rotund, rosy-cheeked gent with a Santa beard and smiley face, knowing I was related to Jack, allowed me a complimentary ticket first house on Monday, every week. If he spotted me he would even treat me to an ice cream in the interval, so I made sure he did.

The touring revue shows in those days were just a delight to my young eyes, even though some of them were crappy nude shows. These are now associated with the end of variety in the 'fifties but they were already around in the mid-'forties. The famed Windmill in Soho didn't have a monopoly on naked ladies at that time, although that was purely a titillation place, with comics in between. The shows I saw were proper variety shows, or what was laughingly called a revue.

Jack alternated between touring revues and variety throughout his career, so before we go any further maybe I should try to explain the difference between the two forms, though the short answer is: not all that much, really.

A revue had variety artists who would do things to

make it more of a show. Essentially, it was like a posh concert party: they would do sketches together, an opening number, and then the close of the first half would probably be a musical routine with the company. So it was more of a running, produced show, and all the words, the songs, everything that was going to be done, had to be presented to the Lord Chamberlain. Acts would then be inserted into that format, like a speciality act and a comic. The principal comedian might do his solo act as part of it, but if he did his double then the feed would also be in the musical routine and they would do a comedy sketch together in the second half.

There were lots of producers around like Hindin, Richards and Hicks, who put on touring revues. Lots of comics used to put their own shows together too, like Terry 'Toby Jug' Cantor, who would do a family revue show with his wife and his son Kenny, who did a little tumbling act, or a juggling act; it would go round and they would be paid for the revue as opposed to being paid for single acts.

Revues could be more lucrative for the producer, though not necessarily for the act, who in effect was working harder than on a normal variety bill. Jack would have to do the double or the single – the 'act as known' – as well as appearing in the sketches.

The term 'revue' may now suggest something sophisticated, but that was only really true of the West End shows; the Number 2 revues in which Jack made his name were really no different in tone from standard variety bills.

I saw the aforementioned Terry 'Toby Jug' Cantor around that time, as well as Cyril Dowler and several of the shows put on by Hindin, Richards and Hicks. Before the grip of television in the early 'fifties, cinema was very popular, but the variety halls were holding their own – so to speak. Nude ladies standing still in a sort of tableau were the norm and

Jane, the popular cartoon character from the *Daily Mirror*, also toured. She was no drawing but, allegedly, the actual model for the cartoon, a blowsy, big-busted blonde who would take a bath on stage and show absolutely ... nothing.

Not that I was interested, as I was far too young to appreciate any sexual connotations and thought it all quite boring – well you would, wouldn't you? I was a seven year old child at the time. I believe I have made up for my naivety since.

GRANDMA Ruth and Jack lived at 17 Pratt Street, Camden Town. I remember the address because in 1947, when I was ten years old, I stayed there for one never-to-be-forgotten month's holiday when they took me to see all the variety shows in and around London. This was when I made my first public appearance at the Crooked Billet in Slough, but there are two other events which stick in my mind from that time.

Jack knew everyone in the business and I remember being taken by him to Sid Field's dressing room at the Prince of Wales. My hero Danny Kaye, a great admirer of Sid's, was there too, and I got his autograph.

The occasion was also memorable for another reason, because Sid gave me half a crown – a tidy sum for a kid in those days – and at the same time I saw Jack being given what I now believe to have been a bung, in the form of notes in an envelope. Sid Field had been Jack's feed in the late 'twenties in various Clara Coverdale revues and it was known in the business that Sid later pinched Jack's mannerisms for his own act, such as an affected little cough which Jack used to accompany with a shaking of the leg and the sound of sleigh bells from the pit.

Later, when I was better able to understand this, I didn't get any sense that Jack felt what Sid had done was wrong. I think he may have been struggling then, coming to the end of his career by the late 'forties. Eight years his junior, Sid's star was undoubtedly in the ascendant, appearing as he was in his third West End show.

Nevertheless, I'm certain I saw money being passed on. I know I was only ten years of age, but it stuck in my mind: I got half a crown from Sid but Jack got notes.

Not that I was too worried about what this meant: a loan, maybe, or Sid owed him the money. I might even have thought that it was a gift, like the hot half crown pressed into my hand – I mean, I didn't know that adults gave money to each other like they did to kids, but if they did it made sense that the sums would be scaled up a bit. If I thought much about it at the time it would have been along those lines; looking back now, however, the clear implication is that Sid was paying for what he took.

Whether it was an unspoken thing, I don't know. I can't say whether Jack was business-minded enough to have made it a formal transaction, but I certainly think that if Sid did bung him, it wouldn't have been entirely innocent, as though this was just another handout for an old pal: he would have known what he was bunging him for, whether or not that would have been openly articulated between them.

I never got the impression, incidentally, that Jack was a huge admirer of Sid's act. Nor was there any particular sense of shared delight in the fact that a comic from the North had hit the big time in a legitimate West End theatre. The only sense I got was that they were in the same business, and whatever happened between them was right and proper.

Readers unfamiliar with the name of Sid Field may wonder why I am labouring this point. The answer is that although his name has slipped into obscurity, those who were influenced by him, such as Tony Hancock and Frankie

Howerd, have not, and I'd like my grandad's role in his success to be acknowledged.

As to why Jack himself never made the big time, that is a tale to be untangled later.

My final memory of that month in London is, technically speaking, a non-event. I mention it here because it continued to puzzle me over the next six decades, and I only discovered the answer to the mystery recently.

At the Casino (now the Prince Edward Theatre), American vocal group the Ink Spots had been flown over for a Bernard Delfont show; he was putting on variety shows in opposition to his brothers, Lew and Leslie Grade, at the Palladium. The group were absolutely huge in those days: one newspaper reported that their opening night at the Casino caused 'one of the biggest traffic jams the city has experienced since pre-war.'

I kept badgering Gran to take me and she eventually relented. We went to see the Wednesday night first house show and the Ink Spots, it seems, had been sent home – it was never publicised as to why. Standing in were – no, not the equally trendy Mills Brothers, but comedy duo Jewel and Warriss, without so much as a 'bomdey do dey' between them. I was bitterly disappointed. And puzzled.

Flash forward to 1983 while I was in Las Vegas on holiday: I noticed the Ink Spots were on a bill with Matt Monro and Johnnie Ray at the (now flattened) Sands Hotel. Only one of the original 'Spots' was still in the group and I asked him in the bar one night what had happened in 1947. He looked at me as if I was stupid and said, 'I can't remember what I had for breakfast, never mind 1947!'

Which I thought was the end of that, until I recently learnt the group had a disagreement with Delfont, who informed them that he expected them to commute between the Casino and the Lewisham Hippodrome, giving extra performances each night for no extra money. The differences were eventually resolved, but it seems to have been my bad luck to have been there on one of the nights when they refused to perform until an agreement had been reached.

So there we are. Not quite as funny as the Vegas tag, I admit, but never mind.

IT may be a little too neat to say that my experience at the Crooked Billet was the catalyst – I always was a cheeky little sod and had been telling jokes at home for some time before that – but that first appearance before an audience undoubtedly reinforced my sense that I was destined to become a comic, and after I returned to Salford I began actively looking around for ways to achieve that goal.

In my teens I became a regular in all the school plays and Sunday School pantomimes which were a big feature at the Pendleton Congregational Church Hall, just a quarter of a mile from Leaf Square. This was where I first appeared in amateur pantomime; as mentioned earlier, I had joined the cubs specifically to give me an 'in.' The producer was Jack Magnall, who became my very first mentor. A stalwart of the Congregational Church, Jack was a police sergeant and a very well respected *Dixon of Dock Green* type of copper. I am still in contact with his son John, who was a friend then; we have met up over the years for reunions with other Sunday School members from those postwar days.

The pantomimes would usually run for five nights and I would normally play a comedy part. I can still recall my very first joke. I was playing the part of a gnome and had to walk across the stage carrying a prop door. The King stopped me and asked me where I was going with the door, to which I replied: 'I have lost the key.' When the King asked what would happen if I lost the door I said: 'I would climb in through the window.'

Meanwhile, I was also visiting as many theatres as I could, travelling by bus and tram to the posher Manchester theatres: the Ardwick Hippodrome in south Manchester, the Regent, Salford and the Grand Theatre, Bolton. Hulme Hippodrome, Moss Side, later BBC North's main light entertainment studio, home of programmes like *The Clitheroe Kid* and *The Al Read Show*, was where I made my first radio broadcast some twenty years later.

I would invariably travel on my own as I was a bit of a loner, I suppose. Not many of the kids I knocked around with really understood about me going on the stage. That wasn't a job, as far as they were concerned, it was just people acting daft, whereas their ambitions lay in going down the pit or getting an apprenticeship in some trade or other and following in their fathers' footsteps.

I wanted to explain that I was doing the same thing: following in my family's footsteps by going on the stage. I knew, technically, that Jack wasn't my blood grandfather, but the connection was as strong as if he were and as I've said, my mother and grandmother had been in the business.

Coming from a theatre-based household, I think I was looked on as a bit odd at school. Kids called me Danny – from Danny Kaye, the big star in the 'forties, although it wasn't done unkindly. In fact for some time I was actually known as Danny, but nobody believed me when I said I'd met the great man in 1947, and I learnt that was not a thing to boast about; you'd get beaten up if you said that.

So there was no point in bragging about the fact that I'd been to London with my grandparents and taken around all the theatres, because as far as other kids were concerned that was fantasy land: I would have been lying. I learnt to keep quiet about that kind of thing and to live an odd, contradictory existence with loyalties on both sides of that very broad street.

I saw some wonderful comedy acts on my travels: Jimmy James and Co, with the lion in the box routine; Jimmy Gay (who wasn't) did a self-deprecating routine about the fact that the theatre was half empty: 'It was so quiet last night that they shot a stag in the gallery.' Anticipating a more recent trend for people putting powder up their noses, he also did a very funny snuff routine at a time when many had this curious habit. He would take the snuff in various ways, spreading it up his arm and sniffing it away, until finally he would blow up a balloon, put a pinch of the snuff in the top and release the air which would blow the snuff up his nose. A very funny man.

I would usually have to sit in the gallery, or 'the gods', as it was called, as the cost of going to these shows was prohibitive. Somehow, however, I managed to pay my way – and it was usually half price for children, so that helped.

I also went to see all the latest films at my local cinemas: the Scala behind Pendleton Church, the Ambassador on Langworthy Road and the luxurious, recently-built Carlton in Cross Lane. Our local fleapit was the Central, or 'the Cent' as we called it, in Gardner Street; I remember once pretending to trip over so I could say my 6d admission had slipped out of my hand and fallen between the floor boards. They let me in, but when they went down to the cellar to check and didn't find the sixpence, they came in and threw me out.

Across the road from the Carlton was the Regent Theatre, where I saw Frank Randle in pantomime. He would take his teeth out and belch over the audience: 'Ee by gum!' He was an alcoholic but a very funny man in his day. He made several films at the Mancunian Studios, although they only gave a hint of his stage presence.

Other great comedians around this time included Freddie Frinton, a great drunk act though a teetotaller himself, whose famous *Dinner for One* sketch has been a New Year's Eve ritual on German TV for the last fifty years.

But it was another sort of act which gave me my first professional engagement – if you discount that whipround at the Crooked Billet in Slough.

Professor Sparks's *Washing the Electric Baby* was another of those eccentric comedy acts touring in the 'thirties and 'forties. A family act with wife and son, the setting consisted of a prop lighting board approximately twelve feet square, with flashing bulbs and large electrical cables attached. The cod 'professor', with long hair, tatty tailcoat and a pseudo-German accent, would open the act with a couple of 'electrical' feats, such as lighting a bulb in his teeth while holding one end of the cable. He would then invite volunteers from the audience to join him on stage – though actually these were his stooges: his son and two others picked up locally each week.

A pal and I became stooges together, sitting in the audience near the front at every show until he called out for 'volunteers'. His son played a goofy character who would do a stage trip up the steps from the side stalls to the stage then generally cause mayhem. What my pal and I had to do was 'wash the electric baby' – a porcelain doll with one of the heavy cables coming from its arse connected to the 'current.' The joke was that when you attempted to wash the baby it would appear as if you were getting an electric shock and wash all the wrong bits, making the doll jump up and down.

For this, my first paid job at the age of thirteen, I received the princely sum of ten bob (50p) for the week. My pal and I had thought we'd be making fortunes – well, a fiver at least.

The experience, however, was to prove priceless. I didn't realise it at the time but when I was watching acts like these I was actually taking everything in and learning. When Professor Sparks's son fell up the stairs and things, subconsciously that taught me how to do it.

And in later years when I would be asked to do something a little bit different in a show – 'Can you go on and do this bit of business?' or 'Can you go on and do this number with these three guys?' or whatever, it didn't seem to me to be difficult. Everything I'd seen was all in the back of my mind. I immediately knew how to do it, I didn't have to think about it: it was ingrained, in my muscles, because I went every week to see these shows. And seeing Jack perform so many times meant that I'd learnt his act (ahem) parrot fashion, as kids can do, so it was second nature to me.

I also learnt from Jack and other performers about timing and what *not* to do. A comedian will usually have his act set out with a big finish that he knows will leave an impression, ad-libs permitting. But there was an odd discipline when I worked on the stage, particularly when I first started. As there were two houses a night, strict timing was enforced – and from a comic's point of view it is always very difficult to time your act to exactly ten or fifteen minutes because audiences change with each show: Saturday second house was always better than first house Wednesday, for example, so it was easy to put on two minutes with pure length of laughs. Managements were totally obsessed with timings - particularly Moss Empires - and you would be taken to task if you went one minute over your time.

So I had to find a way of getting this act of mine a) to do fourteen minutes and b) make that fourteen minutes into an entity with a beginning, middle and an end, which I could then snip things out of when the audience were brilliant, which is what you had to learn to do. It's so hard when they're screaming and yelling, and you know the extra gag you've put in is going to get such a reaction. But you're thinking: 'I've got to take it out because, if I do it, I'll be a minute over and they'll be banging on the side ...' Those decisions are made on the hoof because you never know what it will be like until you actually get on stage.

Apart from Professor Sparks's son falling upstairs, I can't really trace specific bits of business back to individual performers. But I absorbed it all: the funny walks, how to take a call, which is very important, and how to walk on. Things like that became a natural part of me; nobody taught me or said: 'This is how you do it.'

That, in effect, was my apprenticeship, starting at the age of four on the very first day I was taken round the corner to the Salford Hippodrome. When I came to do it myself later, it was very natural for me. I never felt out of place. It seemed the most natural thing in the world to walk on the stage. I never, ever got nerves. Well, I was nervous, apprehensive even, but I have always felt that as long as I know what I'm doing before going on, I'm fine. It all comes together as a natural thing to do.

When I'm performing I suppose I still feel connected to that four year old watching from the wings at the Salford Hippodrome. No, it's not quite as corny as saying I feel more at home onstage than off. But I do feel I'm in the right place when I'm there.

3: Mother

SCHOOL leaving age in 1952 was fifteen and, along with my classmates, I embarked on a job-finding mission.

There was no possibility of further education, though I don't recall feeling any resentment about this because there were too many of us in the same boat: we were very much in an underprivileged working class environment. Nobody went on to further education from my school. Friends from Sunday School may have gone to better schools and then on to the grammar down the road, but nobody else that I knew went to Uni.

Had I been serving some kind of apprenticeship, I would probably have gone to night school, which many of my friends did. But even though I might have wanted to continue my education in preference to finding a job, it didn't particularly rankle because I knew I was going to be a comedian – and you didn't need a degree for that. At this stage I was still formulating how I was going to do it, through amateur shows and what have you, but I knew I would get there.

I was due to learn the tailoring trade – I certainly looked Jewish enough – but my prospective employer, who had rented part of 7 Leaf Square for his business, above the sweet wholesalers, had now moved to larger premises on the south side of Manchester which my mother, quite rightly, felt was too far to travel on a daily basis.

But employment was easy to come by in 1952 and my second option was as a junior salesman at Weaver to Wearer, a large gentleman's outfitters similar to Burton's the Tailors, but in direct opposition – strangely, they usually had stores next door to each other. I used to pay one penny from Frederick Road to Regent Road on the tram bound for Salford Docks. My salary was 32s 6d per week – £1.62 in today's currency. I kept ten shillings pocket money and gave my mother the rest. But ten bob was plenty in those days and I was never short, even though I smoked, as everybody seemed to do. At least, I had enough to exist on, but there were no extras.

I was taught how to shorten and lengthen trousers, something I can still do. A three piece suit was £6 10s and a pair of trousers was £1 12s, but I only served if the manager or the senior salesman was not available. The manager, Eddie O'Reagan, a soft-spoken, slightly built, gentle Northern Irishman, would call me from my position in the back room with: 'Forward, Mr Davies!' whereupon I would leap into action.

After nine months I transferred to the Broad Street branch of Weaver to Wearer, just across the road from Leaf Square, but the manager, Tommy Dunbar, was of a different ilk to the kind yet firm Eddie O'Reagan. I stuck it out until another job came up at the local Co-op. A pal of mine had been working in the grocery office for the Pendleton Co-op and wanted to transfer to the Co-operative coal office (don't ask). Anyway, I got his job, becoming one of the junior clerks who sat at high-slanted Dickensian desks which opened upwards to reveal a drawer for the ledgers. My duties included answering the phone and working the switchboard which was of the very old fashioned type with a separate earpiece on a handle at the side of the speaker.

I still had no idea how I was going to realise my theatrical ambitions but continued in amateur dramatics with the church and joined a local amateur touring variety show playing hospitals and old folks' homes purely for charitable purposes. I used jokes picked up from the other comedians I had seen on my various weekly theatre visits – and, of course, Jack. I did a whiteface 'proper poorly' act, probably copying the comic George Williams, whose opening line used to be: 'I'm not well.' I remember playing at Winnick Hospital, a huge Victorian mental institution, and thinking, 'I hope they don't keep me in because I'm acting a bit simple.'

I also took up ballroom dancing, in particular Old Tyme and modern sequence dancing, which I found a good way to meet the opposite sex, though I didn't have too much success in this quarter beyond the odd fumble in the grass. I thought I was going to get lucky once with a girl called Pat who had buck teeth, but a park keeper shone his torch on us and said that as the park was closing, perhaps we should find somewhere more comfortable.

I would travel to Blackpool for the day and see the shows, waiting outside the stage door for a glimpse of a star and the chance of an autograph. My favourite singer was David Whitfield, who had a hit with *Cara Mia*; he topped the bill in Blackpool for several years. He was later convicted on a charge of indecent exposure and died in a welter of bad publicity; I met him once at the Batley Variety Club and he looked dreadful, as though he had led a life of complete debauchery.

I also enjoyed some of the comedians in Blackpool in the 'fifties such as Bill Waddington, who ended up in *Coronation Street* as Percy, and Joe Church, who became a good mate in later years. Jewel and Warriss were at the Opera House, packed twice nightly every night for twenty weeks … but of course I'd seen them already.

MY call up papers for National Service came, after I'd turned eighteen, in 1956. After extensive medical examinations it was discovered that I had an irregular heartbeat but passed A1, so I was sent to war – at least as far as my mother was concerned. She was convinced that Hitler was still alive and waiting for me somewhere.

That's not quite the joke it might appear as I don't think my mother ever really recovered from the tragedy of my brother Michael's death. She was a very loving, good mum to all of us, but overprotective to the point of exasperation – for us, I mean. She was like that with all of us, but me particularly, because I was her first-born and I don't think she could contemplate the pain of losing another child.

She may have had a point about the hazards of crossing Broad Street when I was younger but she was always neurotic about my leaving the house, fearful I would get into some sort of unspecified trouble. I remember coming back from a dance one New Year's Eve – I was about fifteen or sixteen – and because it was gone midnight she was out on the road looking for me, coming up the street, shouting: 'Where have you been?'

It was very difficult because I knew her concern came from love, but that didn't stop it being annoying at the same time. So, quite apart from wanting to emulate Jack, I suspect another reason I was drawn to school plays may have been that they gave me a degree of independence: a way of being out of Mother's orbit for a while, even though I was doing something she approved of.

My birth effectively put an end to her career, but my mother always considered herself to be still in show business: she would come and help with the make-up at school plays and Sunday School functions. I suppose she was involved, albeit at one remove, because in the early 'forties her mother, my grandma Ruth, was still working, doing the double with Jack; when she retired, Jack reverted to the solo act and the occasional double with Cyril.

She wanted me to go into showbiz. I came home after the army for a couple of months but then left to start my career at Butlins and never really went back again. There were no tearful pleas from her to find a regular job – yes, she cried and didn't want me to go away from home but she knew that's what I had to do.

When I eventually acquired a degree of fame, she was there to enjoy it. She saw my act occasionally over the years and was always very vocal in her praise – not just to me but to everyone around – and I was thrilled when she came to my first recording of *Opportunity Knocks* at the old ABC studios in Didsbury.

My biggest regret, really, was that I couldn't do anything for her, despite my new status. And I really, really tried to help her. I wanted to. But over the years her depression had deepened, and she had become a very sad lady.

She lived in a rather basic council flat, and she hardly ate, she was skin and bone. But nothing I did seemed to help. I would buy furniture and have it fitted, but the next time I went she had no interest in the house, no interest in having a decent living. She would just carry on as she always had done; she didn't seem to know any different. It was such a shame, because she wasn't stupid, just sad.

Whatever I tried to do for her financially was a waste of time. I sent her a monthly allowance, but every time I would get to see her I could never see that the money had been put to good use.

The trouble was that the damage had been done in the early 'forties in a pond in Babbacombe and it was irreparable: she had two children then all of a sudden she only had one. And no husband to support her or share the grief. In those days during the war you were just told to get on with your life, because so many were dying. People were not coming back from the war and it was just normal. You stuck together and got on with things.

That was the theory, anyway. But my mother was never really well and the doctor was never far away. Luckily we had this wonderful lady doctor, Louise Parks, whose surgery was the second house in Leaf Square (in much better condition than ours), so it was not far for her to come.

In 1957, whilst I was doing National Service, Mother got TB. And she was in a sanatorium, close to where she lived. Ironically, it was good for her health in the sense that she got regular meals and put on weight and started to look after herself. There is a photograph of me and her from that time in which she looks well and fit, the best I've ever seen her. It's inscribed: 'From your loving son Freddie.' I was twenty. She was forty. The children had to go into care; they were looked after by a foster mother, who they hated. Mother was there for a year but made a full recovery.

I must stress that her depression never got in the way of our feeling that we were loved, though her overpossessiveness did make things difficult in later years.

Whenever I would go to see her, she was very: 'Oh, my Freddie's come back to me!' She and my first wife, Jackie, never got on with each other and I hardly ever told her when I was visiting Mother in order to avoid conflict.

I did take my mother to Blackpool once when we were living there, and she and Jackie had a terrible row. I'd been to open a fête and came back to find her sat on the doorstep: 'Oh,' she said, 'that cow's thrown us out!' and I had to take her home to Manchester. Very sad; they just didn't get on at all. When Jackie and I got married I couldn't even think about asking her to the wedding.

THERE were two long term men in my mother's life. The first was Burly Lyall, with whom she had two girls and a boy. He lived with us from time to time but I never liked him much as he could be a bit abrasive.

He came from Northwich and had a wife and child there; he was estranged from his wife, but not actually divorced. He would appear at odd times as he was a long distance lorry driver. I was quite young at the time – my half-sister Shirley was born when I was eight – and he would come and stay, disappear for days on end and then come back again. Mother had Peter and June quite quickly after that, and I think it was always assumed that Burly would settle down with her. But he never took steps to divorce his wife and in the end my mother had enough and threw him out.

I feel more unkindly towards him now than I did then. At the time, I think I felt a bit sorry for him when she got rid, probably because he was the only man in our lives; important as Jack was to me, his visits were ad hoc. There may even have been the odd occasion when Burly showed me and the other kids something vaguely resembling paternal kindness, but he wasn't around regularly enough to be considered a dad, although Peter always referred to him as such.

Later, after Burly died, my mother took up with George Butt, who worked nights in the newspaper industry. I think this was more of a platonic friendship, but he did look after her in later years. They lived together – sort of. He would work nights and sleep during the day then go back to work in the evening, as they would print overnight. I knew very little about him, apart from the fact that he'd occasionally turn up if I was working a local theatre or club and ask to borrow money, but he was good to her, as far as I knew.

MY mother died in 1971. She was found one morning by George, who had come back from work. She was usually up and would make his breakfast and things, and then he would go to bed for four or five hours, or however long he slept during the day. I think the cause of death was that old one, pneumonia. She was fifty-four.

I was unable to make the funeral. I was working in Bristol for the week and was struck down with a very bad dose of the flu. I was devastated and my family were naturally very upset at my non-appearance. I know I should have still crawled there on my hands and knees but I never made it. I have regretted it ever since.

It did cause quite a family rift for a while but I am pleased to say this has healed over the years and we enjoy a very happy relationship, talking regularly and with frequent visits. My two half-sisters June and Shirley met their soulmates Brian and Bill and married very happily; sadly, both men are now gone, but fondly remembered. My brother Peter is a happy-go-lucky soul who loves his golf and his wife Rosie and they live in Middleton, Manchester; June and Shirley also live within half an hour's drive of each other.

PART of me was glad to be setting off for National Service – and it wasn't just about escaping the dinginess of those two rooms at 9 Leaf Square. All my of mates had dispersed since school had broken up, and my Co-operative job wasn't exactly a vocation. I needed some excitement in my life, a fresh start. At the time, however, I wasn't really thinking much beyond that: I didn't appreciate, as perhaps my mother did, that this might also be the moment I was leaving home for good. Leaving her.

Which turned out to be true, more or less. I still felt responsible for her and had most of my army pay deducted and sent directly to her, but although I came back for odd weekends on leave, and stayed for a few months after the army, I had grown away: I was a different, more determined, person by then, already actively planning a future beyond Leaf Square. So it feels right to take my farewell to my mother here.

I have so much to thank my mother for. Despite her fragile state she loved and supported us, keeping a roof over our heads through some very difficult years without much help from others. And when the time came for me to make that final break, she understood: she knew that show business was what I was destined to do.

I think of her most days. And whenever I see June, Shirley or Peter that common bond between us is instantly there again: a sadness and a love for a troubled woman who did her best for all of us.

I hope she is at peace now.

4: Excused Boots

I DID basic training for the Royal Army Pay Corps, freezing my balls off in Devises, Wiltshire. I had been told to attend Her Majesty's pleasure on January 20th, 1956, and given my never-to-be-forgotten army number: 23280550.

On my way to enlist I stayed a few days with my cousin Pauline and her husband Bill, who had left Slough and the Crooked Billet, scene of my comedic debut, for a pub in North London, the Pegasus on Green Lanes, Islington, a very popular venue with a large concert room which did 'free and easy' singalongs at the weekend.

During my short stay I went to see *The Al Read Show* at the Adelphi on the Strand. Al's act was quite Northern but his style bridged the North-South divide of those days – no doubt helped by the fact that he was a very popular radio star at the time and had about three sketches which sort of worked on stage. Included on the bill was a young singer making her first stage appearance in London. She did only two songs but was sensational and literally stopped the show. Those songs were *The Wayward Wind* and *Burn My Candle*. Consequently it was Shirley Bassey who was the talk of London, not Al Read!

The intake in my hut at Devises training camp were a motley crew as I remember, but I managed to keep them entertained. With lights out in our freezing army billet I would tell jokes in the dark which were always well received. After the passing out parade at the end of our basic training the lance corporals and sergeant who had been stoney-faced at all times ('*You 'orrible little fucker!*') confessed that they would listen in to my jokes in their sectioned-off portion at the end of the hut but dared not tell me so as to keep up the order of command during training.

I could not get used to the heavy issue army boots and after medical advice, was 'excused boots' and allowed to wear what were called RAF Shoes. I was diagnosed with 'Achilles tendon bonsosa', whatever that is. Anyway, it did the trick and I did not have to do those stupid marching exercises: '*Up and down, up and down, by the left quick march, shoulderrrrr arms!*'

Even as early as 1956, my managerial skills had somehow been divined because I was designated as the platoon organiser, taking a weekly kitty for the passing out party four weeks later. I arranged a coach to Bristol where we all got nicely pissed.

After a short leave I had a month's training as a comptometer operator (a sort of mechanical calculator) and was then posted to Fenham Barracks, Newcastle upon Tyne, where I lived in a barrack room with twenty other blokes from hairy Scots to not-so-hairy English soldiers: we were sharing the barracks with the Northumberland Fusiliers. Every weekday we would be bussed to the Army pay office in Blakelaw, about five miles away. In true military fashion we would all be lined up and marched from the barracks to the bus – approximately fifty yards away.

One of our sergeants, a small wiry man with a huge nose and thick glasses, was named Sergeant Barks. He was a regular soldier and would often march us to and from the bus, left, right, left, right, left, right; we would add a gentle 'woof' in unison to the footsteps: *woof woofwoofwoof*. He would go ballistic trying to find out who was doing this woofing, as we would do it under our breath. He never found out who started the woofing. (Guess who!)

MEANWHILE my real training was continuing. During National Service I took the opportunity to visit the local variety theatres in the North East: the Empire, Theatre Royal and Palace in Newcastle, and the Empire, Sunderland.

One of the comics I saw was Bobby Thompson, the flat-capped 'Little Waster', a prime example of that North-South divide in comedy then. Although Northern comics were the funny men of comedy, they had to soften their accents for mass acceptance – like Ted Ray, who was a Liverpool comic. Bobby Thompson never did, so he could never work south of Newcastle. That is, he could work to his own kind down south – he would often do concerts and they were full of Geordies – but he was too heavy-accented to be generally accepted. A lot of the Scottish comedians were too: the ones that translated and came down were the more gentle, Edinburgh-based comics.

But the divide was as much about attitude as intelligibility. Northern comedy tended to be gentler, more homespun and down to earth, reflecting working class conditions, and Northern audiences didn't like anything that was flash, a bit Smart Alec. Like Max Miller, for example, who stuck to the South. The story goes that when his agent offered Miller a booking at the Glasgow Empire he snapped, 'I'm a comedian, not a missionary!'

Among other comedians I saw at that time were Harry Bailey, a very good Irish comic, and Albert Modley, a lovely Lancashire comic; Modley played the Northern circuit, although he was a big radio star and his act did travel. Almost literally, you might say: one of my favourite routines, in which his drum kit was set up to look like the front of a tram, has been described by Geoff Mather:

> He would stand, squat and jowly, pretending to be a tram driver, using drum cymbals to imitate the controls, juddering his body and calling to someone imaginary on the line ahead: 'What do you mean, where am I going? I'm going' – here the head craning outwards and upwards to glimpse a non-existent destination board on the exterior of the tram – 'I'm going to DU-PLI-CATE.'

I usually went to the theatres with a fellow private from my barrack room, Don Auty, who turned up at Fenham barracks shortly after me. He resembled a scruffy Noel Coward and had already been working in show business as a stage manager before he was called up; his uncle was Jack Taylor, a producer from Blackpool. Don was totally unsuited for regimentation of any kind, hating the army and the discipline with a vengeance. He tried everything in the book to get himself discharged, even attempting suicide by drinking Brasso! But we were good for each other, and very close during our time in Newcastle.

Don's final seven days there were spent in army clink, with me passing fags to him through the bars. He had decided to take a week off and gone AWOL to do some job or other, thinking he would escape the consequences when he returned as he only had seven days to serve. He was jailed in the army lock-up at Fenham Barracks till the bitter end.

We have remained bosom pals to this day. He became a well-respected stage and company manager, although he is still a scruffy bugger: an army friendship goes beyond any looks. In later years Don helped set up the Bill Kenwright Organisation, and had it not been for his liking for the odd drink or two I suspect he would have made more of the theatrical knowledge in which he is steeped. In the 'seventies Don and I put a variety bill together for a week at the Kings, Southsea, during the summer; I topped the bill and the show lost £52, so I worked for the week and it still cost me £26.

Money was also on my mind in those days. A Forces Weekend Return rail fare to Kings Cross for thirty bob (£1.50) allowed me to escape the barracks at Fenham most weekends in order to become a singing waiter at Cousin Pauline's pub. With pay and tips at the Pegasus, I could get between five and ten pounds which would keep me going for the rest of the week as my army pay was only about 28 shillings per week, and most of that went to my mother. I would travel back to Newcastle overnight from Kings Cross, knackered, on Monday, but what the hell, I was just nineteen.

NOT that Newcastle didn't have its own attractions. There was a very popular dance hall called The Brighton, on Westgate Road. Its Thursday dance became a popular army rendezvous as that was when we would get our pay, and there were always lots of girls. That was where I met Jacqueline Olive Clark in 1957. She was a divorcee with a young daughter, Jenny, the result of a disastrous six month marriage to a crap Al Jolson impersonator. (I don't know why

I remembered the Jolson thing, but he must have been bad as it was easy to get into the Black and White Minstrels and he never did.)

I soon fell in love with Jackie, who was my first real girlfriend. She was always very supportive of my ambitions and confident I would make the big time one day. She was three years older than me, very mature and seemed to like the things I did; I had some nice home-cooked food as she still lived at home with her parents.

At the start of our relationship I had no idea she had been married, or about Jenny. Jackie was a nurse at the General Hospital, a very caring person who loved her job, but she thought I would run a mile if I knew she had been married and had a five year old child. I only found out by accident when I was at her mother's house and Jenny kept calling her 'Mummy', which was a bit of a giveaway. But it didn't matter to me that Jackie had a child, and as soon as we married Jenny called me Dad.

BUT before we hurtle any further into the future, I'd better sum up my experience of National Service.

I know that in some memoirs it's presented as a moment of political awakening, the writer's first shocked awareness of social inequality, but I can't pretend that's how it was for me. I had been at the bottom of the heap already so I knew what it was like.

I suppose the most important thing National Service gave me was that it drew a line under living at home, as it did for most people – but maybe, with such a possessive mother, it was a step which was more necessary for me than most. It was a great man-maker: we were boys when we went in, but when you came out after the training, having experienced the discipline of being in the army, it made you wake up and think, 'I've got to do something with my life now.'

Which helped fuel my comedy ambitions. Had I not gone into the army I might have continued to bumble along in amateur shows, vaguely dreaming about the future without doing much about it. By the time I was demobbed, however, it was absolutely clear what I had to do: I had to gain experience in the theatre and the best place to do that was Butlins.

Yet even with my newfound determination Butlins seemed unattainable – until some advice from a former Redcoat turned my life around.

But first – an interlude.

5: A Brief Undertaking

AFTER my demob from National Service in January 1958, I tried to get my old job back as a clerk at the Pendleton Co-op Grocery Office, but it was not to be. On demob your previous employer was expected to take you back, but somebody was already fulfilling that task.

I was, however, offered a job in the Co-op Undertakers on Broad Street, Salford. I had no option but to try it, lasting two whole weeks, during which time I upset the undertaker, Mr Lindsay, by making jokes about the corpses and reducing the coffin bearers to hysteria.

The trouble was that I would see the funny side of everything. I would see the comedic element because it was so sombre. And so serious. So sad. These women would come in and say: 'I'd like to bury my husband' – or father, grandad, or whoever. They were people who knew the undertaker: he'd been burying their families from time immemorial, like he knew all the dead people in the world.

A Brief Undertaking

People don't really think about what undertakers actually do. They arrange everything. Quite apart from the grisly side of things, there are unexpected practical considerations. When you pick up a body you can't stop and have a cup of tea on the road, because you can't stop the hearse: wherever you stop the hearse, people say: 'Somebody's died.' So you have to hide it. If you're going to stop at a transport café, for example, on the way from picking up a body somewhere, you have to hide the hearse round the back. So you go in and say, 'Have you got anywhere I can hide?' Of course, most hospitals have an entrance at the back purely for picking up the dead, so you have to go in that way.

I found all this out in the two weeks I worked there. I remember one case in particular, when a woman came in and said to Mr Lindsay: 'You probably read about it in the paper.' And he was nodding yes – I didn't know what the hell they were talking about – and she said, 'He put his head – ' – and he was starting to finish her lines: ' – in the oven, yes.' It was starting to feel like a Norman Evans routine.

Then she said – and this defeated even Mr Lindsay's predictive powers – 'But the gas ran out, there wasn't enough money in. So he slit his throat.'

I was doing my best to stay suitably po-faced in the background, but thinking: 'For the sake of a *penny*? There's blood all over the place – for God's sake, go and get a penny from somebody – make a neat job of it, at least!'

So perhaps it wasn't altogether surprising that I only lasted two weeks.

Actually, when I came out of the army at the end of January, I'd already been emboldened to apply for Butlins and knew I'd only have a bit of time to fill before the interview, so hadn't really needed to go back to the Co-op at all, apart from the fact it meant getting a few bob.

I remember poor Mr Lindsay trying to encourage me at the beginning: 'You know, if you stick at this job, you could finish up getting fourteen pounds a week,' which was a bloody good wage in those days.

By the time I started, however, I already knew the interview was set for the following week, which didn't help when it came to taking my sombre duties seriously. Luckily for the bereaved of Salford, I auditioned and was accepted as a Redcoat by Billy Butlin.

I was on my way – and, mercifully, the irony that from now on I might be the one doing the dying was lost on me at the time.

6: It Started in Skeggy

MY audition to be a famous Butlins Redcoat was at the now defunct Queens Hotel, Manchester in March 1958. I did my usual magic routine and a few jokes to a panel of five entertainment managers, one from each of the camps. They each had an open folder in front of them and as they lost interest, they would close it, I learned later.

One folder remained open, thank God, and that belonged to Frank Mansell, who employed me at Skegness Camp. I had prayed that I would be accepted as a Redcoat, lying through my teeth that I could organise a table tennis tournament, as Des O'Connor had advised.

I had approached Des for advice in 1957 when he was touring with *The Billy Cotton Band Show* at the Empire, Newcastle; unknown then, he was kind enough to stop and have a chat with me at the stage door. It turned out that he had asked Max Bygraves and received the same advice: go to Butlins and get some experience. But the idea seemed out of reach and I raised all sorts of objections: you had to run sports competitions and I couldn't even swim ... To all of which Des simply replied, 'You bluff your way in – once you're there you can learn.' Which, as I later learnt, was precisely what most people did.

I appeared many times on *The Des O'Connor Show* in the years to come, although when I saw him in Blackpool a few years later he couldn't remember that momentary kindness in Newcastle which had meant so much to me.

Incidentally, Des never made any secret of the fact that he had modelled himself closely on the man who directed him to Butlins. When Max was at the Victoria Palace and Des was at the Palladium, I remember going into Max's dressing room and there was a card from Des saying, 'At least I learnt from the master.'

I WAS issued with a travel warrant and arrived at Skegness station in April 1958. The camp was about four miles up the coast and like a wonderland to me when I first saw it. At the entrance was the Butlins slogan: 'Our true intent is all for your delight.'

I was a very nervous twenty-year-old, but then we all were. There were Redcoats of all shapes and sizes, from large sporty types to tubby, maternal girls who looked after the under-fives kids. The entertainment department consisted of approximately twenty to thirty Redcoats who were meant to smile at the 'Happy Campers' at all times and make them feel special.

Butlins was at its absolute peak in the late 'fifties and early 'sixties. This was before the days of cheap foreign travel, when it was still seen as a great holiday. Somehow I fitted in with this way of life, the 'all for one and one for all' camaraderie.

The Skegness camp attracted families from Nottingham and the Midlands, along with a mixture of Tynesiders and Scots during their annual holiday weeks. Regular campers were proud Butlin 'repeaters' who were treated to a special badge; some people had so many of these little metal badges that they were permanently hunched over, with what looked like a very tatty Lord Mayor's chain round their necks.

Frank Mansell earned great respect from all under him; we called him Mr M. He and his wife, Dizzy, were longtime performers who had been employed in Archie McCulloch's revue show at Butlins Clacton in the early 'fifties; Frank had helped the then entertainment manager, Ron Hayter, with Redcoat scheduling and was subsequently offered the job of entertainment manager for Skegness.

Dizzy put the Redcoat shows together. These were proper productions on the big Gaiety Theatre stage every Wednesday night, and the 1,600 seat theatre was always packed full. By this time the campers knew most of the Redcoats, so they would be a very easy audience to entertain, in the main. I did a silent magic act dressed as a Chinaman in a long coat. Well, almost silent. The first words I ever spoke on the stage at Butlins were: 'You take one piece of sling ...' but I soon realised that, because of the tremendous size of the theatres, people at the back of the hall couldn't see what I was doing. So I turned to comedy – it was safer.

I didn't really try to change my accent when performing: I just spoke normally, obviously with a Northern inflection. I think I was more Mancunian than anything, or a little bit gentler – Mancunian is very *Coronation Street,* very Salfordian. I did try to lose that a bit to make sure I'd be understood.

I regularly appeared in the shows and most of the

comedy sketches with two other comics called Louie Grant and Big Dennis, who were the official 'camp comics' – camp not being the operative word in this instance. They would wander round, go to all the big functions, bathing beauty contests and the like, and generally cause a bit of mayhem; Dennis was like a Billy Bunter and Louie was small, so they made quite a comical-looking pair. I did a double act with Louie for a while outside of Butlins, though we didn't get beyond a couple of working men's clubs in Grimsby.

The top Redcoat stand-up comic that year was Dave O'Mahony, who later became known as Dave Allen. Ringo Starr was drumming in the camp but we never met. He was in the ballroom down the end: officially the Rock and Calypso Ballroom, it was dubbed the Rock and Collapsible.

Dave was superbly funny even then. A little undisciplined at times, but he had star status written all over his face; we all admired and looked up to him. He'd already been there for a year and I gained a lot of experience from his lead, just by watching him work. He was quite different in the 'fifties and did a very frenetic act in the style of Jerry Lewis – he even looked a bit like him. His act's closer was about a man having a bad dream and puffing like a train going mad.

We became good pals. We'd usually get Saturdays off, as this was changeover day, and would try to get away from the camp for a few hours. It was in Peterborough that Dave introduced me to Chinese food, and I've loved it ever since.

Our friendship continued and we'd meet up over the years: if I was working a theatre he'd often be starring at a local cabaret club. He never saw himself as a theatre comic and preferred the intimate feel of cabaret and, of course, television, where he was to become enormously popular, in many ways changing the face of stand-up.

We never really discussed comedy when we got together, though I do remember him telling me, 'You are larger than life, therefore you're more of a theatre comic than me.' It was more than just a friendship, however: it was a Butlins bond, where we'd started together. I didn't ask him about how he'd made the transition from his madcap Redcoat persona to the more confidential bar companion of his TV and cabaret performances, though I do remember the moment I was first aware of the change.

After leaving Butlins, Dave had done the clubs for a couple of years and been encouraged by Sophie Tucker, with whom he'd worked in a show, to try his luck in Australia. He became very successful on television there but decided to come back to Britain, which was when I saw him compering a pop package show at Manchester Odeon in 1963.

This was the kind of presentation, long gone, where each group or singer did a couple of numbers, then beetled off. An up-and-coming group called the Beatles may even have been the headliners, but I had come to see Dave. As well as introducing the acts he had his own spot, and it was a different Dave I saw: wittier, sharper, more in control. An obituary in *The Guardian* fills in the blanks:

> In Sydney, he worked with opera singer Helen Traubel, another woman who profoundly influenced his career. She suggested he replace the corny one-liners with material based on the reality of his youth. Thus was born a style that made the public, and a generation of comics then in its infancy, think a little differently about humour, about the power of words, about authority, and about the world around them.

Mention should also be made here of Dave's brother, Johnny O'Mahony, who was very close to him and encouraged him to make a career out of comedy. Johnny was a Redcoat at Filey. I don't think he had an act as such, but he did a stint as camp comic and was funnier than Dave at the time. He was an academic and a rather private person offstage, a bit introverted, so I never got to know him well. I was saddened to learn that he later committed suicide.

BUTLINS was a happier experience for me than for Dave: he had to get out, and it wasn't until he left that he started to do well. After we were both established he told me, during one of our boozy nights together, that he'd felt stifled and hadn't got the opportunities he ought to have had. I think they knew he was a good comic but didn't realise quite how special he was. That was true for all of us: we were doing a job for very little money and we all had to do other duties as well.

This didn't rankle with me in the same way. As far as I was concerned Butlins was just a stepping stone, giving me the experience of working in a theatre and getting used to talking to people. There was no real training or mentoring: you were left to sink or swim, but you were expected to do it. The experience proved a wonderful training ground in itself, especially where talking to an audience was concerned.

My first job was to be put in charge of the Tombola, or Bingo as it is now called. You had to call the bingo numbers and a cashier from the accounts department was there to take the money. You were forbidden to play for cash in 1958 so the prizes were vouchers which could only be exchanged for goods in the Butlins shops on site, and a percentage was deducted for the Duke of Edinburgh's Playing Fields Fund. This was par for the course, as most of the operations and concessionaires on the site were geared to getting as much money out of the campers as possible. While all the so-called entertainment was 'free', the drinks were expensive and the food was abysmal, giving a whole new meaning to Butlins 'repeater'.

The Tombola took place in the boxing/wrestling arena where there was professional wrestling once a week, with the usual riot of staged falls and throws. And that wasn't the only deception being practised: we soon established a fiddle whereby we would buy back the prize vouchers from the campers at a percentage and exchange them for cash with a friendly shop assistant. This worked well until a Welsh smoothie, who'd taken over the Tombola and the voucher scheme, was found out and summarily dismissed a few years later.

Anyway, that is what I did for six months, calling the bingo. I had a great time and learned a lot. I was able to run the show, so to speak, and built up quite a following with the Tombola crowd. The campers were very enthusiastic and joined in with all the fun – beauty contests, knobbly knees, tennis and snooker with John Pullman, the then world snooker champion who toured the camps doing exhibition games. Visiting variety stars would do Sunday concerts: Jon Pertwee, The Crazy Gang, Bill Maynard, Arthur Worsley – the world's greatest ventriloquist – Billy Dainty and many more. Butlins gave me a great opportunity to learn from established comics as well as Dave, the kingpin of the Redcoat shows.

But the most important part of the whole Butlins experience was getting the chance to perform on large stages and proper theatres in front of people who felt as if they knew me from the Tombola or just chatting to them in the camp, so they were already on my side before I uttered a word. This boosted my confidence and helped shape my comic persona, which was really that of an Everyman when I wasn't in

Samuel Tweet mode - and the spluttering Samuel was still a few years away at that point.

WHEN the end of the season came and we were all unemployed, I went back to Newcastle and rented a bedsit so I could be near Jackie. Our relationship had grown by this time and we were considered an item, although we didn't live together. I knew she had to be at home with her daughter and I couldn't offer her any security in my current position, but it was understood that when things improved we might get together permanently.

I took what work I could get in the local clubs and pubs, trying to establish myself as a comedian. That's a struggle which is going to need a chapter to itself so, for now, let's just say that there were times during those dark winter days when the promise of another Redcoat job next year proved a very warming thought indeed.

There is one experience worth mentioning here, however, as it had the effect of toughening me up, making me more determined than ever to succeed. It's not generally known, but that was the time I made my first television appearance, six years before *Opportunity Knocks*.

I was having a rough time of it in the clubs, as you'll hear later, but things started looking up when I heard on the grapevine that Tyne Tees, the new Independent Television franchise for the region, were auditioning for a talent show to be called *At the Golden Disc*. I managed to get a slot at the studio in Wallsend and did my usual act, a few sleight of hand tricks and into a comedy routine.

This was a strategy which had served me well ever since I'd started doing the rudiments of an act as a teenager in charity shows: start with the magic, get the audience's attention, and then launch into the jokes. It also helped to get me over the fear factor of failing in the first thirty seconds, every comedian's nightmare.

Unfortunately the audition was cold – in more ways than one. Being without an audience is especially hard for comedy: you need the warmth of a reaction to survive. When all you can see is that piece of glass – the camera lens – reflecting your head, it's enough to put the dead hand on any levity you might be attempting. Matters weren't helped by the fact that the studio itself was freezing and only half-built. Still, I did what I could, ignoring what felt like the glacial stare of the producer conducting the audition.

Afterwards he called me over and proceeded to give me some advice: 'Cut the comedy and stick to the magic – you will never make a comedian.'

Now that really stopped me in my tracks. I hadn't been expecting unbridled enthusiasm, but this was a bolt from the icy blue. The magic tricks were a means to an end – didn't he realise that? I had never wanted to be anything other than a comic: it was my destiny, in my blood, ever since I'd been taken backstage at – well, you've read all that.

After the initial shock I was determined to prove this idiot talent spotter wrong. Who did he think he was, anyway?

I now have a sneaking suspicion it may have been the great impresario George Black, one of the foremost producers of big stage shows in the UK and the money behind Tyne Tees at the time. Still, what did he know?

I wish I could say that I gave him a mouthful – whoever he was – and that my innovative blend of comedy and magic went on to steal the show. In fact, I accepted his suggestion and kept to the sleight of hand for the broadcast – not that I had much choice.

I could tell I was doomed as soon as we started rehearsing.

The studio had been done up to look like a nightclub and someone had the bright idea that the acts would perform not in a stage area, but in different parts of the club, with the audience scattered all around. I could see seats placed behind me which, as I couldn't help feeling, might just spoil the illusion a little. I remember saying, 'Er, this isn't gonna work, is it? They're gonna see what I'm doing,' but none of the crew bustling around me seemed to hear.

The show was broadcast live – and no, I didn't win. I was beaten by a singer called David Macbeth, who later changed his name to David North for some obscure reason.

I never seem to win these talent shows.

Thinking about it a little more calmly now, I'm not sure whether he meant I was a particularly good magician or just a particularly bad comic – bit of both, probably. But that little talk with the producer was enough to make me pick myself up and dust myself off on more than one occasion in the clubs that winter, as you'll read a little later.

WINTER and its various humiliations eventually passed and one day in early May my train pulled into Skegness railway station, where I met another Redcoat, Paddy Tomkins. We quickly introduced ourselves, after which I jumped in a taxi and he followed; Paddy, who came from Dublin, had already done a season at the Butlins camp in Mosney in 1958. When we arrived at the camp the fare was half a crown, 2s 6d (12 ½p) and I said I hadn't enough money, as did Paddy, but between us we managed to scrape enough together to pay the driver off. Talk about the big time.

Paddy later changed his name to Mike Newman and was quite a success on television in the 'seventies: he was the sidekick for Simon Dee in his heyday and a regular comic on *3-2-1* with Ted Rogers. Mike came to live in Blackpool and eventually got his act together, working the clubs when Mike Hughes became his agent; Blackpool had many acts working around the North West and it was a great centre for entertainers. Mike had a self-contained flat on the promenade but was invariably round our house for meals.

We worked in many shows together over the years. I appeared with him at the Queen's Theatre, Blackpool, where he met his beloved wife Brenda; they went on to have five children who, with one exception, are all in show business. We have done films together, shared the same jokes on occasion, and remained firm pals for over fifty years.

That second season at Skegness was a lot easier. I felt I belonged by now. In all, I did four summer seasons there, in between stints at other Butlin locations. I continued as bingo caller for the second year, then became a house captain. The camp was split into six houses and each captain had to spur his team on to compete for points and win a cup at the end of the week. It's the kind of thing they do at public schools to foster team spirit, which makes a bit of a change from the usual image of Butlins as a prison camp.

In the summer of 1961, I was back as an assistant entertainment manager / compere, which meant I got to swap the Redcoat for a smart navy blue blazer. This was a real step up – and not just sartorially. The job was an executive position which entailed introducing shows and events like *The Holiday Princess,* a huge beauty contest with a final in London, and *The Butlins Talent Contest,* which had its final at the London Palladium and paid £1,000 to the winner.

In addition to this I had to keep an eye on the other Redcoats and see they arrived for their duties as scheduled. It meant a rise in pay – and a single chalet at last. This was a particular blessing as I'd recently been sharing with the Welsh smoothie who came to grief with the Tombola. He had an indiscriminate eye for the ladies: I'd often be having an afternoon snooze and wake to find the bunk above me heaving in and out – he didn't care that I was there.

Another Redcoat who joined the team in 1961 was Andy King, who went on to become a very respected stage manager. After a fifty-year gap we renewed our friendship in recent years at the Grand Hotel in Scarborough at the annual Butlins Redcoat reunion. Dear Andy, in his eighties, had a wonderful fund of memories that he shared on many websites; I treasure the memory of his friendship and knowledge. Sadly, he is no longer with us. I had the honour of doing a eulogy to him on behalf of his four daughters.

Frank Mansell, still my boss and mentor, always liked to give me a challenge. When we had a wet weather programme all the entertainment moved indoors and Frank gave me a carte blanche show at lunchtimes entitled *Give That Man a Coconut,* allowing me to try out all sorts of audience participation material.

I can't remember exactly what sort of things I did – mainly, I think, getting people up under false pretences and doing a silly trick with them or getting them to answer silly questions – but it was fun to do and I enjoyed being able to ad lib. The experience was to stand me in good stead, making me more resilient when dealing with club audiences.

Along with his wife Dizzy, Frank was a great help in shaping my future in those early days; it was very greatly appreciated and remains a fond memory. Frank rose to become Director of Entertainment for the Butlins group. He became a friend; I'd visit him when in London and we'd go to the theatre together. He died suddenly in 1983, at the age of sixty-seven. I sometimes wonder what would have happened if he hadn't kept his folder open that day I auditioned at the Queen's Hotel in 1958. I shall be eternally grateful that he did.

7: Surviving in the Clubs

DURING the winters following my first two seasons at Skegness, I began to develop an act in the clubs and pubs around Newcastle. As I said, I had practised sleight of hand as a teenager in amateur shows around the North West, making miniature billiard balls, cigarettes and thimbles disappear and reappear, so it seemed like a plan to start my club act as if I were a magician, produce these billiard balls and then perhaps drop one, which would disarm the audience and get me into a gag.

It was uphill work, not least because of the change of environment. Butlins may not have been the acme of showbiz but most of the time I'd been working in a theatre setting – even the tombola had been on a raised platform (a boxing ring). It all felt connected to what I'd been absorbing and studying on my visits to the theatre: I could see from the off how things worked and how I fitted in.

Clubs were different. I had already played a few

when I was in Newcastle in the army, but I never felt I was a club act. They were much brasher than I wanted to be. I always thought of myself as a theatre act, a theatre performer.

I looked up to people like Ken Dodd, as most young comics did: Ken was always very kind and helpful with young comics. I used to go backstage to see him and he always welcomed me: 'Young man,' he called me. At one time I could even feel myself working in his flowpath, but I thought: 'Well, you can't do better than emulate the master.' Ken is very much a theatre comic. He started in clubs but really is a theatre man: larger, more fantastical, with a presence you can feel way up in the gods.

It was hard for the older comics, schooled in variety, to adapt to the clubs. It's a different sort of training. My grandad Jack played a couple of Manchester clubs in the 'fifties, when engagements in variety and touring revues, which had been his staples, were becoming harder to find. As with all the old pros of that era, he was used to a theatre setting where the audience would sit and watch you.

You see, the first thing you notice in a club is that they're not all sitting facing you. And that puts you on a back foot straight away. There's an old working men's club saying that 'a good turn gets his own order,' which means it doesn't matter if they've got their back to you; if they want to watch you they'll turn round. Which is absolute cloth-cap bollocks: they should be turned round anyway, out of manners and respect.

The old comics never seemed suited to working the clubs. They were, to use a modern term, out of their comfort zone. This wasn't to do with a gentleness of approach that wouldn't translate: even Tommy Trinder, a performer not exactly renowned for meekness, used to complain about these audiences not listening. Not his fault: he just came from a different discipline.

On the stage, in the theatre, you have a barrier before you get to the audience: there is that orchestra pit, there is that darkness where you can't really see them, there is the heavy spotlight on you. To go from that into a club, seeing them all with drinks on the table and chatting to one another, must have been a culture shock for the old pros who tried to make the transition, whatever their level of fame.

Yes, you might get applauded coming on but you've still got to make an impact, to figure out a different way of performing for that specific type of audience. This took me time to understand and I had to play a lot of clubs before I felt I had a reasonable act.

Added to the challenge was the fact that no two clubs were the same. There's a kind of consistency when you work theatres, with the proscenium arch and general atmosphere, but the clubs were all different: different stages, different rooms – though you could usually bank on poor dressing facilities, poor backing and poor administration along with the requisite bad sound and worse lighting.

I recall working a club in Wales where I was forced to use the singer's sound system, which was set at the highest reverb level: when I started it sounded like I was shouting down a mine shaft. The singer came on stage to try and adjust it but by then I had lost the plot – I collected my money and disappeared down the fire escape.

There was also the fact that the audience members all knew each other and had sat in the same seats at the same tables week after week, year after year, which didn't exactly make for an optimum working environment. Sometimes even the headline act could feel like an interruption to the main order of business: socialising, drinking, billiards, bingo, hot pies at 9.30 and everything else which made up a night out in a working men's club.

The Northern working men's clubs were notorious for being comedians' graveyards and you had to adapt like lightning to the circumstances you would find yourself in. I recall working a 'noon and night' in a club in Grimethorpe (aptly named), famous for its Colliery Band. You did two turns of twenty minutes each between 12 and 2pm on a Sunday and then four twenty-minute turns in the evening. You wouldn't survive till the evening if you died at the noon session, full of miners with black eye shadow getting pissed while their wives cooked Sunday dinner ... not very conducive for comedy.

It wasn't just the change of setting which could throw you. These clubs all had a committee who ran the so-called business of the club, including the concert secretary, who booked the acts, and the concert chairman, who acted as a compere or MC for the evening, ready to ring his bell for quiet or 'Order!' and introduce the 'turn.' These men were usually miners with no experience of entertainment or any other kind of show business acumen who would literally turn up in suit, tie and flat cap, having just come back from seeing their pigeons land safely. In two words: fucking useless.

I was once introduced at one of these clubs with the words, 'And now the next turn will entertain you.' In another, I was in the middle of a routine when the chairman took the mic out of my hand to announce the raffle or that the snooker table was free.

LATER in my career I was lucky enough to witness a rare example of a concert chairman getting his comeuppance. This was at Greasbrough Working Men's Club, near Rotherham in Yorkshire.

Along with the Scala Club, Doncaster, Greasbrough was an exception to all the other working men's clubs anywhere in the UK. It had a large concert room with a proper stage and curtains (!), two dressing rooms and a stage door. They had a decent variety bill every week with three acts and a star top of the bill: Matt Monro, Frankie Vaughan, Val Doonican and other big names of the day played this venue.

Its success ought to have given a hint to the other working men's clubs as to where they were going wrong, but some just weren't capable of following its lead. Once, when I was appearing there, a couple of becapped brethren from a large club outside Leicester headhunted me for a weekend at their illustrious venue in the middle of a working class estate. I died on the Saturday and slunk away without a word. Along with no stage facilities, lighting or sound, as I recall, they had a blind organist and imagined that booking 'a better class of turn' would be enough on its own to turn the club's fortunes around.

I worked Greasbrough several times, once around 1968 or 1969 with the crying American singer Johnnie Ray, who came with his own self-contained band. He and I were both doubling another club in Chesterfield, and I remember he had a slot machine installed in his dressing room because that was all he wanted to do – play the slots à la Vegas.

Ray had been an international star for almost two decades by then but this cut no ice with the concert chairman, who had a keen sense of the importance of his own role in the proceedings. When Ray's manager told him that Johnnie's intro would be done as an off-stage announcement by him, all hell broke loose: 'I introduce the turns!' was the affronted proclamation. 'No you fucking don't!' said the manager.

'We'll see!' said the chairman, stomping off back to front of house. But as he went through the pass door leading from the stage to the auditorium, the band struck up, and before he could reach his chairman's podium he heard: 'Ladies and Gentlemen, DIRECT from LAS VEGAS – the one and only JOHNNIEEE RAYYY!' – and of course the chairman was well and truly shafted.

My experiences with club chairmen inspired me to take a lighthearted revenge in a TV play which I called *Don't Cry For Me, Johnnie Ray*. It starts with a shot of car headlights in the distance. Then, as they get closer, they become miners' headlamps and we see the men coming out of the pit, getting into the lift, going up and getting washed, then heading home. One is the concert secretary, another the club chairman, and we see them having tea with their families before going to the club to introduce the star of the hour. I was asked if I could make it into a series but it wasn't taken up; I'm still hoping it might be developed.

TO use another modern term, my experience in the clubs, officious or incompetent concert chairmen notwithstanding, was a learning process. When I was in the army I was never far away from the theatre. I used to go every week to watch and learn something. In fact, I never felt I'd seen a good show – and still don't – unless I feel I've got something from it. Even in panto you have to inject a little originality somewhere. However outdated the format, you've still got to watch and think to yourself, 'How can I improve this?'

That thought was enough to keep me going through the early days of developing an act for the clubs. If nothing else, I was learning – at a rate of knots. I would die the death, like all comics, and on the odd occasion when I was able to rescue myself from the abyss I would perhaps do some more tricks.

There's no doubt that the clubs were a great training ground – of sorts. Working on a nightly basis gave you the experience to cope with many unexpected and difficult situations with at least a show of confidence. You got sharper, able to contend with some of the dreadful shitholes you were working.

But there were pitfalls for those who had only learnt their craft in the clubs. Many acts never got out of the mindset of working those dreadful venues and became labelled, sometimes unfairly, as 'club acts.' Some did get away, of course, like Cannon and Ball, Norman Collier, Ronnie Dukes and Ricki Lee, Paul Shane and – for a while, at least – the comedy duo Cheese and Onion, who I'll talk about later.

The trouble for some acts who wanted to escape this stigma was that, over time, their approach to performing in clubs had become ingrained: singers had adapted their style to suit the overloud, echoing sound systems and comics had settled for the lowest common denominator – filth – to get by. It condemned them to a perpetual round of working men's clubs, unless they could rise to the odd TV appearance like *Opportunity Knocks*, which gave lots of 'club turns' a chance. But when they didn't win, many quickly sank back into obscurity.

I WORKED a lot of truly awful venues in those early days, and suffered the indignity of being paid off. One of my worst experiences was during the winter after my first Butlins season, playing some dreadful clubs in the North East with a poor show. Local clubs used to have 'go as you please' contests midweek and, if you did a little spot in one of these and won, you'd get a fiver and the clubs might book you for a Saturday or Sunday night.

That was how I made my first club appearance, in fact, when I was still in the army, though I can't really recall what it was like. I think I just sort of did it: I knew I could tell jokes quite well, putting an act together with old gags and a bit of hypnosis, which worked on some of my more susceptible comrades – a bit dangerous, in retrospect, as they could faint and fall over.

I went in for more of those midweek talent contests that first winter after Butlins, hoping to pick up the odd proper gig afterwards. If the clubs did book you, sometimes they'd ask whether you knew another few acts you could bring with you to make it more of a show. There was also a pub at the bottom of Westgate Road in Newcastle, The Waterloo, that served as a last minute booking venue on a Saturday lunchtime. This was where the concert secretaries met, and all the crap acts – including me – who hadn't been booked, or who'd been let down at the last minute, would congregate, looking for that chance to be engaged for £2 10s.

Which led to my working with a girl ... well, the kindest thing you could say about her was that she resembled a codfish. She was about five feet three, twice the weight she should have been and did a Hawaiian dance wearing a grass skirt ... which conjures up an unbelievable picture. Lovely girl.

She was part of a show I'd put together, which I blush to admit I called *The Showtime Show*. It was like a little concert party, touring around the clubs in the North East. We played at this club called the Sandhole Working Men's Club.

One of the main problems with working in the clubs was that there was no stage entrance, so you had to walk in through the front door of the club, go through the thing about having to sign in as a member and then walk across the stage into the dressing room in full view of the audience.

At Sandhole they let us change in the billiards room, which was upstairs behind the stage somewhere. Then they'd come up and tell you when you were on and you'd go down this back staircase, through the kitchen, or whatever, and then on to the stage.

This particular night we'd done the first half of the show, with the girl doing the Hawaiian dance looking like a codfish, and the concert secretary came up and said: 'I'm afraid, er, we're going to have to ask you to leave.' 'Why?' I asked, in all seriousness. 'Has there been a bomb scare?' He gave me a look and said, 'No, the committee have decided that you should leave.'

So he paid us off, giving me half the money due, which was all of £10. One of the acts, a woman drummer called Nikki, had this drum kit which we had to carry out, then get the bus back to Newcastle. Can you imagine? Going through the front of the club, with all these people knowing we'd been paid off, then standing at the bus stop down the road and waiting an hour for a bus. With these people coming out the club saying: 'Well, *I* didn't think you were *that* bad.'

I'm making light of it, but the experience of being 'paid off' is one of the most soul-destroying, pitiful, never-do-this-again trials you can go through. These terrible clubs should never purport to be anything to do with show business proper: they were just an adjunct to the working men's weekend off – another hobby, like whippets, and the situation in the worst of them was degrading to entertainers who had any kind of pride or dignity in their profession.

At the time I wanted to cut my throat, but in retrospect I think: well, that taught me a lesson. All the clubs and the constant working every night, makes you better and more experienced at what you're doing. Having experienced them, a theatre is easy: the audience are facing you, you have nice lighting, good sound – theatre's a doddle!

Comparatively speaking, that is.

But first, of course, you have to find a way in.

Although I had been improving my club act in those two winters after my Butlins debut, it wasn't yet of a standard which would allow me to break into theatres. I was slowly finding it easier to handle audiences in a club environment, but I didn't have my own comedy identity yet.

There was still a long way to go before I would be ready for my second TV talent show.

8: Marriage, The Metropole and Minehead

AFTER a couple of those euphemistically named 'resting' seasons, Butlins also began to offer me work in the winter at their hotels, so I got some respite from my tough education in the clubs.

I worked the 1960/61 season at Cliftonville, near Margate, where I developed a comedy magic act. Butlins owned around six large but rather rundown hotels spread up and down the main drag in Cliftonville; one had a pool, another had tennis courts, a third a theatre, and so on, so it worked for those who figured it might be better than a camp, though it was virtually the same.

After Christmas I was sent to Saltdean, just outside Brighton, where Butlins had the Ocean Hotel – rather better than the ones in Cliftonville but catering for the same type of punter. When I left to go back to Skegness for the summer, my bunk bed was taken by a young Liverpudlian hopeful named Jimmy Tarbuck, who will feature in this story a little later; Jim's success was to have a profound effect on my own career, as you will see.

After my spell as assistant entertainment manager at Skegness, described earlier, I was sent to the Metropole Hotel, Blackpool, for the winter of 1961/62. A Victorian structure that still stands majestically on the sea side of the promenade, the Metropole was very popular with the regular Butlins clientele all the year round, although during the quiet winter months it could be quite dull. Vince Dimanno became the entertainment manager and I reverted to being a Redcoat for the season.

Jackie and I had been conducting a long distance relationship during this time, surviving the separation with her regular visits to see me *in situ*, but we finally decided to be together and, on Monday the 3rd of October, 1961, we got married at the Central Methodist Church in Newcastle upon Tyne. I'd attended the church during my time in the army and been part of their am dram society; I had struck up a friendship with the vicar, Eric Robinson, who performed the wedding ceremony.

We drove to Edinburgh for our honeymoon in my first car, a 1954 Standard 8, which had cost £325 on HP and was falling to bits. I had purchased it from a snide used car dealer in Newcastle who, when I took it back for repair, told me I had no rights to redress as I had nothing in writing. Bastard! A lesson well learned.

Edinburgh is still one of my favourite cities, but I got food poisoning after a dodgy Chinese meal and was in bed for three days. Some honeymoon, though we did get to see a great Scottish show called *Five Past Eight*, with a comedian called Jack Radcliffe, who I thought was one of the funniest men I had ever seen, and still do.

There was a hop, skip and jump walk he would do

early in the show: he did a sketch where someone was dying with all the family round the bedside, and he did this very funny walk around the bed. I can't describe it better than that – he just had funny bones, and you know what that means when you see a comic like that.

Very happy and in love, despite that less than ideal start, Jackie and I set up home in a holiday flat opposite Derby Baths, as married couples were not allowed to live in at Butlins unless they were both working for the company. Every day I would walk the half mile to work via the windy Blackpool Promenade or sometimes catch the tram that trundled along. I still had the Standard 8 car which wouldn't start and eventually rotted away parked on the front in Blackpool.

The team at the Metropole included comedian Ricky McCabe from Liverpool and Johnny Ball from Fleetwood. Johnny turned up as a comedian and did his act on the Saturday evening. When Ricky arrived the next day, he proceeded to do exactly the same act which Johnny had done the night before: it turned out they had both been at Pwllheli camp for the summer season and Johnny had been drumming in the bar, listening to Ricky's act on a regular basis.

The outcome was actually very amicable as Johnny freely admitted he had just borrowed the act for the night; Ricky charitably let the matter drop, carried on with his act and Johnny was happy to be the drummer for Dave Nicholas, our esteemed organist/MD.

One of our winter Redcoat acts was a blonde stunner called Lorna who did a great speciality act as a limbo dancer. Everyone fancied her, and Ricky tried every trick in the book to get her into bed but, being a bit hamfisted with his approach, was constantly rejected.

Ricky was one of those characters who was totally

useless with his hands. We had to rescue him more than once from getting the sack when he was scheduled to show cartoons with a portable 16mm projector – he just couldn't get it set up to project films onto the screen. I went to see what the problem was and the picture was showing on the floor. I asked him how he had managed to focus the picture onto the floor and he said that was where Mickey Mouse was supposed to be!

He became one of my best mates and later became a very successful theatrical agent. Sadly, he was taken far too young and died in the early 'nineties after suffering a heart attack. I still miss him.

After trying his hand at comedy, Johnny Ball went on to be one the biggest names on children's TV. A BBC radio producer called Geoff Lawrence suggested Johnny audition for a new series called *Play School*, and the rest is history; later his *Think of a Number* show went on to win many awards. Zoe Ball, his daughter from his first marriage, is one of Britain's top radio and TV personalities.

I whiled away the winter playing snooker with Johnny and Ricky, who introduced me to a friend of his called Mike Hughes who had a small agency fixing comedians for clubs and pubs in Liverpool. He booked me for a night at the Blue Ball Hotel for £2 10s and would often book me on my day off from the hotel after that. I was still determined to make it in the clubs and was slowly getting better, but I sure was glad they weren't my only source of income.

At the end of the winter Vince Dimanno was sent to manage the Ocean Hotel and I was asked to stay on at the Metropole as entertainment manager. I was just twenty-five and had a new staff of approximately twelve, which at my tender age was quite a responsibility. The staff comprised a boy/girl twin vocal act, a great Liverpool comic, Mike

Burton, lounge pianist Cherrie, a singer whose name escapes me, another comedian called Joey Boyle, and Roger Milner and John Hewitt, who played organ and drums. Kay Hamilton was our chief hostess, Jack Swann was a balladeer and Joe and Kathy Stead were the ballroom dance instructors.

There were a couple of other people I cannot recall, but we had a great season and I stayed on for the winter. During the summer season I was allowed to have a room at the hotel with Jackie, as she also had a job in the hotel working for the accountant; Jenny went back to stay with her grandmother in Newcastle for the summer holidays.

The manager of the Metropole was Mabel Worrall, a tall, elegant lady who ran it very well. Firm but fair, she was approachable and a very good leader. She had shares in Butlins and an apartment on the first floor of the hotel for life. I found her to be a very good and loyal friend during and after the time I worked under her watchful eye. Her advice regarding management – never cut off your nose to spite your face – has stood me in good stead many a time.

In those days Blackpool was a great place to go if you wanted to have a look at most of the premier acts of the age. On a good day, there was nowhere nicer: you could have a walk along the prom, and see a star-studded show in the evening. Blackpool always enjoyed a longer season than most with the famous Illuminations extending it. And the stars shone bright in 1962 with Doddy at the Opera House, Tommy Cooper and Nina and Frederik at the Queens; all the piers had big stars at the top of the bill.

It was quite a season for us as well, as Smirnoff Vodka was launched on the unsuspecting Blackpool crowds – yes, direct from the Metropole Hotel. Tony Leadley, a young PR man with a glamorous team, descended on Blackpool, and the Metropole in particular. During the launch they had a

Miss Holiday Smirnoff, a Mr Holiday Smirnoff, Smirnoff Bingo, Smirnoff Talent – you name it, they had it. We all got well sloshed nightly on the juice and I received twelve bottles as a gift.

I vaguely recall my son Kent being conceived that week: I remember Jackie begging me to be quiet as her mother was sleeping – no, not in the next room but at the foot of the bed, in a put-u-up supplied by the hotel as there were no free rooms at the inn that week. You can imagine my response when full of the spirit!

I STAYED on at the Metropole for the winter season but then Wally Goodman, overall supremo for the entertainment staff, decided I was wasted there and would be better value in a holiday camp for the 1963 season. I was sent to Minehead, the last camp ever built under the Butlins banner, as assistant entertainments manager.

The entertainments manager was a rather obnoxious gentleman called Al Harris. He really knew how to get the best out of his staff by telling them they were all useless: I recall him telling me one night that I was shit and would never get anywhere. He came to see me in 1972, when I was starring in a pantomime in Torquay, still exhibiting that same distinctive charm of manner. Years later, when I was doing star one-nighters at the Butlins Ocean Hotel in Brighton, he booked me for a gig by telephone only to try and cancel it three weeks later. It gave me great pleasure to inform him that he had made a verbal contract with me and I had to be paid.

Minehead was not in very good condition. Newly built from scratch, it had only been open for eighteen months but was still unfinished: we had the job of trying to keep campers happy as they tramped through building works.

Our son Kent had been born on May 7th that year in

Newcastle and Jackie had struggled with Jenny and him on the train from Newcastle to London, then on to Minehead, all on her own. We had taken a grotty flat in the town and hardly saw one another as I was on duty from 8am till midnight, though we did manage to borrow a van from the bookmaker on the camp when I got a day off so we could take the kids away with the pram on board. It was generally a very bad season – but it became the catalyst for my finally deciding to leave and try my hand as a solo comic.

At the conclusion of that season with the nice Mr Harris I couldn't wait to get away. I was assigned to Butlins Margate Hotels for the winter but, with two children and a wife to support, it was becoming increasingly hard to get by on what the company were offering. Frank Mansell's hands were tied but he suggested that now was the time, with the experience I'd accumulated, to leave and try for some proper professional work outside the Butlins security blanket. This was the final push I needed.

I wrote to Mike Hughes, the up-and-coming agent in Liverpool recommended by Ricky McCabe. Mike had this great idea that comedy was king and he was going to sign all the comics up – and he did, starting with Tarbuck, though he subsequently lost him to a London agent. I had already done the odd one-nighter and other bits and bobs for him when I was at the Metropole, so the natural thing to do was to write to him – only snail mail in those days. He answered by return of post, saying, 'We will be able to fix you from November onwards,' and I never looked back.

And so I took my family – Jackie, six month old Kent and Jenny – for a journey into the unknown, leaving behind the safe salary of £14 10s a week as a famous Butlins Redcoat. What lay ahead for the lad from Brixton?

9: Tweeting

FIRST there was the practical consideration of where to live. We decided to go back to Blackpool as there were friends, fellow theatricals, ex-Redcoats and entertainers nearby. In the 'sixties there were still about ten major summer shows in Blackpool plus big nightclubs and pubs, all requiring acts. We took a small two room bedsit on North Promenade near Derby Baths but quickly moved out to a more permanent flat in a better position in Wyre Grove, off the main drag.

Before Mike's offer, I'd booked a week's engagement for myself at the end of October at the 99 Club in Barrow-in-Furness; I had already done a one week cabaret spot there two years earlier, commuting from Blackpool with a famous old jazz trumpeter, Nat Gonella. I did my first full post-Butlins week, Sunday to Saturday, earning £40, so that was a good start.

On the last night, Tommy Halfpenny, the compere, came into my dressing room to tell me that Jimmy Tarbuck was going to be on *Sunday Night at the London Palladium* the following night.

This came as a bit of a shock as the last time I had met Jim was when he took my bunk bed over at Butlins Ocean Hotel in Saltdean, in May 1961. Jimmy had sat and watched me perform on the Saturday evening he arrived. As we were short staffed I did the bingo, compered the evening Redcoat show, did the main spot, then led a late night singalong in the bar, getting everybody up and singing along and joking, and probably one or two other things, until the early hours – while Jim watched, open-mouthed.

Afterwards he said, 'You haven't got to do all that, have you?'

'I'm afraid you have, Jimmy,' I said, though it was quite normal for me.

'Jesus Christ,' he said, 'I'll never be able to do all that – I haven't got enough material!'

When we talked about it in later years I asked him how he managed. He shrugged and said: 'I got through it.'

When he went on to Pwllheli camp the following season, Jim's Scouse accent failed to find favour with the illustrious Director of Entertainment for Butlins, Colonel Basil Brown, who declared he couldn't speak proper English and sacked him. Brown was really an old 1940s colonel who'd run some entertainment battery in the army, and Billy Butlin employed him to do all the entertainment. He was really up his own arse and it was only the fact that he employed good people, like Frank Mansell, that he got away with it, but he couldn't stand anybody with a regional accent: if you had one of those you were out. He had got rid of Tarbuck like *that* – and now here he was on *Sunday Night at the London Palladium*!

I watched him – how could I not – and he was fine: Liverpudlian, young, modern, with a great cheeky charm about him – just right for that Beatle-mad time in October 1963. It was patently obvious that he had a style and persona, an identity. I knew then that in order to get anywhere at all in comedy I would need my own real comedy identity.

What I didn't realise at that moment was that it wouldn't take me very long. Totally by chance, a great new comedy idea was about to reveal itself.

SAMUEL TWEET was conjured into being in 1963 out of a kind of desperation: the need to gussy up an old joke which I hoped would help me survive in the clubs. I didn't realise how soon he would be taking on a life of his own, and that I would be making TV appearances and starring in pantos in character – or that I would still be associated with him today, more than fifty years later.

It all started with a recently purchased prop for my act, a second hand black homburg hat from a nearly new shop in South Shore, Blackpool, for two and sixpence (12½p). Yes, a homburg, not a bowler: they may look similar but a homburg has a deeper crown and can be pulled further down onto the head.

I used the hat to do an impersonation of Leonard Swindley, the pompous shopkeeper in *Coronation Street* played by a pre-*Dad's Army* Arthur Lowe. He employed the hapless Emily Nugent (later Bishop) and I did his catchphrase 'Good morning, Miss Nugent', in my act, so I already had the hat on stage.

I was playing a wider range of clubs by then. The Gaming Act of 1962 had led to an upsurge in smarter venues which provided entertainment along with blackjack and roulette. The Bailey circuit in the North East had about six very nice cabaret supper clubs, where punters could have a meal and a drink, plus entertainment and dancing to live music. They started out in South Shields, Newcastle and Darlington and then a couple of guys, who had a club in Stockton, opened a big club in Sheffield. Most of the huge cabaret clubs in Manchester had three or four acts on the bill and you would have to double the clubs, one early at 8.30pm and one late at 11pm.

These were a huge improvement on the old working men's clubs: they had rooms with a variety show on, so they really were a move on from the old theatres. No concert chairman on his podium, just a professional compere who was probably an act himself, and most Manchester clubs had session musicians from the NDO (Northern Dance Orchestra) in the backing band.

But while the surroundings were undoubtedly plusher, and it was nice to have such luxuries as a good sound system, most of these clubs were 1,500-2,000 seater ex-cinemas and all too often would be comedians' graveyards. The Southern Sporting Club in South Manchester, the College Club and the Northern Sporting Club were all very difficult to play. The comperes at these clubs, all well known to the regulars, ran the entertainment and could make or break you, but as long as you survived the first night on Sunday, you would last the week.

Having gained a modicum of experience by then, I was never actually paid off in any of these places, but came close several times. They were all gambling clubs and the casino subsidised the cabaret; in fact, to obtain a gambling and late opening licence, the clubs had to have live entertainment. The bigger audiences were usually confined to weekends, and Mondays to Thursdays were fairly quiet – just three or four tables occupied – but the entertainment went on just the same. Midweek there would be wrestling and a show where acts would have to work in a newly erected wrestling ring between bouts; they were usually stag nights and would have a few strippers on the bill as well as comedians and singers.

THE hat and the lisp came quite by chance while working at the humungous Northern Sporting Club, Bury New Road, Manchester in November 1963. Having survived the Sunday show I was travelling from Blackpool every evening to do this monstrosity of an entertainment venue doubling with the Southern Sporting club, both owned by Bill Benny, an ex-wrestler himself.

On the Tuesday night we had approximately thirty to forty people in the huge 1,500-seater room. Fortunately for me, they were sat quite close to the stage. I have always adapted my act to suit the surroundings and, on this night, decided to become more intimate with the audience and tell them all a joke each! I would usually ask for a subject, any subject, then twist it to suit all sorts of silly situations – all very ad lib, but the audiences seemed to like it.

It would go something like this: 'I will tell you a joke about any subject you care to mention and, if I fail, I will buy you a drink – this usually costs me a fortune so be gentle.' The punters would give me subjects which were obscure but this in itself was cause for an extra laugh. If, say, 'A monkey with no tail' came up, I would ad lib until something would come into my head:

> 'So this monkey had no tail, so he could not swing like the other monkeys in the zoo and lay in his bed all day until this man bought him and stuck on a false tail. He had had several tail trials, all to no avail – that is why there is always one monkey in every zoo with a red arse!'

That sort of thing, but much more elaborate. At the end of the session I would combine all the obscure subjects into one final pay-off joke. Ross Noble does something similar, only he rambles on until he eventually gets somewhere.

When it worked it was very successful, especially within smaller, more intimate surroundings. On this particular evening a woman shouted out: 'Tell us a joke about a budgie!', so I told my favourite old joke about the man buying a bird and complaining it did not talk as they were supposed to do.

Grabbing the handy homburg, I made the joke a two character act and situation with the complaining man in a hat pulled down to his ears, like Professor Sparks's son, and with a lisp: 'Budgie'th not thpoke, it hath not thpoken a word, parrotfathe!' so the character got laughs throughout and also had a good punchline: 'After six weeks, the budgie died but it thpoke. With its last dying breath, it said, "Hasn't the man sold you any birdtheed yet?"'

The joke lasted about four minutes and went very well, so I kept it in with the character. And that is exactly how it all started - that night at the Northern Sporting Club in Bury Road, Manchester.

The new clubs may have been intimidating to play, but if you scored in these places you scored big and could gain a following. Manchester sported its own nightclub magazine called *Nightlife* and the character started to get nice write-ups and comments.

The budgie joke was just a small part of my act in those days. I would do, say, forty, forty-five minutes, opening with a song, usually *I'm Gonna Sit Right Down and Write Myself a Letter* which had lots of 'S' words and was perfect for the lisp. I never imagined that the character, who I later called

Samuel Tweet, would become the monster it very quickly did. I also knew that, with the strict regimes on television and radio, I would not be able to use the lisp on air as it would be deemed an affliction, like a stammer.

My first radio broadcast was from the Hulme Hippodrome in February 1964. The producer, Geoff Lawrence, was a very experienced light entertainment producer. I was introduced to him by Johnny 'Goon' Tweed, a very well-liked and popular comedian round the Manchester club circuit doing – you guessed it – goon-type material. Johnny was instrumental in getting me this first radio broadcast and I am indebted to him. The programme, called *New Voices*, was introduced by Gay Byrne before he returned to Ireland for *The Late Late Show*. As expected, Geoff Lawrence told me I couldn't do the lisp, so I left the gag out.

Among our pals in Blackpool were Wally Piggott and Keith Ellam, ex-Redcoats who had formed a double act calling themselves Lester and Smart, a name I had come up with a couple of years earlier. They worked the circuit and the Windmill in London but just could not seem to get that all-important break. They eventually emigrated to Australia where they worked constantly until Keith sadly died in 2001. Wally died in 2014. I miss them both.

In the early part of 1964 Keith came with me in my car to a Monday stag night at the Carlisle Club in Eccles, on the north side of Manchester, famous for its cakes. It was one of those big gambling-type clubs and the Monday stag was very popular – mainly ruder types of jokes, although the 'F' word was never used – well, not then. I did my normal clean routine including the budgie joke with the hat.

On the way home Keith told me how effective the hat routine was and that I should concentrate a little more on it. This gave me pause for thought: at this stage I had not even looked at myself in a mirror. Comedians never rehearse, or rather our rehearsal is effectively in front of the audience, as it's impossible to time a joke without a reaction. After that, however, I made a point of looking at the character in a mirror and realised that he would probably make a good television 'head,' which is what television comedy is all about. Even in those days of smaller screens and fuzzier pictures it was easy to imagine those simple, cartoonlike features standing out, especially when framed by the homburg.

Without my friend Keith giving me this jog things might have turned out differently, but from that moment on I really concentrated hard on the character. And when the time came, a few months later, I took the first step on my way to fame with his comments ringing in my ears.

INCIDENTALLY, the adopted middle name of 'Parrotface' came about by accident. As any variety act will tell you, bill matter, the bit that goes underneath your name, can be very important: Max Miller was 'The Cheeky Chappie', and audiences immediately knew what they were getting. I needed something which would tell the reader that it was me, the man with the hat. People don't know names as a general rule – well, not when you first start. I figured putting 'Parrotface' underneath my name would do it; I was constantly calling the man in the pet shop 'Parrotface' because he sold me duff budgies.

This idea worked fine – until a printer decided to put the word across the middle of my name and it got squashed in the middle, making me 'Freddie Parrotface Davies' instead of:

Freddie Davies
Parrot Face

10: Opportunity Knocks

I HAD only ever wanted to be a comedian, and on August 1st, 1964, nervous yet excited, I was on the brink of fulfilling my ambition: I was about to give my very first television performance as a stand-up comic.

That TV spot was the turning point I had been dreaming of, though I didn't fully appreciate its significance at the time. Mostly I just felt grateful to be in work, as I had recently walked out of a summer season show, with no further dates in the book.

An article in *The Stage* had rather cheekily claimed I was leading my own troupe that summer but the show was in fact ... me. Well, not just me. I did have a pianist called Tom. I was engaged for an eight week season, with two shows a day, at the seaside town of Dunoon on the west coast of Scotland – me, that is, and a pianist called Tom.

I have battled against the odds in my time but this was the summer season from hell. The 'show' was staged at no little expense – none at all, in fact – in an open air theatre on the seafront in a small park by the harbour where the ferries docked. It was called *Fun with Freddie*, and I performed at 11am and 2pm, Monday to Saturday.

It was free to get in – if anybody did come in, or rather sit out. It rained a lot and the seats were always soaking wet. If a few lost souls – kids, dripping wet dogs and some well-known local drunks – did happen along to see what all the noise was about, they would be confronted at the end of the show by scruffy-looking council operatives from the bin department taking up a collection in tins. It's called 'bottling', and I hated it.

Scottish entrepreneur Archie McCulloch had made contact via Frank Mansell, who had suggested me. Archie, married to Kathy Kay of Billy Cotton Band fame, was installing discos – an innovation in 1964 – along the Clyde coast and, in order to get the necessary permission from the local authority, had promised he would provide entertainment during the day in Dunoon, namely me. And a pianist called Tom. He paid me £40 per week – oh, and at the weekend I also had to play rock drums for his son's group at his club in Millport.

I was supposed to do a kind of Redcoat-type audience participation show – when we had a few punters in, that is. I managed to scrape through on a wing and a prayer but it was generally quite horrendous and definitely not fun with – or for – Freddie. I was staying at a local B&B, getting smashed every night on the local golden malt brew, as you do; not a good idea so something had to give.

At 6am on Sunday 26th July, I was on the early morning ferry, a large rowing boat with an outboard motor, chugging out of Millport to Largs, where my second car, a Ford Anglia, was parked. Providing it started, I was driving to Chester to fulfil a BBC radio engagement but had already decided that the 'fun' had run its course. I was supposed to be back on stage in Dunoon on Monday morning but just could not face the prospect of returning to Scotland, however bonnie it might be.

I did the budgie joke this time, though I had to substitute another voice for the lisping Samuel to avoid allegations of mocking an affliction. I opted for a sort of generic old man comedy voice, all whistling sibilants – the sort of thing Kenneth Williams and Dick Emery used to do.

The broadcast I made that day has survived. The gag is well enough received but that voice makes the customer sound browbeaten from the off. The authentic Tweet tones, forever on the brink of apoplexy, suggest a battle between equals, which is funnier. Especially as the pet shop owner is the exasperated Samuel's exact opposite – unflappable throughout. Unlike the old dodderer I'd had to put in his place, you believe that Samuel just might be capable of actual violence if that suave shopkeeper keeps on stonewalling him.

I telephoned Archie McCulloch to tell him I wasnae goin' back. He wasnae well pleased and told me he would probably have to do the show himself – which, apparently, he did. With a pianist called Tom.

I CALLED my agent Mike Hughes to let him know that I was no longer the main attraction in Dunoon. Mike told me I was a stupid prat and there was no work in the book, but he would see what he could do – if anything.

Making the decision to quit the show after four weeks was a big deal to me. I had a wife and two children to support and we were still in our tiny rented flat in Wyre Grove, Blackpool; we needed every penny. My son Kent was just one and stepdaughter Jenny was ten. I fully expected to be out of work for some time but, by the end of the week, my life would indeed change forever.

Mike Hughes called me back within the hour to tell me the headline act had been paid off at the Cabaret Club in Liverpool, a venue notorious for killing comedians at birth. Liverpool audiences will let you live, but only if you talk a bit like them. A heckler I once had at the Cabaret Club was a bastard – not drunk, just stupid. I later learnt it wasn't personal: he heckled all the comics. Freddie Starr was reputed to have jumped off the stage at the Shakespeare Theatre Club, Liverpool and kicked him in the face.

This extraordinary last week of July 1964 began, that evening, at 11.30pm. My act went down well at the Cabaret Club on Monday night, so I knew I would be safe until Saturday. On Tuesday Mike called again to say he had booked me for Friday night at the Candlelight Club, Oldham, which I was to do before travelling to do my spot at Liverpool. Another spot came in for Saturday evening early, at a working men's club in Heywood just off the East Lancs Road, so the week was looking pretty good considering I had just left a summer season with no dates in the diary at all.

The next call from my agent, later that day, changed everything. Mike told me about a new TV talent show that had been on the air for two weeks. I had seen it on ITV in Scotland and it seemed amateurish from the outset, an old lady singing *Ave Maria* winning Week One and Bobby Bennett, a sixteen year old song and dance act from Blackpool, winning Week Two.

Mike suggested I meet the Producer, Peter Dulay, at ABC studios in Didsbury on Wednesday afternoon; ABC Television had the franchise for all network weekend ITV in those days. Son of variety magician Benson Dulay and an old pro himself, Peter said he would not wish to audition me cold and asked where he could see me work. I suggested he came to the Candlelight Club on Friday evening and he said he would be there at 9.30pm, after his rehearsals for this week's show. The shows were recorded, he told me, on Saturdays at 2.30pm and transmitted at 7.30pm the same evening to around (gulp!) 17 million viewers.

In trepidation, I arrived at the Candlelight Club, Oldham, on Friday 31st July at 9pm. Peter Dulay was already there with his PA, Julie, who had also been a Redcoat at Skegness – the skating instructor, in fact. It was good to see a familiar face before I braved the ice.

I did my act, which went well, to quite a small audience. As soon as I came off stage Peter was in the dressing room to say he loved the routine with the hat and the budgie joke, which lasted approximately four minutes. He wanted me in the studio at 9am the following morning for that week's show which, he told me, was called *Opportunity Knocks*. When I asked about the acts he had already rehearsed, he told me he was going to take someone out to put me in. Now there's show business working at its ruthless best!

No mention was made of the lisp possibly causing offence so I went on to use the proper Tweet voice on television. Ironically, that radio show on which I'd had to use a substitute voice wasn't broadcast till a month after *Opp Knocks*, doubtless confusing listeners who'd grown accustomed to my rasp.

I travelled to the Cabaret Club on cloud nine, performed in a daze and eventually arrived back home in Blackpool around 3am. I woke Jackie up to tell her I would sleep on the sofa for a couple of hours and get my music together, but I was actually much too excited to sleep.

Arriving at the studio tired yet still very excited, I handed my meagre band parts for the act to 'Uncle' Bob Sharples. I had ten-piece arrangements in those days and the band in the studio consisted of about 25-30 musicians, so they had to augment my meagre band arrangements to encompass the extra musicians. Somebody must have earned a few bob for that.

'Uncle' Bob, who was quite an arrogant man, said that my musical arrangements were like tatty music hall parts. I told him I was a tatty music hall comic! (Boom boom!)

Actually, I probably didn't say anything, as I was quite nervous – yet strangely confident at the same time. I knew it was make or break time – this was it, my chance to do it, to come up with the goods: Red Light Time, the thing I had wanted all my life. I knew what I was about to do was funny, tried and tested; I had done it hundreds of times in the past eight months, and six days ago I had even done the budgie joke on that BBC radio show which had covered my escape from Dunoon. Even better, now I didn't have to compromise with that doddery-old-man voice I'd used in the radio broadcast: I could do the act as intended, let fly with untamed Tweet.

Bobby Bennett performed first, having won from the previous week, and I went on about fourth with no sponsor. Presenter Hughie Green introduced me himself, saying that the person who was scheduled was unfortunately taken ill at the last moment and they had brought me in as a replacement – well, some of it was true. I had seen the poor unfortunate act, another comedian, in the canteen earlier but somehow could not bring myself to speak to him.

I opened with the song *I'm Gonna Sit Right Down and Write Myself a Letter,* followed with a gag with a baby's dummy, and I was up and running.

I'd actually forgotten all about the dummy gag, which I used to use in the clubs, until I was sent a clip of my TV appearance, the only fragment which has survived of all the hopefuls in that first series. It all came from my son who was very young then, because he used to cry and we would stick a dummy in his mouth, like you do with kids – 'MMMMM!' – which stopped him crying. I used to do it for him to make him laugh and that gave me an opening. Then I had a big one made with a bigger rim on it so the audience could see it from the stage. I totally dismissed the gag probably within half an hour of doing the show, but that's how I used to open my act: I would sing a bit of *I'm Gonna Sit Right Down ...*, start babbling uncontrollably then stick the dummy in my mouth to pacify myself.

I closed with the budgie joke. Here it is, just as I delivered it that night, although you'll have to imagine the hat going on and off:

> I must apologise, folks, that isn't really my real self, that's my other half. He's a zany, wild character, and the other week he walked into a pet shop. Something like this.
>
> 'I thay. Ah thay! Come 'ere, Parrotfathe!'
>
> The feller behind the counter said: 'Are you addressing me, Sir?'
>
> He said: 'Yeth, you, Parrotfathe! It'th not thpoke! It'th not twittered, and it'th not barked – nothing!'
>
> The feller behind the counter said: 'What hasn't, Sir?'
>
> He said: 'That budgie you thold me latht week. That budgerigar you thold me 'ath not opened itth beak. Parrotfathe.'
>
> The feller said: 'Well, what have you got the bird in?'
>
> 'What have I got the bird in? That little box with the 'oles in.'

'Well, that's the box I sold it you in. You see, you have to put the bird inside a cage. You must put the bird inside a cage.'

'A cage?! You never said anything about a cage when you flogged me the budgie. How much is it? [*Here I started babbling again and pacifying myself with the dummy*] How much are the cages?'

'Fifty bob.'

'Fifty bob?!! You must be joking! I'll have one.'

So he sold him a cage, fifty bob, he took it home, and he went back the following week.

'I thay! Come 'ere! It'th not thpoke – again. Two weekth on the trot, now. Now, fair dooth. Faaair dooth.'

'I can't understand it, Sir. Tell me, doesn't it twitter when it's on its little swing?'

'What thwing? What are you talking about a thwing, Parrotfathe? You never uttered a thwing. You didn't utter a thw – one word. How much ith a thwing?'

'A dollar.'

Ah, we won't go through all that again. Anyway ... he sold him a swing and he went back the following week.

'Ah thay! Thith hath gone too far. Parrotfathe. It'th not opened itth beak again!'

'Well, I can't understand it, it should have got used to you by now. Tell me, doesn't it go mad when it looks in its little mirror? You, know, the budgie's mirror.'

'How much are the mirrorth?'

'Seven and six.'

Well, to cut a long story short, he sold him the mirror, and he took it home, and he went back the

> following week. 'Ah thay now, come here. Four weekth ago, you had the audathity to thell me a budgerigar. Three weekth ago you thold me a cage. Two weekth ago you thold me a thwing. And a week ago you thold me a mirror. And thith morning the budgie died. It patthed away! And apart from that it'th dead.'
>
> 'Well, I'm very sorry to hear it, Sir. Tell me, did the budgie say anything before it died, did it speak at all?'
>
> 'Oh yeth. Fair dooth. It thpoke. It looked up at me from the bottom of the cage and it thaid: "Hasn't that feller sold you any birdseed yet?"'

My act seemed to go very well. Viewers had to send a postcard vote in – no telephone voting in those days – and the result was announced on the following Thursday. I was tipped to win, but didn't. I was beaten by Bobby Bennett, though he was beaten the following week by the musical muscle man Tony Holland, a bodybuilder who flexed his muscles to a tune called *Wheels*. He was a bit of a one trick pony but still went on to win for the eight remaining weeks of the series; I suspect he had a bit of a gay following even though he himself wasn't.

It did not seem to matter a jot that I failed to win – people saw me, probably around twenty million. With a grand total of two channels to choose from the power of the box was incredible then, more so than now.

In one sense not winning was a relief as I would, in truth, not have had a good enough follow up spot so quickly. It was always easier for singers as they did not have to find fresh comedy material. I arrived that evening at the Working Men's Club in Heywood to find it had suddenly filled up once the word had gone round that 'that man with the hat' was on – and in Liverpool, too, the fact that I had been on TV at all was a tremendous boost.

That one appearance on ABC Weekend television at 7.30pm on Saturday August 1st, 1964 is probably why I am still recognised today, over fifty years later.

AS it happens I was brought back for the last show in the series anyway, as the all-winners show could only muster Tony Holland, Bobby Bennett and the lady who'd sung *Ave Maria* on the first show. And that wasn't the end of my association with the programme, as I'd come back occasionally over the years and was there for Hughie's final show in 1978.

I got to know Hughie after I had done the programme. He wasn't a close friend, but he was always kind to me and about me. He was very supportive of all his protégées, in fact, and would plug our latest record or mention where we were appearing in panto.

Hughie Green was a child star who had gone on to become one of television's biggest names with quizzes like *Double Your Money* as well as *Opportunity Knocks*. I really only knew him as a sort of uncle figure, although they hated him in the studios as he was arrogant and tetchy, and they couldn't wait to get rid of him – after which the door effectively closed on his career. He owned the title so they still had to pay him when *Opportunity Knocks* returned nine years later with Bob Monkhouse as presenter, but when the original show finished I think that was the finish of Hughie, really.

In 1997 he was in the news when a journalist revealed at his funeral that Hughie had been the father of Paula Yates. There had been stories of his philandering, and I knew Yvonne Marsh had a very longstanding affair with him – he turned up to see her in Bristol in 1970, when I was starring with her in pantomime – but that truly came as surprise to myself and most of the others at his funeral. That scandal has overshadowed Hughie's achievements on television so I'd prefer to leave the last word on Hughie to Les Dawson, another of the guests on that final edition of *Opportunity Knocks* on March 20th 1978. He said, quite simply: 'You gave a lot of people a chance.'

MY exposure on *Opportunity Knocks* probably happened at just the right time for me. By the time I left Butlins in 1963, I'd already had a lot of experience and humiliations in clubs, died a death and become stronger. So when I was taken on by Mike Hughes and began to work clubs full time, I had a reasonable act. Not long after that, Samuel Tweet had been born and, prompted by Keith Ellam's advice, I'd had a few months to perfect him. Tweet had been a real boon, allowing me to get the attention of clubland audiences without being aggressive about it.

Over the previous six years, in between those educative stints at Butlins, I had been able to move along, working particularly in Manchester and Northern clubs, gradually developing a persona for the clubs; by the time of *Opportunity Knocks* I had a forty-five minute act. I was experienced enough to know exactly what I was doing on the programme, and I was only telling one joke, in effect, with a sort of an in and an out. I was new, young and, hopefully, not a bad comic – although when I look back on it, I don't think I was that great, but only with hindsight.

Other acts with whom I used to work the clubs, like Syd and Eddie (Little and Large), all seemed to get away round about the same time, doing better material and TV work ... our time had come, as they say. It was the era of the

Beatles and working class heroes, so having a regional accent didn't hurt – especially if you were a Scouser like Tarbuck.

Being part of Liverpool-based Mike Hughes' stable also helped. He was in at the start of the 'sixties when Liverpool was the buzz word: lots of groups came from there and the Cavern was a big deal, so by association we were 'of the time'. In fact, if you screw your eyes up when you look at the publicity shots of Johnny Ball, Mike Burton, Mike Newman and me staring moodily into the camera we could almost pass for some half-forgotten Merseybeat combo.

The newfound success that comics like me were enjoying was also about that burgeoning scene of smarter cabaret clubs in which we could learn our trade. Clubland may not have been my preferred environment but there was no doubt it had knocked off the rough edges and given me that second chance on television.

BUT I came down to earth with a bump quite quickly. Two weeks after *Opp Knocks,* Hal Monty, an ex-comedian and agent who had seen me on the show, got in touch. He thought I would be great for American servicemen and booked me for a two week stint at US military bases in and around France, with Paris as a base.

Hal Monty could not have been more wrong. On the first night I died a death. As the pianist/driver had got in quick to drown his own sorrows, I had to round off the evening as his chauffeur for the long journey home – left hand drive, right hand side of the road and a five hour drive back to Paris ... took my mind off things, I suppose.

Afterwards they wouldn't let me even try another base. I stayed in the hotel in Paris, sweltering in the summer heat for the duration of the two weeks – but I did get paid.

Things were better back in the UK, where my

newfound fame led to more TV shows, such as *Comedy Bandbox* and *The Good Old Days*, and several better cabaret bookings over the next few months.

But I still had the sense I was treading water. The real breakthrough came in November that year, at a showcase arranged by 'Whispering' Mike Hughes. Mike had cornered the market in comedians by now, and we were all signed to him: Mike Burton, Johnny Ball, Mike Newman, Johnny Hackett, Freddie Starr, Russ Abbott and Ken Goodwin to name but a few. He knew absolutely nothing about show business per se, having given up a very good job as a quantity surveyor to be a comedian's agent, but he sure knew how to negotiate a deal – and he knew that the comic on the bill was probably the most important commodity.

Most agents ran an annual talent showcase for prospective bookers but this one, held at a small private venue called Neptune Moorings, near Altrincham, was special. Mike had invited the top movers and shakers in the industry, along with several big London agents and impresarios. After the showcase I received enough offers of significant, prestige work to last me for the next three years solid.

This, for me, was the real turning point: work in theatres, the focus of my hopes and plans for so many years. At last I could really tell myself I was following in Jack's footsteps, stepping squarely onto those stages which I had studied so long from the wings.

And try saying *that* in character.

11: The Big Time

THIS new phase of my career began in March 1965 when I toured with singing group the Bachelors, who were chart toppers at the time. A successful harmonica trio from Dublin, the Bachelors had put a few songs in their act and become a middle of the road attraction appealing to young and old alike. Con, the lead singer, was a tall, handsome tenor; Dec, his younger brother, played guitar and harmonized while John Stokes played double bass and added to the harmonies, although it was really Con's voice which sold the act.

Their managers, Philip and Dorothy Solomon, came from Belfast and were active in setting up the pirate station Radio Caroline in the early 'sixties. They were well experienced in show business management, having managed Nina and Frederik in the late 'fifties. Philip Solomon set up Major Minor Records and I later recorded several albums of comedy, children's songs and quite a few singles for the label; these sold well but, with clever accounting, I never received a royalty payment. Dorothy was also to become my London agent.

I had first met the Bachelors when they were second top to Al Read at the Central Pier in Blackpool in 1962; they'd had their first big hit, *Charmaine*, then. But we really got to know each other during this tour, which played ten weeks of one-nighters and weeks in major towns like Bristol, Gloucester and Liverpool.

The show had an amazing line-up, with Paul Gadd (Gary Glitter) whose act was cut to one song as he was so bad. Second top was Susan Maughan (*Bobby's Girl*) and, as she could not do Sundays, Dorothy Squires stepped into the show, closing the first half. The show had two orchestras: one in the pit and fourteen musicians on stage for the Bachelors and the rest of the bill. There were also ten dancers, Mike Preston, a young pop singer, Hal Roach, a comedy magician from Dublin, and brother and sister vocal act Elaine and Derek. Only sixteen then, Derek Thompson later found fame as Charlie Fairhead in the BBC hospital soap *Casualty*.

All the theatres were in the region of 1,500 to 2,000 seaters and generally we played two houses, 6.15pm and 8.30pm. But thanks to my Butlins experience I didn't have a problem at all, working those big theatres and cinemas. I felt I was right for it as I had quite a strong act by then. In this show, as in later summer seasons, I just picked the best fifteen minutes from the act: I'd open with a bit of hat stuff, take it off, do a lot of other types of gags, and then finish with the Samuel Tweet thing. (Later, however, when I was offered panto, I never used to do an act, if I could help it; I would just play the character and do stuff within the panto.)

I appeared just before the Bachelors, which was to become the norm for about ten consecutive seasons. I became known as 'the Bachelors' comic' – although, offstage, I could also be their fall guy if I didn't have my wits about me. The boys had a very dry but somewhat juvenile sense of humour and would contrive to wind me up with complex deceptions – which amused them, at least, no end.

One was the case of 'Ivor Silverstone', a so-called agent of Shirley Bassey. They informed me that he wanted me to tour with her and go into the West End. They kept up the story for weeks. Eventually this man turned up in their dressing room and I was introduced to him. He was smartly dressed and I really thought he was genuine ... until he burst out laughing and said he couldn't keep it up! All part of showbiz, folks. My real moment of disillusion with the group would come some years later, in the wake of a notorious court case ... but more of that anon.

The Bachelors were hot in 1965 and the tour opened in Gloucester at the ABC cinema and ran for six nights with twelve sell-out shows. Its final week, at the Odeon cinema in Liverpool, which seated 2,500, followed the same pattern – in everything, that is, apart from the sell-out bit.

I will never forget first house on the Wednesday evening. In the middle of my spot an emergency exit door burst open near the stage, two cheeky Liverpudlian kids appeared, saw the stage all lit up and shouted: 'Fuck off!' before quickly exiting back through the doors. What made the incident more memorable was that the words echoed all round the virtually empty auditorium: 'Fuck off! – Fuck off! – *Fuckoffofofofoffff*!' The pit band broke into hysterics and I replied with the classic line, 'Sorry, I don't do requests.'

That apart, it was a wonderful time. Playing those big theatres with the Bachelors' show was just what I had needed and had been building up to all my life: I had honed my act to be just right and, with my few appearances on television up to then, was just starting to become known. The tour gave me the opportunity to really get my act together, putting all the valuable experience I had gained up until then into practice: I really felt at home on these huge stages and never regretted it for one moment.

SUMMER season at Great Yarmouth followed the tour; I was to be with the Bachelors for this show at the ABC this year, and many more to come. Variety hadn't died with the theatre closures of the 'fifties, it had just relocated: summer seasons were, in effect, fixed variety bills which lasted for sixteen weeks instead of one and in the 'sixties they nearly all featured big names at the top of the bill; Matt Monro was at the Wellington Pier with Mike and Bernie Winters and Jimmy Tarbuck on the same bill, while Norman Vaughan had a big variety bill at the Britannia Pier with Joe Brown.

I was scheduled to do a *Blackpool Night Out* TV show but Mike and Bernie Winters put a stop to my appearing as they thought I detracted from Bernie's hat act. In fact my hat joke was nothing like Bernie's and our characters were completely different, his persona being very much that of a silly-billy character, a bit daft, whereas Samuel Tweet was a more pompous, obnoxious twit. But comics are a jealous breed and we hate to think anyone is funnier or in competition.

Our feud was short lived, however, and we became friends until Bernie died in the early 'nineties. Later I employed and directed him in a panto and a summer show. I knew the boys well, and they were good fun till they split up; for a while Lionel Blair worked as Bernie's feed, and did a good job of it, but it could not last. Bernie later found a new partner, of sorts, in a St Bernard dog called Schnorbitz. Mike moved to Florida, where he owned a nightclub and was also a boxing promoter; he died in 2013.

AFTER the summer season of 1965, the next show was *The Birthday Show* at the huge Coventry Theatre for Sam Newsome, a rare solo theatre owner who eventually went broke trying to keep the venue open. In those days they would produce all their own shows and this was yet another great bill with three comics on the show: Derek Dene, Mike Yarwood and me.

Mike Yarwood is no longer in the business after succumbing to some kind of a nervous condition which prevents him performing. In his early days, however, he was the best mimic around and Harold Wilson was, of course, his finest impression, although he could do anybody. Unfortunately Mike was a very nervous person even in those days, and had a rather unfortunate manner, stopping rehearsals to declare that he was not going to be subservient to people whom he considered lower than him on the bill.

Finale walkdowns, or 'Who's Best', as Eric and Ernie called them, are notorious for bringing out the worst in artists who think they deserve a better position/dressing room/ billing etc, and Mike always insisted on his position, even though it is actually the producer/director who has the final say. Any other grievances after that should be sorted by the artist's agent.

The pantomime season of Christmas 1965/66 was also with the Bachelors and Mike Yarwood, at the Bristol Hippodrome; Mike and I were due to play the brothers in *Puss in Boots* originally played by Mike and Bernie Winters at the London Palladium. Mr Yarwood insisted he would not walk down with me at the finale, even though we had been playing a double act throughout the show. He wanted me to walk down first but I was equally adamant and told him in no uncertain terms that if he didn't have the grace to walk down with me then he certainly wouldn't be walking down after me.

It was eventually resolved by us taking turns walking down last: him one week, me the next. Stupid, I know. The result was a rift which has never really healed. We never spoke socially, only on stage, which was a shame as I thought he was a great talent and we should have been good pals.

AFTER the pantomime season I went back to working the big cabaret clubs around the UK, usually topping the bill. I enjoyed this period as I was in an environment I understood by now. Yes, I preferred the theatres but they were not available fifty-two weeks a year. By the mid 'sixties, variety was no longer viable and had moved into the big cabaret clubs; nowadays you will find it on cruise ships.

TV fame undoubtedly helped my act. Every audience is different but once you become successful the people come in to see you, so there's less chance of you dying. You'd have to be very poor or very pissed not to make it work, because they're coming in, they've seen you on the telly and you feel the excitement. Even before *Opportunity Knocks*, the Samuel Tweet character had started to draw club audiences, but now there was no longer an uphill battle to win them over.

Well, most of the time, anyway. I do remember dying on my arse once in a club in Sunderland when I was quite well known. It was a Whit Monday and they'd put a special afternoon show on, starring yours truly. I walked on … to silence. For twenty-five minutes. Embarrassing silence. Nothing I said got through to them at all; they just sat – staring at me. It was a weird feeling. It wasn't even like they were talking and I'd lost them: there was just no reaction. In the end I said something like, 'I'm obviously not entertaining you so I'd better go.'

I came off and the concert secretary said to me: 'That didn't go very well, did it?' So I said: 'No, it didn't, and I didn't quite know how to deal with it – it happens so rarely these days that I wasn't prepared for it: I usually go out and kill 'em stone dead.'

When I was hit with that wall of silence and they just stared at me on that first gag, I'd gone into the second, thinking: 'this always gets a reaction' – you know, WALLOP! – I'd put the hat on and – nothing. Nothing worked at all. All I could tell him was that it was just so rare. I didn't take the money.

Dying a death is every comedian's nightmare. It knocks your confidence, there's no doubt about it: you have to move on to the next one, like getting back on a horse again after a fall. It happens to every comedian at some time or other, and it can be quite hard to work out just what it is that's going wrong. Several factors are involved – quite apart from the performer's innate ability.

To perform as a stand-up comedian certain things have to be in place. The audience has to be facing the stage – or cajoled into doing so in a club environment – they have to listen to what is being said, be able to see clearly and hear distinctly, with the sound being loud enough to enable the performer to be 'in command'.

Established stars, name acts and those who think they are, can demand these elements to be put in place before they perform, thereby lessening the possibility of not getting the attention required. With comedy, the performing situation is even more critical because the audience are always wary of the newcomer: they have not yet gained confidence in knowing that this comedian is going to make them laugh, so the comic has to grab the audience immediately.

Sometimes in a club, you have no choice but to

bludgeon the audience, but I prefer to think in terms of winning them over, especially in theatres. Many of you will have been in a theatre audience when the artist will try and get the audience to talk to him. I think audiences hate this, being forced to say 'hello' when they are sitting anonymously in their darkened seats. I always felt this was an embarrassment and tried not to do it. (Pantomime, where audiences usually expect to join in, is the only exception I'll admit to this rule.)

I suppose fame – knowing that people have come especially to see you – makes you a little more complacent as a performer. But then a comic has to appear confident: you have to give the audience that confidence. Once you show it's gone, you – are – lost. You cannot get it back. At least, it's very hard to regain, once you've lost it.

It's also hard to make running repairs once you've 'lost them' and started going down badly. That clever line which might save the situation usually doesn't come to mind quickly enough. When you're getting no reaction you don't have any thinking time, because you have to keep talking; if it's not working there are no gaps, and your timing goes completely.

You do have a bit of breathing space before the audience are aware of it. An audience doesn't know that you're dying a death – only you know it, because only you know where the laughs usually come. So, up to a certain point in your act, you can actually bluff them into thinking that it hasn't started yet.

It might seem odd to be talking at such length about 'dying' in a chapter devoted to my growing success, but that gig in Sunderland really stuck in my mind: a reminder of mortality, I suppose. TV doesn't make you invulnerable.

Incidentally, I know several comics who work on the

premise that they're dying a death. They will do one gag and then say: 'Oh, it's going to be like that tonight, is it? D'you know, I never get laughs.' Only trouble with that is, if they do get laughs right away it kills the idea, so all the gags coming later, like: 'I got more laughs at my mother's graveside', don't actually make sense.

When I asked one particular comic why he was still working as if he was dying on his arse all the time he admitted that he didn't know: 'It's just become my act now.' Weird. I suppose it could be a self-fulfilling prophecy because, if you keep using gags which no longer fit, then sooner or later your act *will* die ...

I APPEARED at the ABC Blackpool in the big summer season show of 1966 starring – you guessed it – the Bachelors. The show also starred Cilla Black, the Rockin' Berries, Canadian comedian Frank Berry and Ray Fell, another very slick Liverpool comic. Ray went to work in Las Vegas in the mid 'seventies and never returned.

The Blackpool show was directed by Albert J Knight and produced by Leslie Grade. It was a lavish, classy production by anyone's standards, the sort of show where if you shone, it would be noticed in London. All the big guns came to see the shows in Blackpool and I really felt I was getting somewhere.

I was living at home in Blackpool in our first house, a new dormer bungalow bought for £2,275 a year earlier, on the strength of my upcoming contracts. I had a Nat West mortgage and the bank manager (those were the days when banks had managers) actually came out to see the proposed plot where the house was to be built. It all felt a long way from those two shabby rooms in Salford, although I didn't really reflect much on my newfound wealth; I just accepted it for what it was. I was moving on, never thinking it was going to end; I felt as if I was becoming part of the establishment.

I don't know about genius being 99 per cent perspiration, but during that season I developed a new routine which undoubtedly benefited from the opening of the Davies pores. Every Monday afternoon most of the Blackpool showbiz fraternity would congregate at the Derby Baths Sauna and Turkish Baths which, after a sweaty session, resulted in a sort of washdown by the resident attendants. Nothing gay – in fact, quite the opposite. I found the relaxing atmosphere conducive to concentrating on new material for the act, and it was here I came up with a comedy routine about the latest blockbuster film *The Sound of Music*. Just about everyone had already been to see it more than once and I was no exception. The routine was a twist on an old joke but with *The Sound of Music* it became, in effect, something new.

With a restricted time on stage, adding new material is always risky, so when I arrived at the theatre that Monday evening before the first show, I tried out my idea on Ray Fell who was in the next dressing room to me. He said to me: 'If you don't do it, I will.' That was it! I figured that if I put it close to the start of my act I could still recover if it failed.

It was first house Monday, 6.15pm, with not one empty seat and a great holiday audience. As I went nervously into the routine the place went wild, and I knew I was onto a winner. Each line got such a tremendous reaction right up until the end that I actually had difficulty following it with my usual act. By the time I came off stage most of the company had come down to the wings to see what was happening as they had heard the huge reaction from their dressing rooms. I had no option but to close the act with this routine from then on, which gave me a very strong finish.

It went like this:

> I have just been to see *The Sound of Music*, it has been on at [*I'd name the local cinema*] for six months, it's been on so long now it has affected all the staff working at the cinema. I went to buy a seat and the girl behind the pay box gave me my ticket and sang [*Climb every Mountain*]: 'Climb up the staircase, until you meet, a woman who tears your ticket and shows you to your seat.' I went up the staircase and the lady at the door took my ticket and sang [*Sixteen Going On Seventeen*]: 'I am forty-nine going on fifty'. During the interval, all the usherettes came out singing [*Favourite Things*]: 'Ice cream and lollies and peanuts with salt on.' I thought: 'This is becoming a madhouse!' so I went to find the manager. I said: 'What is the matter with your staff?' and he sang [*Edelweiss*]: 'They're Idle-swines, Idle-swines, and they're leaving on Friday.' Outside I spotted a policeman – I said: 'You need to go in there – they have all gone crackers!' and he sang [*Maria*]: 'How would you like to get in the Black Maria?'

It was planned to be used on a *Blackpool Night Out* in mid-July, not compered by Mike and Bernie Winters this time but Tony Hancock, broadcast from the ABC Theatre where I was also appearing nightly. Unfortunately, I was barred from using the routine as it was parodying the songs and they couldn't get clearance from the music publishers; I don't think they were bothered about my doing it on stage but not on national television.

I can't grumble, as what I did on TV went well anyway. I did some material from my current act because I had actually taken some stuff out in order to put *The Sound of*

Music in. So it sort of worked because it gave me a new slant with the act.

I recently got the chance, some forty-five years on, to watch my performance. I'd forgotten how the audience used to laugh at the character all the time, as opposed to the gag: the gag was a bonus but Samuel Tweet got laughs all the way through; I'd forgotten just how strong it was at the time. The basis, as mentioned earlier, was that he was a very good television 'head': the camera could come up close and I could make full play of the eyes. Quite often I would work with two cameras, in fact, facing one without the hat, then turning to another with it, making it like a double act. But this wasn't wise for live transmissions: they had to cut very quickly and, if they got the cutting wrong, it was terribly screwed up.

It's interesting to watch Tony Hancock's performance from this distance. One thing Hancock wasn't was Blackpool; he could never have done a summer season there. They didn't understand him, even though he was getting sympathetic laughter. I remember him doing it and really hating it: 'Bloody people up North!' – they just weren't him. I was working on my home ground so I had that confidence behind me as well: I was working on the same stage I was working on every night.

The downside to my off-air success with *The Sound of Music* was that so many comics knocked the routine off. So-called good mates and big stars stole the routine in one form or another. One scriptwriter, who shall remain nameless, had it in his portfolio of scripts so people could pay *him* for the use of it.

In those days very few comedians wrote their own material, whereas nowadays it is the norm. Jokes would be bandied around and twisted to be used by anyone who could make them work. Luckily, my budgie joke with the hat was difficult to steal without it looking like an impersonation of me – and believe me, many tried.

In fact, my newfound fame was due, in large part, to my impersonators. Even when I wasn't on the television – I was. It was easy to mimic, a black hat and a lisp; schoolkids throughout the nation could splutter like 'Parrotface'. I would get hundreds of letters a week from a cross-section of the public and formed the Parrotface Fan Club, run by an old Butlins friend I had known since her childhood, Dorothy Elmore.

The Elmores had been at Butlins during my very first season; Dorothy and her brother Richard helped me with the Tombola and had followed my career ever since. I became friends with the family and used to stay with them in Kettering when I was on tour. I was very touched recently when Dorothy and Richard turned up to see me perform at the Ashcroft, Croydon, fifty-five years on from Skegness.

My fame was so far advanced by 1966 that I was even approached to do a television commercial. Oddly enough, it wasn't for birdseed; that came later. No, this was for the Blackburn-based Thwaites Brewery and a milk stout they were trying to put on the map. I played two parts: the barman and the punter with hat and catchphrase: 'THWAITES THTOUT – THMASHING!'

The television onslaught was accompanied by a huge poster campaign with my head on it all over Lancashire: everywhere you looked, yet another beaming Samuel Tweet would be proffering a pint of this dubious nectar. I had an unlimited supply of Thwaites Stout in my dressing room, but nobody would drink the stuff.

The commercial was written, directed and conceived by fellow Salfordian Ken Bowden, who also became a friend and mentor. A former RAF pilot, Ken had formed the largest advertising agency outside London – Bowden, Dyble and Hayes – in 1964, and was responsible for some very big accounts including Solvite the wallpaper adhesive and the Cyril Lord carpet ads ('This is luxury you can afford...'). He celebrated another Cyril in the song *Nice one Cyril,* which began life as an advertising jingle for Wonderloaf but became a novelty hit in 1972 when reworked as an anthem to Spurs player Cyril Knowles.

Ken was also an accomplished theatre technician who gave me lots of invaluable advice over the years regarding stage and theatre presentation, the art of standing still on stage and directing the attention onto oneself. He was very fond of a routine I used to do in the clubs around the word 'knickers', and would bring parties of advertising executives to hear it. A very Lancashire sort of routine, it started like this:

> Knickers are sold by Marks and Spencers and it's a normal, everyday word. Depending on how you say it. Because you could say [*here I'd put on a deep voice*] 'KNICKERS' and then it becomes very rude.

And then I'd go through all the bloomers, briefs, panties and bikinis and the whole rigmarole of them:

> And in Lancashire they call them 'kecks', so from being a sexy word they become unsexy, because to be asked to 'get yer kecks off' is not terribly sexy.

I can't remember it all now, but Ken used to dine out on it and when I saw him not long before he died, he kept begging me: 'Do us the knickers routine! Do us the knickers routine!' I had to say: 'I can't remember it, Ken.' He sadly passed away in 2007 and I miss him.

I WAS offered a pantomime in Coventry for the 1966/67 season. As this was away from the Bachelors stable, I grabbed the opportunity and appeared in *The Pied Piper* with Frankie Vaughan and Norman Vaughan (no relation). Norman had found fame as the compere on *Sunday night at the London Palladium* in 1962, and Frankie had been one of our biggest stars since the early 'fifties. Frankie played the Pied Piper and giggled his way through the show, kicking half the chorus to death (joke). He was one of the nicest men in show business, also one of the kindest. One small gesture was characteristic: on the opening night of *The Pied Piper* I had had a particularly good reception and Frank rang Jackie at home to tell her.

It was a great season, during which I took Frank to see a matinee performance of *The Sound of Music* in Birmingham; he sobbed his way through it like we all did. I worked with Frank on many occasions and he always gave one hundred per cent. The last time I saw him was just before he died in 1997, when he came to see a show I was in at the Wimbledon Theatre; he had just turned seventy. I loved him and miss him.

Probably because I'd had such a good press in Coventry, Sam Newsome offered me the starring role of the Pied Piper for the following season at the Alhambra Theatre, Bradford. Before this, however, there were cabaret and TV shows, including Tom Jones and Cilla Black, as well as a summer season.

As it was the last show of Cilla's series they had a party at an Italian restaurant called San Lorenzo in Beauchamp Place, Knightsbridge, where I met Paul McCartney, who was with Jane Asher at the time. Paul told me he often sang *Yesterday* with a lisp in rehearsal. I was sat next to Frankie Howerd, a big friend of Cilla's, but all he could talk about were his tax problems.

I met Frank several times over the years and always found him a rather morose sort of character. A few years later he was starring in a panto in Chichester when the supremo called to ask if I would stand by for him as he had a very bad leg and there was the possibility he could be off. 'But whatever you do, don't tell him that you're doing it.'

I went down to see it once and he said to me, 'What you doin' 'ere?'

'I've just come to see you, Frank.'

'*Why*?'

He never got so bad that he had to be off, so I took the weekly money, which was quite good, to not do it. It was *Jack and the Beanstalk* and he was playing Simple Simon; he was alright, the same as usual, though I don't think he was ever one of the great panto performers.

The last time I saw him was in Great Portland Street, waiting for his friend Dennis. He was always very pleasant, but it was a case of comics that pass in the night, really. There was never any kind of power play, but we were nothing alike, anyway, so we were never in competition.

Odd though it sounds, given his fame – and he was a huge radio star when I was growing up – he didn't entirely escape that North-South divide I mentioned earlier. I saw him struggle a couple of times in Northern working men's clubs in the late 'sixties – they didn't quite get him. I went over to see him at a club called the Garrick, in Leigh, and he just about got away with it, but he was still very much what you'd call a Southern comic: more sophisticated.

THE 1967 summer season was at the Futurist Theatre in Scarborough and, once again, played to packed houses. I was back with the Bachelors, the Kaye Sisters, my old pal Mike Newman and Mike Burton, a great Liverpudlian one-liner comic who I had employed on my staff at Butlins Metropole in 1962.

I was really attacking on all fronts at this time, making more appearances on television, including several on *The Des O'Connor Show* plus *The Good Old Days* and *Comedy Bandbox*, not to mention my regular comic strip in *Buster* and the novelty records I'd recorded for Major Minor Records which were being played by the hour on Radio Caroline and other pirate radio stations owned by Philip Solomon.

And if all this mid 'sixties media saturation drove you to drink, well, you only had to look up at the nearest billboard to see that I had that covered too – in the Lancashire region, anyway.

12: Panto Star

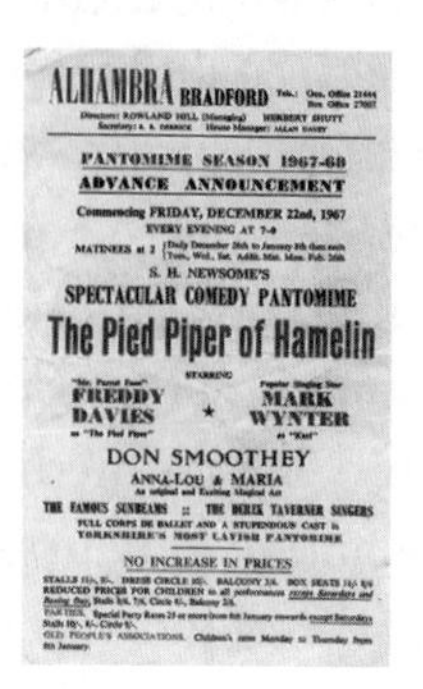

FOR all this success, there was still one hill left to climb. In the winter of 1967 my first starring role in pantomime was looming at the Alhambra, Bradford, one of Britain's premier pantomime theatres since the 1920s; it still is. I even felt a kind of family connection with the theatre as HT Butler, Jack's uncle Harry, had worked with Francis Laidler there, stage managing pantos which were said to be the most spectacular in Britain, before launching into production for himself.

Panto is often praised these days for its ability to bring children into the theatre for the first time. True, though that doesn't necessarily mean they'll keep coming back. I think panto's main appeal for a performer is that it's a rare chance to play to a real family audience: you know you're going to get Mum, Dad, kids and grandparents there, so you have to be aware of that and work to that order. They all know the story, so your challenge is to make the bits in between interesting, exciting and comedic for everyone.

When you do that, and a panto is going well, it feels as though theatre suddenly matters again. It can never be the same as in the 'forties and 'fifties when people regularly went, of course, and it clearly doesn't matter as much as it used to, because the runs are now a lot shorter. In the 'sixties we used to start later, around the 22nd of December, and go into March, whereas nowadays you're lucky if you get five or six weeks out of it, usually closing at the beginning of January.

The Bradford panto normally ran for fourteen weeks. I was very happy to be working with Mark Wynter, a good looking young pop singer who had had some success with recording, and we made a great team – so much so that the show was reproduced the following year at the Theatre Royal, Nottingham with equal success.

The experience of appearing in pantomime is second to none; it brings together the best of variety performers and members of the acting profession. Comedy routines are handed down through the years and I developed several routines which I featured only in panto.

In Bradford, I played the title role as the Pied Piper which, I have to say, suited me a lot more than it did Frankie Vaughan. I made a character of the Piper and, while it was a serious role, I was able to have great fun with the juveniles who were part of the show. Bradford always called their juveniles 'The Famous Sunbeams', a throwback to the lavish Francis Laidler pantomimes of the 'twenties and 'thirties; in fact there is a 1924 review in *The Stage* which gives Jack's uncle particular credit for coaching 'Laidler's Little Sunbeams.'

The 1960s juveniles came from a local dancing school and were very well disciplined. If you remember the story, the Pied Piper lured the children away from Hamelin – I doubt whether you would be allowed to stage the show nowadays – but one boy who was crippled was left behind.

He was played in our production by a young actor called Dominic Jephcote, who went on to a very good acting career which I have admired through the years; I was able to remind him of his first professional role when I bumped into him forty-five years later, at the Groucho club in London.

Living in Blackpool, I could get home every weekend but stayed in a hotel during the week. Mark Wynter and I obtained a show business deal at the Frederick Hotel in Bradford and they kindly afforded me a suite, which led to many late night parties with friends who would pop in to see me during the run. Mark was always very professional, both on and off stage, and we struck up a warm friendship which lasts to this day. He is now a very accomplished actor and tours the UK in fine plays and musicals.

That panto season at Bradford was a very happy experience for me. Looking back, I can see it's because I was exactly where I wanted to be for the first time: top of the bill in that most delightful of entertainments, the culmination of my hopes and dreams since I first set foot on stage in one of Jack Magnall's long-ago Sunday School pantos.

But I didn't think about it like that at the time. My career had been moving along and I accepted this latest development as part of the picture, though there's no doubt I was excited about doing it, because you are regarded differently when you're topping the bill. That recent Bachelors show may have been a prestigious production but I was only part of the package; Bradford was the proof that I was indeed a draw.

My abiding memory is of the absolute roar of welcome I would receive at every performance; it's just the best feeling for any performer, and made it an easy ride – even if that meant it was also easy to be a little undisciplined. I do believe all performers should have an in-built warning system not to take advantage of their very important and privileged position in front of the public; I am always surprised and annoyed to see this privilege so often abused.

That said, I have to admit I did take occasional liberties with the *Pied Piper* script, but I felt the end justified the means as the director would approach me with furrowed brow and say: 'Freddie, Freddie, Freddie, that was naughty – *but for God's sake leave it in*!'

I have several favourite moments, purely ad lib at the time. During the scene in which the Pied Piper takes the children away from Hamelin they would ask me where we were going. I had to say: 'To a land where there are no worries, no taxes, no school, children are free to enjoy themselves all day long and live in happiness.' 'Where's that, Mr Piper?' one of the kids would ask, and I was scripted to say: 'A magical land far, far away – to the Hall of the Mountain King.' But on one occasion when the innocent child posed his question, I could not resist replying: 'Heckmondwike.' The laugh was worth it and I did do the correct line next.

I HAD occasion to cause a corpse during the matinee of a pantomime in Torquay in 1972. I was playing Jack in *Jack and the Beanstalk*, waiting in the wings to go on. The Princess was played by a stunning dancer, singer and actress, Mary Dunne, who later formed and choreographed the international vocal and dance group Wall Street Crash. She was in the throes of being captured by the Giant onstage and her line was: 'Oh Jack, where are you? I need you to come and rescue me!' From the wings I said, just loud enough for her to hear: 'I'm just here, love.' At which she started to laugh uncontrollably – so much so that she had to leave the stage in hysterics.

The director, Robert Marlowe, who was also playing 'Fleshcreep', the Giant's henchman, stormed to my dressing room between the shows and proceeded to tell me off in his very camp manner for causing the corpse. This was extremely hard to take seriously as he still had his full green, sequined makeup on and I started to laugh – which didn't help matters.

Many performers and actors try to make their fellow actors laugh and I am very bad at corpsing. But one such occasion really did leave me helpless on the stage. It was during my Comedy Band routine when I was fortunate to have the Dallas Boys as the band members, but with my road manager Percy as the 'White Face Scotsman.'

The routine was a front cloth sketch. The conductor, playing the straight man or feed, would introduce the item as the 'Village Band' and would announce 'the Raistrick and Brighouse Wind and Pipe Ensemble, augmented by the drummers from the First and Last King's Own Highland Regiment. And here they are – the Pig and Trumpet Town Orchestra!'

At this, five bedraggled looking musicians would march on to the Laurel and Hardy theme from stage left with various instruments, trumpet, sax, etc, followed slowly by a limping Scotsman in full kilt and regalia, sporran etc, with a huge, bandaged, gouty left foot. He also carried a sousaphone and had a white face and tam, and would stand at the end on the right of this line-up of favour facing the stage.

The conductor would then count the band and say, 'Where's the drummer?' The pit band would play *The St Louis Blues* and the comedy band members would look offstage left, a spotlight would hit stage left entrance, and I would enter stage right with a big Salvation Army drum wearing a loincloth, green tights, size 12 hobnailed boots and a busby – don't ask! I would then take my place next to the Scotsman, to whom I'd sing: 'The minute you walked in the joint' – *Bang! Bang!* on the drum, then I'd look at the big gouty foot

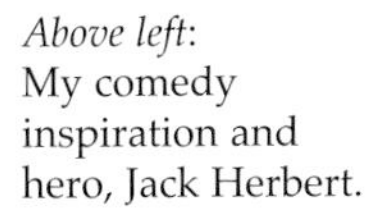

Above left:
My comedy inspiration and hero, Jack Herbert.

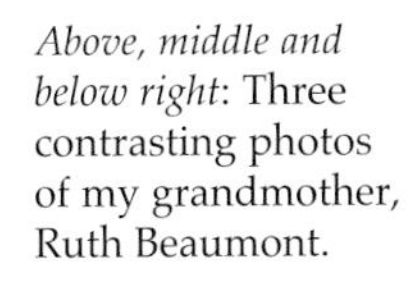

Above, middle and below right: Three contrasting photos of my grandmother, Ruth Beaumont.

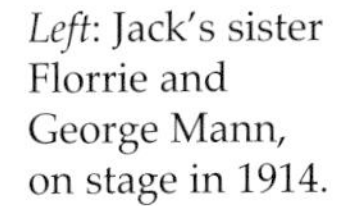

Left: Jack's sister Florrie and George Mann, on stage in 1914.

Left: John Street School, 1945. I am doing my first yoga class, front row, third from left, aged seven.

Above: My first stage appearance in pantomime at the Pendleton Congregational Church, Broad Street, Salford, 1950. Can you spot me? No! Not the Goose!
Below: My first name-check in a panto programme.

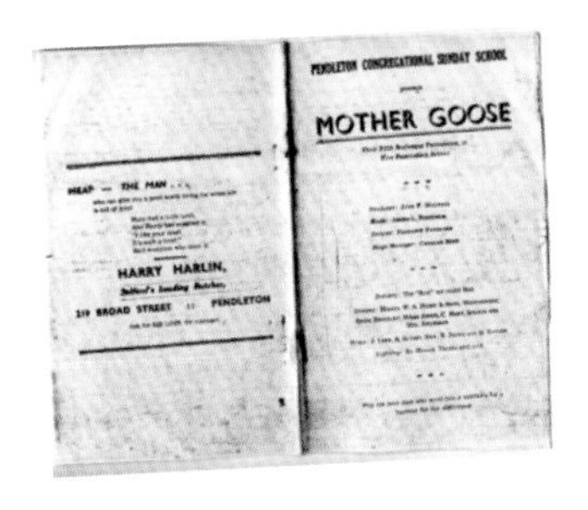

HEAP — THE MAN . . .

HARRY HARLIN,

219 BROAD STREET :: PENDLETON

PENDLETON CONGREGATIONAL SUNDAY SCHOOL

MOTHER GOOSE

Right: An Army course for the purposes of skiving.
Below: 'B' Company, 26 Platoon, 181 Intake, 1956. Yours truly: middle row, second from right.

Above: With ex-Butlins colleagues Mike Burton, Mike Newman, our agent Mike Hughes and Johnny Ball. Notice who has the smile?

Below: Standing - Dave Nicholas, Kay Hamilton, myself, Lorna the stunner. Seated - Roger Milner, Wally Piggott, Keith Ellam, Mike Burton, Mike Newman, unknown.

Above: Who said I had a big nose? Life as a Redcoat, Skegness, 1958.

Above: My illustrious entertainment staff, pictured at the Metropole in 1962.

Above: My son Kent steals my act.
Right: In at the deep end.
Two fellow Redcoats, undressed ...
and me with my flies open!

Above: Me and a Glamorous Granny. *Right*: Dave Allen enjoying his day off.
Below: The 1958 'ents' staff at Butlins, Skegness. Frank Mansell is centre, with me and Dave O'Mahony (Allen) circled. Don't ask me to name the others!

Right: Introducing my bird to a child with Sooty and his mentor, Harry Corbett.

Below: The last of the original *Opportunity Knocks* shows with Hughie Green. How many star names can you spot, all discovered on the programme?

NEWS 21

howbiz genius who let Opportunity Knock for thousands

iewers as his wise-guy grin and, right, the galaxy of comedians, singers and cabaret acts he discovered on his talent show

HE was the man who

Y NICOLA DAVIDSON

His son Christopher, who lled his wedding to be at s bedside at the Royal Hospital, in

way into the office of the BBC's head of light entertainment and demanded an audition. He was given his own radio series.

In 1949 he was asked to

Left: Jackie - my first wife - with daughter Jenny and son Kent.

Right: An early publicity picture when I still had my own teeth.

Left: I found him abandoned in a huge nest. *Above and below*: Bachelors shows at the Victoria Palace in 1969 and Coventry, 1965

Above left: With my old mate Jimmy Tarbuck.

Left: Visiting the police, when it was okay without a warrant! The Bachelors and Cilla Black at Blackpool in 1966

Above: A Royal Command and Water Rats function at the Lakeside Country Club. 'King Rat' Cyril Dowler introduces HRH Princess Anne - now The Princess Royal - to Arthur Askey, myself, Hughie Green and Russell Harty.

Above left: Mike Yarwood and me being pushy with a pile of coins for charity.
Above right: On the Isle of Wight at another charity event with Earl Mountbatten. 'Oh, you're the chap what spits!'

Above: The launching of Smirnoff Vodka, 1962. Roger Milner, myself, Freddie Frinton (who never drank) and Tony Leadley hit the bottle.

Below: My very first publicity shot before Samuel Tweet was born.

Above: Anita and me in *Aladdin* at the Palace, Manchester, 1971. 'No, you are rubbing the wrong lamp!'

Above: Scarborough, charity cricket, 1972. I was bowled out seven times by the West Indies and proud of it!

and give the impression that I might kick it with my hobnailed boots.

After several very funny sight gags we were supposed to be playing the *Poet and Peasant Overture* with me, the drummer, getting it all wrong and being chastised by the conductor. The tag of the sketch was that the exasperated conductor would snatch the drumstick from my hand, throw it down on the stage strategically between the Scotsman's legs and demand that I 'pick it up.'

I would then go down on my knees and, while picking up the drumstick, would look at the audience and then glance up the kilt. I would then slowly stand up, look at the Scotsman, wink, take my big drum, which was side on to the audience, and turn it round to reveal, on the opposite skin, the letters 'NO'. It would get a big laugh and we would then go into the final portion of *Poet and Peasant*, ending with my hitting the gouty foot with my drumstick – beat – blackout!

That was how the sketch ended ... until Christmas Eve 1971 in the Palace Theatre, Manchester, with the Dallas Boys as the band members. We had got to the part where I had to go down and pick up the stick, but as I went on my knees there seemed to be a strange illumination coming from up the kilt. I didn't normally look up the kilt but, on this occasion, being understandably intrigued, I rolled over on my back, moved the kilt with the drumstick so I could see up … the Dallas Boys had rigged some flashing fairy lights around Percy's private parts with a note which said, '*Happy Xmas Fred.*' I could not get up from the stage and they just played it out and did the blackout.

BEING top of the bill, on TV and being recognised by the public is quite strange in many ways. You tend to get treated with a kind of deference which can be a problem if you wish to be anonymous. You cannot do the things you normally would do: when you are out, people stare at you as if they know you, something you have to learn to live with. It can be a problem when you are in Tesco's, and I still am not totally used to it. People say the oddest things: 'Are you who I think you are?' 'Aren't you on the telly?' 'The wife loves you, but I can't stand you.' 'Why are you not on the telly anymore, then?' 'My grandad used to laugh at you.' 'Fancy seeing *you* shopping!'

It can also be difficult to make close friends once you are well known, which is why I, and I am sure many other well-known people, tend to favour old friends who knew them before the fame. Nevertheless, I loved being top of the bill and always tried to include the company as a family, offering my help if any of them had a problem.

PANTOMIME in Bradford ended in March 1968 and I then embarked on another round of TV shows and personal appearances before a summer season at the Queen's Theatre in Blackpool, which was to run for some twenty-four weeks. The show starred the great Irish tenor, Josef Locke, and I was second top.

Joe was making his big comeback after several years in the wilderness (Ireland) for alleged tax evasion. I got to know Joe quite well during the season and we chatted most evenings. During the 1950s he had been one of the biggest names in Blackpool and regularly starred for a season. His mentor was Beryl Formby, the formidable wife of George. Joe often appeared with George at the Opera House in Blackpool, but it was Beryl who secured a recording deal for Joe which led to him becoming a bill topper in his own right; George was already a huge recording artist, so all Beryl had to do was put a bit of pressure on the powers that be at George's record company.

Joe was very astute and showbiz savvy. His tax evasion had happened by accident when he went back to Ireland for the winter: his tax assessment had been delivered and lay on his hall carpet in Blackpool uncontested, and if you didn't appeal the assessment, it became a demand. He either refused to pay or couldn't pay and, consequently, could not come back to the UK as a warrant was issued for his arrest.

As the years went by, however, his popularity never seemed to wane and another act, mysteriously called Mr X, toured the clubs as a lookalike. Whether this was the real Josef Locke or not was never revealed – it wasn't, of course, but what a great gimmick. On one occasion two detectives and an Inland Revenue officer swooped down on a performance at the Theatre Club, Accrington; it took twenty minutes for the officials to be convinced of his innocence. The real Joe, safe in County Kerry, was reported as saying: 'I hope he pays my tax.'

Erik Ellison, Mr X, later appeared on *Opportunity Knocks* and made a great living out of the mystery as he not only looked like him but sounded like him too.

In the mid 'sixties, the real Joe eventually did a deal with the Inland Revenue and came back to work in the UK. He never told me what the deal was but you can bet it was in his favour. Peter Chelsom made a lovely movie loosely based on his life called *Hear My Song* in 1992, which brought Adrian Dunbar and James Nesbitt into the spotlight, although it took several years for James Nesbitt to gain the leading man status he now has.

BLACKPOOL was, as usual, awash with stars in 1968 and the theatres all played twice nightly. I was also recording a weekly radio show called *The Golden Parrot Club*, a variety-based concept produced by Geoff Lawrence and recorded at the Co-operative Hall in Blackpool. I played the owner of the club and my character, Samuel Tweet, was a sort of obnoxious twit who kept popping up. The show had a one hour slot on Saturday evenings and music was from the fabulous Northern Dance Orchestra, with guest stars and acts from the Blackpool shows.

I introduced Mike Craig and Lawrie Kinsley to the BBC, two Yorkshire lads doing their first professional radio show, and Gary Knight who, over the years, wrote most of my television and radio shows, and a lot of material for my stage act. Various voices were provided on the show by Colin Edwin and Barbara Mullaney (later Knox). Barbara went on to play Rita Fairclough on *Coronation Street* – where she still shows her skill as a feed in the more comic scenes – and Colin did a lot of work with Les Dawson and later with me on my own TV series *The Small World of Samuel Tweet*.

Mike and Lawrie later wrote quite a funny routine with Samuel Tweet where the straight man was a hypnotist who asked: 'Does anybody need any help with a problem?' Samuel would come out of the audience and say: 'Yeth, I've got a problem', and the hypnotist would say: 'What's the problem?'

'You haven't notithed?' I'd say.

'No,' he'd reply, 'what is your problem, Sir?'

'You *thtill* haven't notithed?'

'I haven't got a clue.'

And I'd say: 'I've got one leg shorter than the other.'

It was a classic double act where he would hypnotise me to get rid of the lisp – and the tag was that he would finish up with it. I first did it with Ronnie Hilton on *The Good Old Days*, because Ronnie could do a very good impression of Samuel Tweet. He used to do it in his act and even looked a bit like me when he put the hat on.

The radio show ran for twenty-four weeks and some

of the later shows were recorded at the Hulme Hippodrome in Manchester. One of our bill topping acts was Eartha Kitt, who was due to do a sketch with me as Samuel Tweet; she had great difficulty reading the lines and kept calling me 'Samula' instead of Samuel. There was one unforgettable line in the sketch where I offered Eartha a cup of tea, saying: 'Excuthe me, Mith Kitt, but would you like a bithkit, Mith Kitt?'

Mike and Lawrie were good with the sketches, but Gary Knight was the feller for one liners. His real name was Peter Colby and he was a chartered accountant, of all things, with an office in Hindhead, Surrey. He kept it totally separate, never talked about it: that was business, that was Peter Colby; the writer was Gary Knight.

He'd written to me, asking if I needed any material; I told him I was looking for budgie jokes, and he sent some, then began writing for me on a regular basis. He and Wally Malston wrote comedy material together. I think Wally was more a situation writer but Gary was very much a gag writer: I had him on a retainer and every week he would supply me with a page of topicals which I'd use as I felt fit. As well as writing material for *The Golden Parrot Club*, Gary wrote the *Samuel Tweet* TV series, which I'll discuss a bit later, and my sketches for *The David Nixon Show*. He was always on hand, someone to talk stuff over with, and I am still in touch with him.

He wasn't the only writer I used: lots of people used to write to me with gags, which was a mixed blessing. There was a woman from Newcastle and a showbiz editor from *The News of the World*, who also did some stupid things like printing a story that I was looking to buy a parrot; I got to the theatre one night and found this long line of people outside the stage door, all because of the article. Then he put it about that I would pay £5 for a good budgie joke. I got thousands –

gags that I'd already told, or old chestnuts. But the woman from Newcastle wrote to me with five fresh one liners that I use to this day. She came to see me when I was working in Newcastle at La Dolce Vita, but they wouldn't let her in. I've still never met her.

That piece asking for gags comes back to haunt me even now. I got a nasty letter just recently from a man in South Yorkshire claiming he'd sent me a joke – one of those thousands – and that I'd stolen it from him and used it without permission. 'I don't suppose I'll ever hear from you,' he finished. I wrote back and said, 'I'm sorry you feel that way, but probably hundreds of people sent me that one.' He did write back and apologise.

SUMMER season in Blackpool was followed by pantomime at the Theatre Royal, Nottingham 1968/69. This was with the same cast as at Bradford including, once again, my dear friend Don Smoothey, a great revue comedian and the comic in the duo Smoothey and Layton (bill matter: 'Laughing at life'). Don, who also worked with his brother Len Lowe, was part of a great show business family, including Jeannie Carson, who went on to gain fame in the USA. Len was very helpful to me in supplying some great pantomime comedy material. Nottingham is a great Midlands town which has, like Bradford, a tradition of long pantomime seasons; we ran well into March of 1969.

April 1969 saw the Bachelors and yours truly in a six week television series for ATV, followed by a sixteen week sell-out variety show at the Victoria Palace in London, staged by Dick Hurran, with sixteen Tiller girls. Dick Emery was second top of the bill and did not like the competition. It seems odd in today's comedy world, with comedians following comedians and all doing well; back then, however, it was the source of great friction and it was quite difficult to follow a comedy act who had done well.

I followed the magic act Johnny Hart, who used to feature budgies and macaws, and I'd had this huge six foot parrot made out of polystyrene which I'd bring on under a cover. I'd walk on with this thing and it was so obvious it was a bloody great parrot under there – it used to get such a yock!

It was made for me in 1966 by Peter Pullen, who was prop lad at the Coventry Theatre. He only charged me for the materials – £13 – and it actually started him off: he became a very sought after professional prop maker, set up a studio and for twenty years directed commercials, because he was making props for them. Peter makes the best ventriloquist dolls in the world but it all began with my big parrot, which used to sit on my shoulder, turn its head and blow an earsplitting raspberry.

Dick Emery had some difficulty following me – though he was, to all intents and purposes, the bigger star. I had the spot just before the interval musical routine and he did the spot before the Bachelors, who closed the show. I really pissed him off on one occasion when I 'blacked up' for the first half finale number; as the Black and White Minstrels were the show we had replaced for the summer at the Victoria Palace, it looked as though one of them had been left behind. Everyone in the show and the audience were in on the joke and laughed out loud – everyone, that is, except Dick Emery, who went bananas.

Being in the West End was great, and we took a rented house in Esher, about forty-five minutes' drive from London. I also had to do twelve Sunday concerts topping the bill at the Winter Gardens, Margate, so never got a day off, though I do recall seeing the moon landings on my birthday, 21st July, 1969, at the house of Jack Green, entertainment supremo for the Margate theatres.

Dick would also go off and do Sunday concerts and I later found out that he was doing most of the gags in my act. I had some very good lines as well as the Samuel Tweet thing, and somebody came to see me and said 'I saw Dick Emery on the Isle of Wight last Sunday and he did all your bloody material!' He was never a stand-up, Dick; he was a comedy actor, really. By the same token, when Freddie Starr, who was new to London audiences, stood in for him, I had difficulty following *him*.

With so much driving at this time I had to employ a roadie, an old chum from my early club days in Newcastle, Percy Barker. He called himself Paul Baker when he worked the clubs and spoke with a Scottish accent – which was odd, because he came from Chorley. The story – and there are many – goes that he left his wife Mary for a Scottish girl and, in order to avoid undue attention, spoke with a Scottish accent which he found hard to get rid of when he went back to Mary after ten years away.

Percy was indeed a great pal and, unknowingly, quite hilarious. He'd had an unfortunate accident at the age of 14 when his left hand was severed. He occasionally wore a false hand but would usually drive the car changing gear with his stump, which was fine. We were driving down the M1 on one occasion when I could not help saying to him: 'Percy, it is difficult to believe you only have one hand.'

'Oh,' he said, preening himself for a compliment, 'how?'

'Well,' I said, 'sometimes you drive as if you've got no bloody hands at all!'

I had a huge flash Mercedes 600 which was one of the biggest cars Mercedes ever built. It did 8 mpg and was an enormous expense, almost bankrupting me in pure upkeep: the only mechanic who could work on it with any knowledge was at Mercedes HQ in London.

This silly purchase came about because, once I could afford it, I had bought a Rolls Royce – a status symbol, really – and Bernie Bresslaw had said, 'It makes you look like an old man!' (This was the swinging 'sixties, remember). Needing to get rid quick, I swapped it for the Mercedes, though I eventually got rid of that when I part-exchanged it for a more sensible BMW in 1972.

This was my only real indulgence with my new earnings, but I really enjoyed having such a good car: we couldn't afford a car when I was growing up and, as a child, I had hardly ever ridden in one. Sadly, my mother was unable to share in this unaccustomed luxury: whenever I took her out she was an absolute nightmare to have in the front passenger seat and was totally neurotic.

BUT I can't end this chapter without referring to a blessing bestowed on me by a truly great star, which seemed to set the seal on my panto-prime.

Pantomime 1969/70 was at the Hippodrome, Bristol, with my dear pal Bernard Bresslaw playing Abanazar, in *Aladdin*, with Joe Black as Dame. Aladdin was played by Yvonne Marsh (sister of Jean), the Dallas Boys were the Chinese policemen and I played Wishee Washee.

The pantomime was directed by Eddie Espinosa, from the famous Espinosa ballet family. He really understood comedians and introduced me to the famous Comedy Band routine described earlier, originally done by Sid Millward and the Nitwits. I was able to add lots of great sight gags to this routine which was a bonus to me for years to come; I would sometimes put it into summer shows as well. Joe Black was a great Dame in the true tradition of 'A Man in A Frock.' In variety he had a very funny act, slightly camp in his gentle, Yorkshire way.

Halfway through that season in Bristol, I had a visit from the Company Manager, Ray Lamarr, to say that Cary Grant was in the audience for the Thursday matinee with his young daughter and her nanny, and had asked whether he could come round and meet me after the show. Yes, I know, even reading that sounds like some kind of joke. Cary was visiting his mother, who was in a home in Bristol, and he came to see the shows at the Hippodrome when he visited.

Thrilled to bits, I told Percy to tidy the dressing room, open the door and then make himself scarce: 'And remember, Percy, his name is Mr Grant.'

Matinee over, there's a knock on the door; Percy puts his fag in his mouth (one hand, remember), opens it, sticks out his right hand and says: 'Hello, Cary'. I thought about killing Percy there and then but decided to wait till later.

I have to say he was lovely to meet: charming, very natural and absolutely sincere. We chatted about the show and he made some nice comments. During pantomime I always feature a scene where six children from the audience come on stage to sing a song with me; I then present all the kiddies with a little hat like mine. On matinees full of pensioners it can be difficult to find six children, but Cary's six year old daughter came up on stage. When I asked her where she came from she said 'Beverly Hills, California' – all the other children had come from districts around Bristol.

Skip forward twenty years to the next and last time I saw Cary Grant – it was at a Water Rats Ball at the Grosvenor House Hotel in London. The first thing he said was: 'My daughter still has the hat!'

13: Ups and Downs in the 'Seventies

THE 1970s started in a similar vein to previous years with summer seasons, cabaret clubs, television shows, pantos and one-nighters in places as far away as Spain providing me with stable and consistent pay packets. Each year the work kept coming in, just as before, and it seemed like this run of success would never end.

But it was all getting a bit too comfortable, a bit samey, somehow. I longed to move on, to do something different, although I had no idea how, or even what that thing might turn out to be. It was to take ten years before I realised where I was eventually to be led.

Pantomimes aside, some work from this time has blurred together, although there are still many non-panto engagements which stick in the mind – not always, I admit, for the best of reasons.

There was, for example, a one-nighter in Spain in the summer of 1970 which rapidly descended into farce. I was booked as part of a variety bill for the final night of an ABTA (Association of British Travel Agents) annual conference and jolly in Majorca. The yet-to-air Capital Radio had set up a commercial selling booth at the conference and were paying for the closing night cabaret, which consisted of Sandie Shaw, Kristine Sparkle, Terry Seabrook (a great comedy magic act, now sadly passed on) and yours truly.

We arrived at the huge venue where all the delegates were to assemble for the farewell dinner and dance – and cabaret. Unfortunately, nobody told the ABTA organisers they had a cabaret booked, and when we arrived for the so-called rehearsal at 2pm on the day we were told that we would not be required: we would be paid but the show was off.

For some inconceivable reason, Sandie Shaw went ballistic and insisted in doing her act that evening. In disbelief, the rest of us tried to reason with her but she would not listen to our appeals; the fact that we were getting paid anyway and could have the night off was of no consequence to her.

Eventually a compromise was reached: we would do a thirty-minute show in total which I would MC, doing one longish joke; Kristine Sparkle, an impressionist, would do five minutes; Terry would do one trick and Miss Shaw could do a medley of her hit. We were all getting small fortunes for the gig as money seemed to be no object: they had the Majorcan Symphony Orchestra (all forty-five of them) as the accompaniment although Sandie had her own drummer, bass player and musical director flown over with her.

We did the show, which was ignored by the audience, as expected. They were well smashed by 9.30pm, having been wined and dined by the Spanish tourist board, and we went on at 11.30pm. Need I say more?

We were flown back to the UK on a Freddie Laker DC 10 and Mr Laker himself was on the flight. On every seat was a self-build DC 10 small scale plywood kit as a gift. During the flight Freddie Laker made a speech to the assembled travel agents outlining the advantages of using his services for charters, etc. At the end of his speech he asked whether there were any questions. Tongue in cheek, I asked him how the plywood kit fitted together, to which that future knight of the realm graciously responded: 'Piss off.'

Which seemed an entirely fitting end to proceedings.

THE rest of 1970 was taken up with TV, cabaret clubs and a summer season in Skegness at the end of the pier. This was a smallish show but very well paid, I recall. The trouble was the owners of the pier were stagestruck and wanted to play at show business: they put on shows which couldn't help but lose money because the capacity of the venue was too small. They did about four or five summer shows with big stars – Ken Dodd, The Barron Knights, Norman Wisdom etc. I was supported by Clinton Ford and the Kaye Sisters.

I also played Sunday concerts at the Floral Hall, Scarborough. I used Bob Monkhouse's dressing room, as he was doing the season there, and every week he would leave a cartoon drawing for me – all superb; I only wish I had kept them now, as they would be worth a fortune. Bob was a great comedian and friend who was also very bright and probably one of the best game show hosts we have ever had; I still miss him.

THE Floral Hall also sticks in the mind for a less happy reason. An ex-choreographer, Ken Martyne, was allegedly directing a summer season show I did there a couple of years later, but he stood about for an entire week and did absolutely nothing. He got to the 'who's best' finale and didn't even set the walkdown or give any kind of simple instruction along the lines of: 'You come on now and stand there' – it was just shambolic and we had a dreadful row about it.

But I can't blame Ken Martyne for another disaster visited upon me in that show – though I wouldn't say it was entirely self-inflicted either.

It started – as so many things do – with the best of intentions. When I began topping bills in summer season, I didn't want to be one of those performers who just popped up at the end. I hadn't been allowed to do sketches when I'd been supporting the Bachelors as the director, Dickie Hurran, thought they were old-fashioned and just wanted a variety bill. So once I became a headlining act, I seized the opportunity to give my own show more of a revue feel, and insisted on doing sketches throughout. I'd do a warm-up after the opening, and then I would do a sketch and close the first half, invariably with a musical item, and then do my act at the end. Whatever else holidaymakers or critics might find to say about the show, I was determined that at least no one could complain about an insufficiency of Davies.

Which is what led to my hiring Norman Barrett's budgie act.

Norman is a world famous ringmaster and a very old pal. He used to do Blackpool Circus in the summer then wouldn't have much work in the winter so, because he could train animals, he had developed an act with about ten or twelve actual live budgies who would do tricks on a little stand, which was great for cabaret.

The birds used to stay in his caravan all summer, so one day I said: 'Would they do the act for me, the budgies?' So he said: 'Well, try 'em,' and he got them out and they did their little bits and bobs.

I was instantly captivated, thinking how great it would be for me to do a budgie act in the show – because, of course, my whole thing was budgies. I sealed the deal with Norman on the spot, already hearing in my mind that first roar of delighted surprise from the audience as they caught sight of my acrobatic feathered friends.

Having watched Norman put them through their paces so showily, however, there was something I hadn't really considered: the implications of a change of master.

It used to frighten them when I put the hat on because suddenly there was this figure looming over them: as one bird, they would back away, as though to say 'I'm not doin' this for *you*.' Like an HM Bateman cartoon. Only with budgies.

Every night I would come out, take the budgies out of their cage and put them on the perch – and they all used to turn their backs on me. Then quite often they would fly off into the audience and I'd have to go out front and get them back.

They just wouldn't perform for me. I'd take them back to Blackpool for the weekend and Norman used to get them out and say: 'Now listen. You *will* do this act for Freddie!' They'd sit on the perch, looking at him. And he'd say: 'Come on now, we'll do it now.' They'd do it perfectly for him – but they wouldn't do it for me.

I wish I could say that it became one of those comedy-from-chaos situations – a sort of anti-budgie act which, against all the odds, made the audience laugh even more uproariously than the conventional routine, eventually becoming the cornerstone of my summer shows. Actually, it was just awful – especially when I had to keep finding a reason for scrambling offstage to get them back. Luckily *The Stage* seemed to think it was all part of the act – unless they were just being kind:

> His budgie act is very popular, especially when one flies into the audience and another won't do as he is told.

I stuck with it for about four weeks and then just gave them back to Norman, paid him a nominal fee and put the Comedy Band back in the show.

You could say that comedy of a sort eventually emerged from my onstage shambles. At least, I told the story to Peter Chelsom and it became a line in a draft of the movie *Funny Bones*. It didn't make the final cut of the film – maybe because it's almost a private joke – but in the original script Lawrence, the solicitor who is helping the young American comic, Tommy, to find material tells him he used to be in the business himself and did a budgie act. 'Cute,' says Tommy. 'Can be cute, yes,' Lawrence replies. 'My budgies were ... bastards.'

TALKING about novelty acts reminds me of the Liverpool comic Jim Cooten, who used to do an act with a dog. It would howl when somebody sang, and that was the end of his act.

He was a good comic, Jim, but it was well known the dog was a big part of the act. Anyway, he was about to be booked on a kids' TV show from Granada in Manchester, and I happened to be in the producer's office as I was doing one of the shows. He said: 'Stay with me, I've got to ring this agent to get Jim Cooten.'

The agent's name was Dave Forrester, and he handled Mike Yarwood and Ken Dodd – a few good acts. A very astute agent-manager. And he had a very whispery, hoarse voice.

His office was in Brighton, and the producer, Rod Taylor, got hold of him and he said: 'Hello Dave.'

''Ello, er, Rod.'

'I wanna book Jim Cooten.'

'Hang on – I'll blow the dust off his date sheets.'

Dave comes back on the phone: 'What date do you want him for?'

'21st of April.'

'He's free – how much?'

Rod says: 'Seventy-five.'

There was a slight lull in the conversation, just a slight pause. Enough for Dave to know that he could get more money. And in that twenty seconds' gap he said: 'D'you want the dog?'

Rod said: 'Of course.'

'One and a quarter.'

I CAN'T date them precisely but I also have a couple of memories from the City Varieties, Leeds which may as well go here as anywhere else in the book – though readers of a nervous disposition may wish to look away for the next few paragraphs.

At the City Varieties, you had to bang your foot on the stage to get the MD back. His name was Johnny Rocket, and I knew him from Butlins Skegness where he had the Number Two pit orchestra and had done several musical arrangements for me. John would sit on an upright piano underneath you in the pit, and he'd play you on: *da dadadahh, da dah, da dah dah*! And as you got to the microphone he and the other two musicians would disappear into the hole under the stage.

One matinee we had a crowd of students in from the university. They were never a good audience. And as John was going into the hole, I banged on the stage, and he came back and said: 'What?'

'Don't leave me!' It got a big laugh from the audience.

'Please don't leave me, John – I might need you, soon!'

I did the City Varieties a few times. Backstage it's quite small, but there was a dressing room with a little balcony where you could look down on the stage – an open balcony, like a fly tower, quite high up. I'll never forget Michael Joseph leaning over this one Monday morning, calling down to a stripper onstage: 'Look, get a bit of plaster that's flesh-coloured – although I suppose you could make it up. If you get a plaster that isn't flesh-coloured then put some powder on it, so you can't see it.'

I did warn you.

BOLSHY budgerigars notwithstanding, 1972 was a very good year for me. I became David Nixon's magic assistant for a ten week series for Thames Television at Teddington, directed by Tony Parker. David Nixon had been a television celebrity ever since I could remember, and as well as being an accomplished magician featured in many a television panel show; he had established himself long before that cheeky chap Paul Daniels emerged from the clubs and eventually took over his mantle.

David had his own show for many years and, with his writer George Martin, discovered and wrote the material for Basil Brush. My job on the show was as his silly assistant, riding disappearing motor bikes and having my head screwed round, plus a sketch with David and the guest artist and a spot of my own. The guests, people like Ronnie Hilton, Matt Monro or Gilbert O'Sullivan, were usually plugging a record, and the programme went out at 6.45pm on Monday evening, just before *Coronation Street*.

The show was recorded on Sundays and as I was appearing at the Floral Hall in Scarborough for the summer season, this meant my having to travel to London overnight on Saturday after the second show, arriving knackered at Teddington for 9.00am rehearsal with the recording at 7.30pm.

Getting there became the biggest problem. Thames TV arranged to have a private charter aircraft bring me back on Mondays, but there always seemed to be some hitch on the outward leg.

I got an overnight sleeper from York to Kings Cross but my car failed to turn up. The firm who had the contract with Thames were almost fired, but were given a chance to redeem themselves. I was to be chaffeured from the theatre on Saturday evening to London, put into a hotel in Richmond then picked up for the studios on Sunday at 8.30am.

The only limo they could find came from a local funeral car firm. The driver thought he was taking me to Richmond, Yorkshire, until I corrected him. A nice lad, he then insisted on talking to me all through the journey so I could not get any rest at all; I was just nodding off around 4.30am when we arrived at the North Circular and he woke me to ask for directions. After another post mortem at the studio, the car firm's contract was well and truly in the mire.

One happy result of this debacle was that I met the man who would eventually become my new manager and agent. All I had asked Thames for was a comfortable car with a driver who would allow me to sleep on the journey and actually knew his way to Richmond, South London. The next Saturday arrived, and halfway through the evening I was informed that my car was at the stage door. It was a large Volvo estate with everything I could want: a blanket in the back and pillows, a flask of coffee, a range of sandwiches and several miniatures. The driver said that his name was Paul and he was Anglo-Indian, originally from Karachi. He was also the best chauffeur I have ever known as, after volunteering that information, he did not speak to me for the whole journey and woke me only when we arrived at the hotel in Richmond.

He was waiting to take me to the studio later and on Monday morning drove me to the airfield for my flight back to a location near Scarborough. He never spoke or looked at me the whole time unless I asked him a question. He turned up the following week at the stage door and repeated the journey: no contact, just driving.

When I did eventually get him to talk, he confessed he had been under strict instructions not to speak to me as I was some kind of monster who had got rid of every driver who had been sent to ferry me if they so much as uttered a word during the journey.

It turned out that Paul was an associate of the owner of the car hire firm who were about to lose their lucrative deal with Thames if I was not accommodated as requested. The story had somehow got twisted out of all recognition by this time and Paul had been dispatched to Scarborough as a last resort – not, of course, that Scarborough *is* a last resort.

Paul was actually a very successful businessman who was doing his friend a favour and not really a chauffeur at all, but he agreed to drive me during the following summer as I was going to be doing late night cabarets for the Butlins organisation. He had a Rolls Royce which he'd occasionally use; I may not have wanted to own a Rolls, but I certainly didn't mind being ferried around in one.

We became friends and I soon realised that he was very astute in business: one of his main pursuits was that of consultant turf accountant and he would often provide information and advice to a horse racing advisory service. I asked him to represent me when I decided that my time with the Mike Hughes organisation had reached its end.

Paul was unknown in show business circles but soon

overcame this and established himself as a likeable but shrewd negotiator. We entered into several business ventures together, one being to record all the groups playing at the Butlins Holiday Camps during the summer season of 1974 and sell their records on the camps to a captive audience. Ultimately, we hoped to find a star group – we didn't, but we did record some bizarre acts in studios up and down the country and in all made about twenty-five EP (Extended Play) records with four tracks per disc. One of the better groups was Black Lace, later to find fame – or infamy – with *Agadoo*, though they recorded a version of *Bohemian Rhapsody* for us.

I DID a bit of singing myself in 1972, which led to my becoming an international star – well, sort of.

The story really starts the year before, when I was doing a summer season at the Wellington Pier in Great Yarmouth. Also appearing on the show was a newly found *Opportunity Knocks* act called New World - three boys from New Zealand who had one major hit record. Fortunately it happened during the season, so we benefited from some increased business.

Their manager, John Grossman, played double bass on stage with them. A very astute man, he saw the potential in my recording something other than silly ditties with a lisp. It was a period when Ken Dodd, Max Bygraves and even Jimmy Tarbuck were putting out straight records and selling them and if they could do it, why couldn't I, John asked.

To sell a comedian as a singer you need a lorra, lorra luck, and I knew I didn't have an operatic voice like Doddy or Harry Secombe to bolster my chances. But John persisted, so I challenged him to find me the right song.

After the season he arrived on my doorstep in

Blackpool with several ballads in demo form. The one which stood out was an Italian song called *Sempre, Sempre.* John had already fallen in love with the song – which had been given English lyrics and renamed *So Lucky* – and soon I did too. I had a bash at singing it and seemed to be able to handle the top notes, so it was decided that we should have a punt and pay for the recording ourselves – that is, John, my agent Mike Hughes, and me. We had a three way share which cost £810 in total for studio, arrangement and orchestra ... well, it was 1972.

We booked two sessions in the studio. The backing track was all sorted out on the first day, but when I tried I found I just couldn't sing it. It was too high, it was too *everything* – studio nerves kicked in and everything was wrong. As John recently recalled: 'It just wasn't happening, no matter what you did.'

I got home, put my head in a corner, and rehearsed it for twenty-four hours. I went back the following day and the improvement, John said, was unbelievable: I just was able to sing it.

John later told me that he put more effort into this one recording than for the average album. He arranged, produced and took an entire day to mix it before he got it right. But it turned out very well, much to the delight of the English lyric writer, a Mr Bill Owen (Compo from *Last of the Summer Wine*); Bill had been a songwriter for years and had written the musical *Match Girls* and songs for Cliff Richard and others.

We only took the finished product to one company, Pye, but they loved it – ate it up, you might say – and released it almost immediately. And lo and behold, it became an instant ... miss. It got loads of BBC Radio 2 plays, but nowt. It almost made the Top Fifty but didn't.

One to chalk down to experience. Or so I thought.

Fast forward three years to 1975, and John got a letter from Pye Records with a huge cheque. He rang them to say there must have been some mistake but they said no, there was no mistake. It was for about seven or eight grand, so that was lucky.

It turned out that the song was a major hit in Brazil. The record company used to send everything out to their reps there, and as luck would have it a new rep had played it, liked it, and got requests for it, so Pye had sent over the matrix from London.

Then we started getting cheques from the Philippines, where it was the first track of a compilation album of big ballads and had got a lot of airplay. We only received half royalties as it was a foreign 'pick up' but it more than paid for the recording. As an added bonus it became the biggest selling English record in Brazil that year, and I was summoned to the Brazilian Embassy in London to receive a gold record!

So Lucky remains a favourite song for many of a certain age and, some forty years later, it's still selling via the internet. There have been other versions: my pal Ken Goodwin covered it, as did Morris '*Feelings*' Albert, but it still seems to be associated with me, which has to count as a great tribute to John Grossman's production.

I use the song in my act even now. Not only is it a powerful closer, it's also a source of great personal comfort. When shows are less than full or critics less than kind, I tell myself that it doesn't matter. I'm big in Brazil.

Where the nuts come from.

THE year 1972 was also when we moved from Blackpool to Beaconsfield in Bucks, which was much nearer my work, and as I was now a member of the Grand Order of Water Rats I was able to attend the fortnightly meetings when I wasn't away working.

The Water Rats were formed in 1889 by variety artists, mainly comedians, who formed a fraternity or brotherhood similar to Freemasons' Lodges with the object of helping members of the profession who had fallen on hard times.

How the Grand Order was formed is a lovely story and worth telling:

> This great organisation was first formed in the late 1800s when Dan Leno, Harry Freeman, Wal Pink, Cinquevalli, Little Titch, Chigwin, and other great names, were topping the Music Halls.
>
> The name of the organisation came out of an incident when several of them got together and bought a little trotting pony, which was originally known as 'The Magpie.' It was won in a bet in Newcastle upon Tyne and brought down to London in a train and walked back to its intended stables.
>
> On the way, however, it poured with rain, and they were soaked to the skin. The little animal looked so bedraggled that a bus driver opened his window and shouted: 'What have you got there? It looks like a bloody water rat.'
>
> After the laughter subsided, they began to think a little deeper on the subject, and the result was 'The followers of the Water Rat' which developed over the years into the Grand Order of Water Rats.
>
> There was a good deal of serious thought attached to this name for the idea was to name themselves after the lowliest of animals and try to uplift to the highest in their ideals and aims.
>
> Take the word 'rats' backwards and you have the word 'star' and each member, regardless of his

> aim, should endeavour to be a star in the firmament
> of conviviality, good fellowship and charity.

When I joined the Rats in 1970 I had my emblem, a small gold rat, pinned on by Mike Yarwood who had overcome his ill feeling towards me – well, he had for the moment.

This was a golden period for the Water Rats. Past King Rats sat at the top table during the meetings, and what a top table we had at this time: Wee Georgie Wood, Terry 'Toby Jug' Cantor, Ben Warriss, Tommy Trinder, Ted Ray, Bob Pearson (of Bob and Alf fame), Jimmy Tarbuck, Frankie Vaughan, Henry Cooper, Roy Castle, Matt Monro, Max Bygraves, Harry Secombe and one very special evening when Peter Sellers was made a Water Rat and we had a private dinner afterwards which resulted in much banter between him and me and lots of laughs.

At a Water Rats Lodge the jokes would come thick and fast. If you told a good one you got to wear the Jester's Medal on a chain round your neck and everyone had to pay into the Collecting Rats' Plate. If, however, you told a terrible pun or story you had to wear the large golden Egg and pay a fine. All good fun. King Rat serves as the final arbiter – which, in the right hands, can be hilarious. Both the Jester's Medal and the Egg were donated by Rats Laurel and Hardy, who toured the UK variety halls in the 'fifties. Only two hundred 'Rats' are allowed at any one time and it is rare that this figure is reached.

Ray Alan used to tell a very touching story about touring with the great comic pair in 1954. At the bottom of the bill, his dressing room was correspondingly rather high up in most venues, and one night he was surprised to hear much panting and clumping on the narrow stairs leading to his door. It was a beaming and perspiring Oliver Hardy, asking him to sign his and Stan's autograph book; it simply hadn't occurred to that good man to dispatch someone else to do it.

Thinking about the Water Rats also brings Max Wall to mind; now he *really* had funny bones. I used to meet him quite often, Max – not socially, but by accident. He lived down in St James's somewhere, and when I went to the Water Rats' meetings, which were at the Eccentric Club on Sunday evenings, I would walk through St James from Green Park tube and often bump into him, quite by chance.

He became quite a serious character in his old age. I asked him, 'Why don't you join the Water Rats?'

'Oh, I'm not a bleedin' joiner, I don't join anything,' he said, 'I really don't join anything.'

A marriage scandal in the 'fifties effectively killed Max's career until he was rediscovered in the 'seventies. This was partly thanks to a rock group with the unlikely name of Mott the Hoople, who booked him as their support on a 1972 tour. As Max succinctly put it in his autobiography: 'Thanks a lott, Mott.'

ALL stage performers strive to play the London Palladium and I was no exception. I had done *Sunday Night at The London Palladium* on several occasions, the last time with the legendary Judy Garland. Sadly she was almost at the end of her career: she had moved to live in England and was appearing, or not, at the Talk of the Town, at times refusing to go on and more often than not unfit to perform through drink or drugs.

On the morning of what was to be her final appearance on television, Judy had read an horrendous review of her performance at the Talk and had vowed never to appear on a British stage again, so ATV had a problem.

Jimmy Tarbuck, who had been standing by and performing for her at the Talk, had formed some kind of relationship with Judy and was dispatched to the Savoy to persuade her to appear. It was touch and go, but when her six minute overture finished she did walk on – to a tremendous ovation – and of course stormed the theatre.

In 1974, for a spring season of five weeks, I was fortunate to be on the bill with Cliff Richard topping and packing the venue to the rafters. He has always been a huge draw, and rightly so. He is kind, thoughtful and one of the nicest men one could ever work with. Also on the bill were Little and Large, who I had worked with in the pubs and clubs around the North West in my early days. Eddie Large, as he is known, now lives in the West Country and we often correspond.

I have two abiding memories of the famous London Palladium. My act was fourteen minutes long, just before the first half closer and one evening, having just come off, George, the stage door keeper, called me to say there were three men to see me at the stage door.

As I approached them it was obvious to me that these three men were not for real: they looked like a caricature version of the Mafia, right down to the hats, broad shoulders, black ties – the lot. The spokesman introduced himself in a Brooklyn accent: 'Hi, Mr Davies, we thought you were just great and we want you to star in our big show coast-to-coast broadcast in the States – are you free on Sunday?'

Approaches like this aren't made every day and by the look of these guys I was sure it was a wind up. I looked at George the stage door keeper in his box, but he just shrugged and carried on watching the TV.

I stared at the three guys and waited for the smiles to come. They didn't. I asked for some kind of ID. Still no laugh.

Eventually one of them pulled a wallet from his inside pocket like a gun and took out a gold American Express Card on which was printed 'Universal Pictures: *The Dean Martin Show.*' Now *I* started to laugh. The show was filmed at the Cambridge Theatre and every comic and his dog was on it! I did a spot with some girl who was standing in for Dean Martin on this 'summer replacement show' and I got $525.

My second memory is of taking the whole Palladium Orchestra – well, twenty of them – to play me on at a Masonic ladies function I was performing at after the show at the Eccentric Club dining room (which the Water Rats shared). Usually all you get at these functions is a three piece band – piano, bass and drums. I arrived and said, 'It's OK, I bring my own musicians,' then they all trooped in, taking up most of the dance floor space. The audience of approximately 150 people could not understand what was happening: I think they thought Sammy Davis Jnr was about to walk on and it was only me with my silly budgie stories – a wonderful, one-off indulgence.

MY Samuel Tweet character took centre stage in the 'seventies for a television series. *The Small World of Samuel Tweet* was a children's show which ran for two series between 1974 and 1975. It was recorded at the famous old church studios in Dickinson Road, Manchester, site of the early broadcasts of *Top of the Pops* and once home to Mancunian Films, who produced low budget comedies with such great Northern stars as Frank Randle and Jimmy James.

The show came about when Gary Knight wrote a ten minute sketch for me as a pet shop owner which was shelved until a suitable situation reared its head. Later, when I was appearing at the famous Batley Variety Club in Yorkshire for a televised charity gala, the producer for the BBC, Tony

Harrison, asked me whether I had anything which might be developed into a series for children's television. We had a meeting and I showed him the ten minute idea that Gary had previously written.

A pilot was commissioned and filmed, then we were given the green light to proceed with the first series of six episodes, to be broadcast on BBC 1 on Fridays at 5.15pm. Cardew (the Cad) Robinson, Damaris Hayman, Prue Clarke and Colin Edwyn were engaged as the regular cast, and a very young Christopher Biggins, who had just left drama school, made an appearance in one episode. He was, of course, soon snapped up and very quickly became a popular entertainer. Cardew played my nemesis Lord Chumpton, a silly-ass squire forever getting in my way, and vice-versa.

I have to admit I found it a bit of a strain trying to sustain the character of Samuel Tweet for twenty-five minutes at a stretch. Important as he was to my act, I had only ever featured him in the odd gag. Impresario Derek Block later approached me to do a stage version but I turned it down as I couldn't see it lasting ninety minutes – though nowadays, of course, just about every kids' TV series goes on tour regardless.

Considering the show was recorded with no editing time, I think it stands up pretty well, although there's no doubt it was of its day, and I now know that is not the way slapstick should be filmed. Slapstick comedy is a particular art form and when performed should be done with strict timing and almost to a steady beat: this – to that – to this – to that – to surprise, bang! You can't mess about.

Film can be easier to edit to get the correct rhythm; unfortunately the *Samuel Tweet* series was mostly recorded 'as live' on video and as the sight gags had in most instances been under-rehearsed, camera cuts would not always be on time, thereby screwing up the gag. This is difficult to explain on paper, but a slapstick gag will only work if the tag is a surprise, as with all humour.

According to James Towler in *The Stage*, I 'displayed an almost Chaplin-like charm' in the film sequences in the first episode, but he was struck by the 'complete difference in style' between film and studio and wondered whether it would have worked better with an audience. Actually, we'd tried kids in the pilot and it hadn't worked: they couldn't see what was going on properly because of the cameras.

One of the more successful episodes featured Samuel and Lord Chumpton as rival candidates in an election, and this undoubtedly benefited from several substantial filmed inserts showing their inept attempts at canvassing. It was an episode close to Gary's heart because he was a member of the Liberal party and used to help them in their campaigns, so he knew all about the electioneering process; he even went up for the council once.

That's probably why that show was better than some of the others, though I don't want to give the wrong impression here: they weren't all bad – just most of them. But it was very difficult because they didn't allow any editing time at all. It was all done with five video cameras. Once or twice I did stop and say, 'This is not going to work.'

The producer/director of the series, Tony Harrison, gave me a classic criticism after a dress run for one of the shows in which I had had a lapse of memory and was fluffing the lines somewhat. He came down from the control room and said, more in sorrow than anger, '*Why is it never the same once*?'

Of other television I did around this time I particularly remember a lovely series for BBC 1 from Manchester called *Let the Children Sing*, featuring an audience entirely made up of children singing. The programme featured the Northern Dance Orchestra, a superb outfit featuring the cream of northern musicians. The children were seen in close-up singing all types of songs, well rehearsed from their schools but a very heart-warming, popular and simple concept nonetheless. A well known presenter would talk to the children during the show. I actually telephoned the producer directly, asking to present one of them, and finished up doing four in all.

MOVING back down to earth for the final story in this chapter, I have particular cause to remember the 1978 season in Hastings at the White Rock – or White Elephant, as it came to be known. I was with Peter Goodwright, in a very poorly attended summer show.

At the time it seemed like a blip – just a bad season. Looking back, however, it was something of a milestone: my first major setback since *Opportunity Knocks*, fourteen years earlier.

It wasn't entirely unexpected, I suppose, in that I had been slipping down the bill a bit in pantos – by the late 'seventies I would be second or third on the bill rather than top – but they were bloody good panto bills, and my cabaret dates were still going well.

But that season offered the first indication that audiences might not come in on my name alone anymore. And when you top the bill in theatres you feel responsible for the business: as Dickie Henderson once very wisely stated, 'you can't take it out of the stage door if it is not coming into the box office.'

I became quite depressed at what seemed a sign that perhaps I had flogged the parrot a bit too much and that now was the time for a change – though I still didn't know what that change was to be.

I also wondered whether *The Small World of Samuel Tweet* might have lost me some of my adult audience, that I was in danger of becoming perceived solely as a children's entertainer. I was happy to play Tweet in panto, but my regular act was aimed at an adult audience.

There was nothing wrong with the White Rock show – though I must declare a personal interest as I'd also been invited to direct it by Clive Stock, who I'll introduce in the next chapter. I thoroughly enjoyed doing it, loved the artistic bent of it all, and we did a very unusual opening. The dancers came on and did a warm-up in their practice tights and then at the call 'overture and beginners' the house tabs were dropped and they did it all again in their glitter and their glam. I just loved the theatricality of that opening – I mean, it didn't bring anybody in, but we loved it.

And nobody – ever – mentioned it. People tend to remember what happens at the end of a show, like when you watch a film; the beginning is only a vague memory. I set it up as carefully as I could: the usherettes were asked to tell people the show was going to start any second. There would be no indication of it, but we still did the overture – *It's Not Where You Start, It's Where You Finish* – and we closed with it as well.

The show was good entertainment, but Hastings does not have a theatre-going holiday audience in the way that, say, Eastbourne has. During the day the town and beach would be deserted and in the evening, the theatre even more so.

The whole summer season thing was coming to an end around that time generally, but I also have to say that the White Rock, Hastings really wasn't a very good venue. The council were treating it as an amenity: they felt they had to put something in this monstrosity of a venue, and yet they didn't want to spend a lot of money on the show.

Whatever the reasons, I felt a personal sense of failure over that disastrous summer. And a few years later, when the opportunity arose to turn things around for the White Rock, it became a kind of badge of honour to try.

SO there we are: a brief selection of the highs and the farcical, or unexpectedly painful, lows of a very busy decade.

Pantomimes, which I'll discuss in the next chapter, were a more dependable pleasure for me during these years – well, most of the time, anyway. Even some of the panto experiences which were less than wholly enchanting at the time were to have a positive effect on my career.

And in 1979, the year after that disastrous summer season at Hastings, a pantomime was to change my life in more ways than one.

14: More Pantos - And a Change of Direction

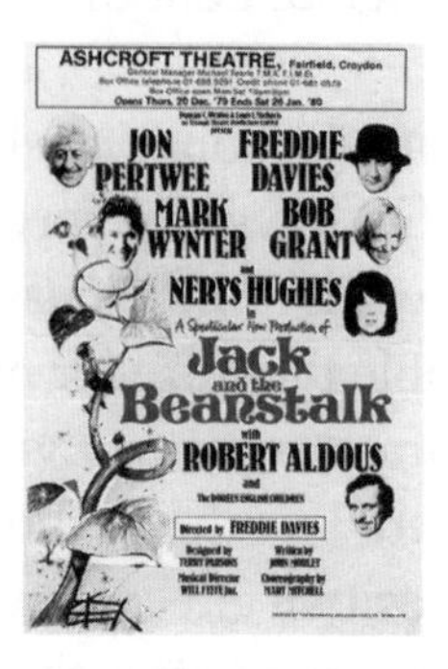

MY first panto of the decade was *Dick Whittington* in 1970/71 at the Birmingham Hippodrome with Anita Harris. I played Dick to Anita's Alice Fitzwarren, Bernard Bresslaw played the Captain, Billy Dainty the Dame and the Dallas boys were ship's crew.

It was a great show. Anita Harris is a stunning singing star who has had some success in the recording industry but I feel she should have pursued an acting career sooner, as she is a fine actress as well. During this season I fancied her like mad – who wouldn't? – but it was not to be, and she eventually married her manager, Mike Margolis.

The following year at the Palace, Manchester, the same team came together for *Aladdin*, but it was an odd season with the three day week and power cuts not helping. The season ended early, and on the last night we were taken off at the interval because of an IRA bomb scare. They cleared the theatre, leading us all out onto Oxford Road, Manchester, freezing in January. Still clad in green body make-up and skimpy costume, the Genie of the Lamp sought shelter in the pub next door. When a drunk said to him, 'What have you come as?' he camply replied: 'I'm a bleedin' leprechaun – what's your excuse? Now piss off!'

Jack and the Beanstalk followed at Torquay, with Richard Murdoch as Dame, then Robin Nash, a very well known BBC producer, called in 1973 to ask if I could assist with the annual BBC Christmas Day pantomime, which was recorded early December at the Wimbledon Theatre; that year it was to be *Babes in the Wood*. I helped with the writing and casting, which was a joy as you could ask for anyone and the Beeb would get them. Robin Hood was played by Anita Harris, Maid Marion the Irish Eurovision star Dana and Dame Trott was played by the wonderful and sadly missed Billy Dainty. The robbers were Terry Scott and Hugh Lloyd and I played a character called Samuel Tweet.

I had heard that Terry Scott could be difficult to work with, but we immediately hit it off. I had admired him in pantomime for some time, and his Dame was indeed to be envied. But he was just as enthusiastic with me, and I found him a joy; he even offered to be the feed for my Comedy Band sketch and was just great.

MY next panto, in 1974/75, sticks out because it finally allowed me to try my hand at something new. I was contracted to play Buttons in *Cinderella* at the Gaumont Theatre, Ipswich, for Mervyn Conn. Mervyn had not found a director who was acceptable and I offered to do it. My experience with Ken Martyne and others had taught me a lesson, namely that the director really had to be The Director: had to order proceedings, not be airy-fairy about decisions, and most of all had to know what they were doing.

I was not a director in the true sense of the word, so went into the project with my eyes wide open – though I was not expecting the problems to be quite so many, hitting me out of the blue. But I very quickly learned, from my many mistakes, what not to do.

One of the many constraints in producing non-subsidised theatre anywhere is time. Rehearsals have to be budgeted and paid for out of projected box office takings, so rehearsal time is limited: pantomimes usually get thrown on and you all hope for the best. I did not want this to happen under my direction but try as I did, it is near impossible to put on what amounts to a small-scale musical in seven to ten days.

Knowing how easy it is to fall behind, I planned a comprehensive rehearsal schedule, starting with the read-through and ending with the final dress rehearsal, which I believe is an invaluable guide to where one is in the full picture. But I wasn't prepared for all the other things that cropped up during this period – and I was supposed to be the star of the show as well! When you have a reduced rehearsal time, homework before the event is essential. My motto is 'Never Assume': always check, double-check and then check again.

The Gaumont, Ipswich, was a disgrace as a venue: the backstage area was inches thick in dust as it was a cinema for forty-six weeks of the year and was never used. After the filth was sorted I learned that the stage was very shallow and the back wall was not straight but at an angle, so all stage cloths had to be hung in front of the angle, making the stage area – the depth from front to back – even shallower. The scenery did not fit the stage as it should, so certain pieces of scenery had to be left outside in a stable behind the theatre.

We had hired the stable for two Shetland ponies to live in during the run of the pantomime; they pulled the glittering coach to transport Cinderella to the Ball. In addition to the ponies we hired a donkey which hardly ever appeared on stage: another mad idea of mine was to have a real donkey which would come on and 'talk,' becoming Daisy the Magic Donkey. Daisy was supposed to announce all the special parties who would give their names for a mention during the show. It was a great spot in the show, as livestock always goes down well on stage, and the donkey was able to live with the ponies as they are great companions.

Unfortunately the bloody donkey would not go on stage. It would set its legs in that straining position and would not move, whatever we tried to coax it with. Carrots, apples etc, had no appeal for this bastard: he just would not budge.

Actually that's not quite true. He did make an entrance once. He was kept tethered in the wings until the Shetlands had made their entrance, then went back to the stable with them in the horsebox. However, he must have got loose on this occasion, as he wandered on just as the glittering coach was entering – and promptly deposited a steaming shit on the stage. The audience were in hysterics as the fairy godmother waved her magic wand because it seemed like a cue for the donkey to have a shite.

This, however, was just one of the many problems a director has to deal with. We had been rehearsing for approximately seven days with all hell breaking loose around me, such as props not being made properly and orchestra leaders throwing wobblies and refusing to do new arrangements or key changes.

The choreography was by Mary Mitchell, who worked on most of my shows over the years; like most good choreographers, she was a great help in putting the show together. We had ten professional dancers and ten juvenile dancers from a local dancing school in Ipswich. There were two teams as the children were only allowed to work so many hours and needed to be licensed to perform on stage. But local dancing schoolchildren are usually good for business as they bring in all their families to see the show and that can amount to quite a few over the run.

I usually ban parents from the backstage area and employ professional chaperones, but on this occasion my rules were flouted as a certain father did get past the stage door keeper and banged on my dressing room door just after curtain down one evening. I opened the door to find a tall man in a pinstripe suit, bowler hat and black overcoat, holding a small child by the arm. Seething, he spluttered out in his fury: 'This child has just torn my child's pixie hat!' and he lifted the kid's arm up to indicate 'this child.' It took me a while to fully comprehend what he had said. Seeing that I was not taking him seriously, he roared: 'And what are YOU going to do about it?'

I was so taken aback by his attitude that I just waffled on about how these things happened, we would get his child another pixie hat, and perhaps that it might be an idea to put the other child down.

He turned out to be a top QC and sent me a very threatening letter stating he would sue the pantomime company for allowing such a disaster to happen to his child. He never did – but it gave me a very good anecdote.

Patience was needed with some of the cast as well as irate fathers. Ken Barnes, who played one of the Ugly Sisters, would open a bottle of port during the interval and get progressively smashed during the second half of the panto, staggering down in the walkdown well out of his skull. I had several words with him but it made no difference: how could he break the habit of a lifetime? He had been doing it for forty-five years and it was ingrained in his work ethic.

Not, I admit, that the rest of us were professional all of the time. Our musical director was Colin Norman, a fine

MD, who also happened to have a speech impediment. We soon got used to his manner of speaking, although he did make some very strange noises at times. During the dress rehearsal for the show, the Prince, played by Mike Rowland, was due to sing *She,* the Charles Aznavour song. Unfortunately he missed the note from the piano and started in the wrong key. From the orchestra pit Colin shouted / sang the right note for him: '*Schnee may be the voince ...*'

I am afraid we lost the plot on stage. We did eventually recover but every night at the same time I could see our Prince physically exerting himself not to corpse as he launched on that most tender of ballads.

Nevertheless, I learned so much from putting this pantomime on and can now keep my calm when the stage crew screw up a scene change time after time. And the experience was to have a longer-reaching effect on my career than I could possibly have imagined at the time.

Twenty years later the movie *Funny Bones* was filmed in Blackpool but the idea had been conceived, although we did not know it, backstage during that season at Ipswich. A young Blackpool actor called Peter Chelsom, then aged eighteen, was spending the season cleaning up after the ponies and being a general assistant, stage manager and flunkey in the show. He soaked up the backstage life, listening to all the old pros' tales and my talk of Jack, putting it all to good use when he eventually became a film director in the late 'eighties. More of this later.

ON the subject of corpsing (giggling when one shouldn't), the worst time I can ever remember was when I, along with several very fine straight actors, had the laughing fit to end all laughing fits – not in a panto, but while making a film written by the rock star Chris Rea.

Funny Bones

The Corpse to End All Corpses happened during a scene when Paul Shane, Jack Smethurst and about four other actors and myself were standing round a table in a factory setting. Door behind Jack opens and woman comes in with tray of tea, simple enough. Camera on Jack: close up. Action. He starts to speak, door opens and in comes the biggest woman you have ever seen with the tray of tea – only she gets stuck in the door and can't get through.

Now, only we, the actors, can see this on the set as the director, John B Hobbs, is closely watching the monitor of the film being shot. As this poor woman struggled to get through the door I could see the other actors starting to go and then the tears started. We were now shaking – in silence, of course.

Jack could sense something was wrong but he had his back to the door; he glanced at me but I was helpless. As the director did not get the expected line of dialogue he shouted 'CUT!' and we just – went. The director stormed onto the set and we tried to explain what had happened; the poor woman extra was extracted from the door and it was decided that she should start from inside the door next take.

Action. Jack starts his line and the woman with the tea starts to move. She is on a six-inch raised platform and with the next step she takes her right foot goes through the wooden platform and gets stuck, poor love. We were all in a state of hysteria by this time and were broken for lunch early, with an irate director yelling in the distance. I think we laughed so much that we became weak with laughter; people were coming up to us in the canteen and asking us what we were still laughing at a full hour later.

The film, *La Passione*, is a story about a young boy obsessed with motor racing. It was partly based on Chris Rea's own childhood in the north east of England; he was born into an Italian ice cream family, loved Red Ferraris and owned several. I believe Chris could not get anybody to back it so he made it himself. It did not get a general release but can be found on DVD.

SUNDERLAND Empire 1975/76 was my next pantomime: *Cinderella* again, with my dear pal Clinton Ford playing the Baron. I played Buttons and am pleased to say I did not have to direct this one as they had engaged a proper director, Geoff Reed, who did a great job. I had worked with his brother Jack Reed, a very funny ventriloquist, at Butlins. Joe Black was the Dame and Vicky Lane choreographed and played Dandini; Vicky later married Ken Goodwin. *Cinderella* is one of the best pantomimes for comedy and pathos.

To my delight I was offered Bradford Alhambra again, this time with Barbara Windsor in *Aladdin*, for the following year – and what a great show this turned out to be. Michael Bates, a very funny comedy actor from the sitcom *It Ain't Half Hot, Mum* was in the pantomime along with several other actors from the show, but it starred Barbara and me, and we had the lion's share of the action. She is such a marvellous performer and always gives 100 per cent, however she is feeling; even after a fall she continued with her arm in plaster. On the minus side she can let the language out a bit: during rehearsals the theatre chaplain paid us a visit and she blurted out: 'Oh fuck, the vicar's here!'

At the curtain call on the opening night she turned to me as the curtain came down and shouted: 'Hey, you never told me you were going to be fucking funny!' – which I suppose is a compliment. We got on like a house on fire ... and no, I didn't!

Harry Ramsden's fish and chips were a local delicacy in Yorkshire and the cast of the show had an open invite for free meals at their original shop near Ilkley. Barbara and I were invited to the Harry Ramsden staff Christmas party and I wrote a silly little song for it. The managing director took a fancy to the ditty, and the cast and I went to make a recording for the Queen's Silver Jubilee year, 1977. The record, *The Ballad of Harry Ramsden*, was sold in their gift shop and included such deathless lines as:

> We're all going to Harry Ramsden's,
> Harry Ramsden's for our teas,
> We're all going to Harry Ramsden's,
> And we're 'aving mushy peas.

The recording finished up as quite an epic, featuring the string section from the Halle Orchestra – along with the Hammonds Sauce Works Brass Band, appropriately enough. I thought a Yorkshireman should sing the lyric, someone like Ronnie Hilton, but they insisted on my doing it. The only trouble was that when working out the recording costs, I completely forgot to factor in for my efforts, and I was the only person on the entire recording who received nowt. But we did get a great last night pantomime party out of it – and all the chips we could eat.

Not that there was always such a spark with my co-stars. One of the pantos I would rather forget was *Jack and the Beanstalk*, at the New Theatre, Oxford at the end of 1977/78. The director was Malcolm Goddard and playing Jack was Joyce Blair, Lionel's sister. I am sorry to say we did not get on, and as Malcolm was trying to produce two shows at the same time – the other one was in Leeds with Dick Emery – we saw very little of him and sort of cobbled it together in his absence. Joyce insisted on singing every time she appeared and Malcolm was browbeaten into not cutting any of her songs so the rest of us had to suffer.

We hardly spoke off-stage, and on one occasion when we did it was to bark at one another in the wings just as we were about to go on. The song we had to do together began: 'Friends, isn't it rather nice to have friends?'

THAT new direction I'd been looking for since the start of the 'seventies came closer when I did a panto for Bunny Baron in 1978. The show would ultimately lead to a change of focus in my career: in less than two years' time I would control many aspects of the Bunny Baron Organisation, which led to forming my own theatre production company in the early 'eighties.

Bunny had the small seaside shows around the south coast sewn up, presenting up to five summer shows and a similar number of pantomimes. By 1978, however, he had been in ill health for some time and had handed the management of business over to Clive Stock.

A true man of the theatre, Clive met his lovely wife Gwen when they were both appearing in the original London production of *Oklahoma!* at Drury Lane in 1948. They toured the world in various musicals and Clive Stock and Gwen Overton later became one of the most in-demand after-dinner, show and concert attractions in London.

Clive was also an entrepreneur and agent who had established himself in partnership with the organist Robinson Cleaver as 'Mr Show Business' in Llandudno, North Wales. He presented shows, concerts and summer seasons at just about all the venues in this holiday resort and eventually settled there. The arrangement with Bunny was that Clive would spend his weekdays in London with the Baron organisation and weekends in Llandudno.

I also directed the show, *Dick Whittington,* at the Civic theatre in Slough – a home booking for me as I was just up the road in Beaconsfield. The theatre in Slough was newly built, with state of the art lighting. As I had responsibility for the whole production I enlisted the help of the great lighting designer Francis Reid, whom I had seen in action lighting several shows I had been in in the past. He kindly came to the Bunny Baron HQ in Marylebone and gave me a crash course in lighting design for which I have been grateful ever since. Delighted that I had thought to ask his advice, he would not take any payment from me – although, being a Scot, he did graciously accept a bottle of malt.

The pantomime was good fun and I was surrounded by good performers and good friends. Jenny Kenna, who I'd met when she was a Windmill Girl in the late 'fifties, played the title role and I was Idle Jack.

Just before the season started, however, Bunny sadly passed away at his home in Brighton and his wife Lisa was left with the business, which Clive continued to run.

THE panto of 1979/80 was a huge turning point for me as I was asked to perform in and direct *Jack and the Beanstalk* at the Ashcroft Theatre, Croydon for the premier producer Duncan Weldon and Triumph Productions.

I had worked for them on and off for years and known Duncan when he was married to Helen Shapiro. A hard man who knew how to negotiate, he had assembled a great pantomime cast with Jon Pertwee as the King, Mark Wynter as Jack, Bob Grant as Dame, Nerys Hughes (of *The Liver Birds*) as Fairy, and me as Simple Simon. I was naturally nervous directing this stellar line-up but had cobbled together a good script with lots of comedy and it was a big success.

Jon Pertwee had his own dresser, a stunning red-headed young lady who would sit in the wings waiting to help with his costume changes. We struck up a flirty, chatty relationship on my twice daily sketch entrance; dressed as I was for my Comedy Band routine in green tights, hobnail boots, loincloth and busby I must have looked quite fetching. Her name was Vanessa and she was married, but there was a definite spark between us – me with my green legs.

The Ashcroft, Croydon pantomime broke all box office records that year. It was great fun to do, and a real boost to my morale after the failure of the White Rock summer show the previous year. The success of my additional role as director in this prestigious production seemed a reassuring sign that there might, after all, be life beyond the parrot.

And there was more reinvention to come. Clive Stock eventually found running the Baron office too exhausting in tandem with his own Llandudno operation. After he left at the end of 1979, Lisa asked if I would help out. Finally, as a new decade dawned, I was being handed the challenge I'd been searching for since the early 'seventies.

More importantly, however, I had met Vanessa. Very soon I realised that this girl was part of my life I could not live without.

15: The Other Side

I JOINED the Bunny Baron Organisation as associate producer, working with Bunny's widow, Lisa, at their Head Office in London. This was a very nice flat in Luxborough Street, just off Marylebone, which was also Lisa's home and the little back bedroom became my office.

The Baron Organisation, or BJB Productions, was a relatively small-time operation. There weren't the panto producers then that there are now. The biggest name was Delfont, who had virtually all the dates; Howard and Wyndham had about three or four, including the New Theatre, Oxford, and a couple in Scotland, where they used to do very good quality pantos with Stanley Baxter, but there were very few producers on the fringe. Other producers were Johnnie Spillers, Duggie Chapman, Denis Critchley, Duncan Weldon, and there were lots of repertory productions – which could be rather arty farty – which left a space for Bunny Baron.

After the war, Bunny had been principal comic in his

own summer shows and pantos before he moved into producing full-time in the late 'fifties. Over the years he had made a niche for himself, building relations with local authorities and their entertainments officers. He knew what they wanted: not lavish Palladium-style spectaculars but competent, quality pantos and summer shows, done to a certain budget, in places like Felixstowe, Lowestoft and Weston-Super-Mare. He used to say, 'You can't cut the quality but you can cut the number' – meaning there might be a few less dancers than in other shows, but councils knew they were getting a reliable product and came back for repeat bookings. *The Stage* dubbed him 'the municipal producer.'

It was six months after Bunny's death that Clive Stock decided he couldn't continue to run both the company and his own operation in Llandudno. I don't think he really wanted to be in London every week and it was affecting his Llandudno business. He missed his beloved Gwennie and felt he had done all he could for Lisa in the circumstances. He wished me luck in my undertakings with her and engaged me to do regular shows, topping the bill at one of his many venues at the Welsh resort. It got me out of the office for a few hours and I was able to supplement my salary somewhat.

Lisa wasn't very good at negotiating and putting deals together. Bunny used to do all the booking and she would look after all the costumes and the dancers – that was her side of it, which she continued with when I joined. We did auditions together and it was still the Baron organisation.

It was a very good working relationship – and that's all it was, although everyone assumed we were having an affair. Absolutely not true, although I always thought she was a nice lady. Besides, that spark between Vanessa and myself at Croydon had already well and truly ignited by then, though it was to be a long time before we were together for good.

The atmosphere in the office was complemented by the presence of one of the nicest gentlemen in the business, Gordon Holdom, who provided back-up and sorted all the admin. A veteran of the London concert circuit, beekeeper extraordinaire and all round good egg, nothing was too much trouble for him, and he told the most engaging stories.

One tale had him working a Masonic dinner at the Connaught function rooms in Covent Garden. He performed the *Master's Song* at the start of the evening and went away to change for his next spot which he did dressed as a chimney sweep, with a black sooty face, singing *Chim Chim Cher-ee* from *Mary Poppins*. The Connaught rooms have over twenty function suites and all of them are occupied most evenings. Gordon walked in on a private board meeting where his opening '*Chim chim-i-ney …*' was met with a stoney silence. Realising his mistake, he backed out the way he had come, still gaily crooning: '*Chim chim-i-ney, chim chim-i-ney, chim chim che-roo ...*'

IT soon became known that I was now in management and every act I had ever worked with or known contacted me for work. I was in a position to employ some very good artists and actors and was often pointed in the direction of many up and coming stars, some affordable, some not.

One was a schoolgirl from Rochdale, the home of Gracie Fields; this was in 1980, my first year with Lisa, when we were putting a pantomime into the Middleton Civic Hall. Bob Parsons, entertainment chief for the Rochdale council and an old friend, had engaged me to produce and direct the show and asked me to see this sixteen year old girl who had, he said, an astounding voice.

I went to the school she was attending and her music teacher, who appeared to be a mentor and manager of sorts, played for her to audition for me. I thought she had a sweet voice, but nothing special, and her accent had a broad Lancashire/Rochdale twang – not quite what one would expect a fairy to use. I turned her down. She left school soon afterwards and got a recording deal. Her name? Lisa Stansfield.

The Rochdale pantomime starred Lenny Henry in *Jack and the Beanstalk* with Alan Randle as the king. Lenny was only twenty-two but already well established by then, with plenty of theatre experience to complement his TV work. He'd spent four years with the stage version of *The Black and White Minstrel Show* and had just come from a summer season in Blackpool with Cannon and Ball. He'd been in a couple of pantos before but this was the first time he'd played principal comic role, in this case Jack's brother, Simple Simon.

He had a very protective manager in Robert Luff, who was well respected in the business. Robert called me a few times to say 'You *will* look after him, won't you? You will make sure he does the right stuff?' I did some funny walks with him and showed him how to fall upstairs like Professor Sparks's son – it always goes back to the Salford Hippodrome.

But Lenny was the least of my worries about that panto, which sticks in my mind mainly because it was a production nightmare. Despite my efforts to keep to a proper rehearsal schedule for a ten-day period, technical delays on stage meant it had to be continually put back. The venue was basically a multi-purpose council hall which had never had such a large professional production within its walls so, as well as directing the show and trying to force the set-up onto a stage on which it couldn't fit properly, I found myself saddled with having to teach the amateur staff what needed to be done.

One problem followed another: all the hanging wires holding up the scenery were virtually destroyed when one wire snapped and wound itself round all the others: it was a thick hawser which could have killed a person if they had been in the vicinity. It took about five days to get it fixed and in the meantime we couldn't put the scenery up or rehearse on stage. We had no stage manager, no stage crew as such – it was absolute chaos.

In the middle of all this I had to go to a very important Masonic meeting and was away for one day. At that meeting a very good friend of mine, Jimmy Jacobs, was making a speech when he collapsed and died. I had to travel back to Manchester overnight on a sleeper in tears, and was back at the rehearsals the next day, tired out and in dread of whatever was going to happen next.

Despite all that, the show opened on the scheduled Monday night. I have two memories of that evening. One is of the young lighting operator sat at the board at the back of the auditorium, shaking so much he couldn't put the sliders into place for the opening lighting cue; I had to do it for him.

There was also a silly girl who was supposedly doing props and acting as assistant stage manager. Her initial task was to smoke up the stage using a smoke machine, as the opening scene was to be a misty morning. As the house curtains jerked open, this stupid girl was still in the middle of the stage squirting her fog about as the lighting came up. She took one look at the audience and fled, bewildering a full house and almost ruining the opening of the show.

I ran from the front of house round the side of the theatre. By the time I had reached backstage the girl playing the fairy, lovely Lisa Crann, was waiting in the wings to go on stage for her first entrance. 'Where is she?' I hissed, knowing she must have seen the incident. Lisa just looked at me and said 'She's gone, but don't worry – I kicked her in the crutch!' We never saw her again.

The show went on and did great business for six weeks – and Lenny was great, though there was no time to bask in this as I had to travel overnight to direct another pantomime at the Lewisham Concert Hall with Bernie Winters and Michael Robbins plus the *It Ain't Half Hot Mum* team (they came as a package deal) in *Robinson Crusoe.*

THAT'S a fairly typical example of the pace of things, but I had no regrets about my change of role. I loved it – loved the creativity of it all, loved seeing a show coming to fruition and being able to see the big picture in a way that hadn't been possible when I'd been centre stage. I wasn't all that keen on theatres collapsing around me, but it was exhilarating, as well as exhausting, to be working at full stretch, immersed in a new set of challenges. When I had a spare moment to think about it I began to feel a real sense of achievement in this new career.

It also gave me the chance to get to know some of my fellow comedians a bit better, though Bernie Winters was already a mate. We'd had some issues in the past with the hat thing, but now he was a solo act and quite vulnerable – and more than a little childlike. Having been so many years with Mike, he was finding it difficult to adjust and develop a version of himself which would work in this new situation.

In Hastings the previous summer, he had done a few weeks' early season, before the main show starring Lena Zavaroni, and had berated me for not helping him enough. He got quite possessive of me, actually: on the opening night he said, 'You could have helped me more.' He was right but, unfortunately, I didn't have the time, as I was doing too many other things in the show.

Robinson Crusoe had mainly actors playing the parts, which made it easier to direct: actors do the lines as per the script and don't mind the rehearsal process and the idea of finding the character. Comedians and variety folk don't understand this discipline of rehearsing full out: they just go on and do it, which can make it hard for a director to see how they're coming along in the rehearsal process. Coming from that background myself I understood, but many directors don't.

Bernie was fine in this situation, however, because he had a script and his own little panto comedy items, so he knew where he was. And don't worry – he always remembered to claim for Schnorbitz.

Robinson Crusoe was played with affectionate charm by Jenny Kenna, the vivacious Windmill girl who'd played Dick Whittington at Slough in 1978. As mentioned earlier, I had known Jenny since she was sixteen, when she holidayed at the Butlins hotel in Margate in my youthful Redcoat days. Jenny has developed from a soubrette into a very artistic lady with *The Windfalls*, a stop-motion animation TV series designed to teach children about the countryside; it's ingeniously done, featuring characters made up from bits of garden twigs and flowers. She now lives in south Wales with her husband Brian Lidstone, one of London's foremost act doctors and drama coaches, writing cookery books.

The following year I returned to Lewisham to produce and direct Charlie Drake in *Aladdin*. I have to say I approached him with trepidation, but found him an absolute joy. We became quite good pals actually, probably because we were two old comics working together, and I knew what he was after. There is a kind of kinship among comics – provided you're not in competition.

Charlie did some very stupid things in the business. He was involved with a dancer in panto at the Alhambra, Bradford, and insisted that she be made up to play the part of the fairy, even though she'd only just got her Equity card. Equity didn't want it to happen, the producer didn't want it to happen, but because of his stature as top of the bill he made it happen: 'Either you do this or I go'. He was subsequently fined by Equity and banned for twelve months from working in provincial theatre.

In many ways he was quite bitter. But he was always very professional on stage, I have to say, and had some very funny ideas. He said: 'Get me a bit of elastic and a bit of fluffy material.' My son Kent had been put through just about every backstage job with me and was very good at props, so I got him to make exactly what he wanted and Charlie invented a very funny rabbit sketch for the kitchen scene.

The Dame, Billy Whittaker, would tell Charlie to go off and get a rabbit to make a pie. Charlie would come back with a toy one which had an elastic line attached to it, and as soon as he put it on the table it would fly offstage and he'd have to go and get it again and so on and so on.

Finally he would bring it on without the line and they would put it in the pie, lay the crust on top and put it into the oven. After some preamble, the oven would begin to smoke and the kids would shout: 'It's burning!' The Dame and Charlie would open the oven door, remove the burnt pie and take off the crust to reveal a real live rabbit inside the tin, sitting up and blinking in the spotlights (as they do). It was a great gag on every level and it was very funny with the whizzing off, the baking, and then the surprise tag: brilliant.

He was very ingenious, Charlie. He would climb on top of a wardrobe to get a three tier cake down, and just when you were sure it was going to fall in a certain way it went another, so his head and shoulders came through the cake and out the top.

Then the wardrobe, which was quite a tall one, would

come away from the wall with Charlie hanging onto it, supported only by three stage crew behind it holding it with a rope – it was quite dangerous, actually. But that was what he wanted to do, so I thought: 'Let's try and make it work.' And he didn't want any mattress there to land on, either.

What makes this all the more surprising is that he had already hurt himself once very badly at the BBC during a live broadcast of *The Worker*, fracturing his skull when a stunt went wrong. But there he was, no mattress: 'I'll do it.'

Later on, when he left his fifth wife, or she left him, he came to stay at my house in Beaconsfield for about six weeks – couldn't get rid of him in the end.

HASTINGS was one of Bunny's longstanding dates and booking the summer shows there finally gave me a chance to exorcise the ghost of that poor summer season at the White Rock Pavilion in 1978. Hastings Council still had the venue and I knew the entertainment manager, Roger Dennett, who seemed to like the idea that I now had such a major role in the Baron Organisation. I told him: 'You've really got to put a better standard of entertainment in here,' encouraging him to book acts like Tommy Cooper, and good Sunday concerts, with groups like the Searchers and the Seekers. 'If you're doing a week's variety,' I said, 'Let's put *names* in. They might be old-fashioned names, but give 'em something of value.' That was to work better for them than just throwing a summer show together.

Even so, the venue never made money. I was to be associated with the White Rock for quite a few years and booked several very good shows, paid for by the local council tax, all to no avail. Even Tommy Cooper didn't sell out completely – there were odd seats at the ends of rows – though probably as full as the White Rock could manage.

Booking Tommy was always a nightmare as he had an enormous capacity for alcohol and might not make the show if he'd been on a binge. But, though he was notorious for last-minute cancellations, he did turn up for me and was sensational.

The last White Rock summer season I appeared in was in 1982 with Lena Zavaroni, the child star from *Opportunity Knocks* who never grew up. Sadly, she was a chronic anorexic who seemed to take advice from the wrong people. Her manager, Dorothy Solomons, planted the seed very early on when Lena was a little girl and very impressionable, telling her to watch her weight; I think Lena was a bit in awe of her.

The show also featured Dougie Squires' Second Generation Dancers and I was directing as well as performing, partly to keep my eye on Lena. Her problems were already evident by then, although they never showed onstage or in her ability to take direction. She was still a great little performer though so painfully thin she'd be covered up onstage and given loose sleeved costumes: a little waif of a thing who didn't have a pick on her. I used to keep giving her Mars bars for all the good it did.

I had encouraged Roger Dennett to book her – hoping she would bring a younger crowd in – for only five weeks, so that it wouldn't overtax her. But although it was a very good summer show, it still did poor business. Hastings was not ready for Lena – or anyone else for that matter.

Hastings Council gave up on the traditional variety-style summer show after that and parted company with BJB Productions. Two summers of weekend shows also ran at a loss, despite some very big names, and eventually they bit the bullet and revamped the theatre, which is a much nicer hall now. But it was run on such old-fashioned lines when I knew it – it had a resident stage manager, two stage crew and a resident cat, called Omo. An article in *The Stage* aptly entitled 'Leaving Purgatory Behind' summed up what had been the main problem:

> The White Rock Pavilion was built in the days when municipal orchestras thrived and light entertainment was still the end of the pier ... The advent of radio, revues and summer shows demanded larger audiences ... and the 1,400 seater pavilion soon resounded to the patter of variety. As an orchestral concert hall, the acoustics were second to none. As a theatre, they were poor. Generations have sat in the circle with cupped ears, straining to listen to the whispers of a pantomime fairy or the vague deliveries of a fading thespian.

See? So it wasn't all my fault.

AS well as booking all the pantos and summer shows, my job as a producer meant travelling around the country to see as many new acts as possible, so I could see what was happening in the provinces, not just down south. Which leads me to the painful story of an opportunity missed – and this time there's no doubt that I have to bear the blame.

I found what I considered to be a very funny double act in Rotherham, when Angle Entertainments, a Doncaster club agency, put on a special showcase of their acts for me at the Rotherham Trades Working Men's Club. There was an audience of twelve, including me – well it was an afternoon show – but I genuinely laughed out loud at one double act who had the dreadful stage name of Cheese and Onion. The comic had a good sort of cheeky look about him – a bit Bobby

Ballish, though Bobby was more Lancastrian. But the act was original. They had a screen onstage, a three-sided thing, and the feed brought out a terrible, tatty vent doll and sat it on a chair. Every time he went behind the screen the comic would go and turn the head of this doll and go: 'AAARGH!' It was a very funny running gag. The feed would go: 'Don't touch the doll, just leave him alone, alright? He's got nothing to do with you.' It made me laugh, and I thought: 'That's a good bit of business, they can develop that.' Then they did a thing behind the screen, throwing things up in the air, which was funny visual stuff.

I hadn't intended to become an agent as I had already made the decision to be a producer, and the two don't really mix, but I was asked to try and find some TV work for a couple of friends – Dave Butler, a West Country comic I had worked with at Butlins, and Adam Daye, a very good comedy impressionist who needed TV exposure. And I thought that I might manage the career of the pair I had seen, Barry and Mike, alias Cheese and Onion (ugh). That they were funny was in no doubt, but they were a 'club act' and that was as far as they had come. What they needed was experience: proper stage work away from the working men's clubs.

The first thing Lisa Baron asked me about the boys was: did they have any class? Now that was a valuable lesson learnt. What Lisa was referring to is now almost dead and gone, but theatre performers used to have to have a certain style about them: a way of dressing, presenting themselves, behaving – a discipline. On stage, one was expected to be clean and immaculately turned out; even now, I would not dream of going onstage without looking smart. Sadly, it appears that, since the 'eighties, the opposite has become the norm.

So did Cheese and Onion have any class? The short answer – apart from the name – is that the potential was there. They were wanting to up their game; they had the capability; they were young enough (thirty-ish) and more than willing to learn. For my part, I loved the idea that I could pass on some of my knowledge to the younger generation in the form of these two eager and ambitious volunteers. I thought Barry, in particular, had funny bones and intended to give him every assistance.

In hindsight, however, I did not keep my promise, and threw them to the wolves.

It happened in stages, beginning with a visit from Alec Fyne, a talent booker with ATV and Lew Grade; I knew him from my days doing *Sunday Night at the London Palladium* and all the ATV shows I had done in the past. His office was quite near Luxborough Street, where I was based, and in 1981 I had been booked to do a variety show called *Starburst* for ATV.

Alec called in at the office because I had asked him to look at Dave Butler and Adam Daye with a view to their appearing on the show. I had a photograph of Cheese and Onion on my desk, and before I could whip the picture out of sight he asked me who they were: 'I haven't heard of these – can we see them?'

I protested that they were too rough as they stood, and that I would bring them to London when the time was right. But he insisted, saying all he had to do was make a couple of calls and he would find them anyway, so I reluctantly got the boys to London and told them what material I thought they should use at the audition.

They arrived at ATV's Elstree studios the following week and several producers attended the audition in a rehearsal room. I don't know to this day why I didn't hold them back as they had unbelievable potential. The act was a bit Yorkshire in dialect, but Barry had a very infectious comedic presence on stage, and they had developed a fairly good comedy rhythm, although they needed to get a lot more proper experience before they could really capitalise on their talent.

The audition went almost too well, as they did the cream of their material over about ten minutes. The producers who attended just fell about and I was immediately offered a spot on *Starburst*. This was naturally a result for them: all of a sudden, I had become some kind of miracle worker as I had only seen them two weeks before and was still mulling over the prospect of becoming their manager; nothing was signed and they already had an agent in Johnny Stvan, who was Angle Entertainments of Doncaster. I figured that a spot on *Starburst* wouldn't do them any harm; if presented and shot to advantage, it could even give the boys a lift.

They were booked onto *Starburst* for the last show of the series, which was recorded about three weeks before transmission in November 1981 on a Wednesday evening at 8pm on ITV. They gave the boys a top spot in the show and the flexibility to do about fifteen minutes' material. They brought the house down: there was a buzz around the studio, all about Cheese and Onion. The boys took it well, kept their heads down and left all the decisions to me.

The show went so well for them that I thought I might have been wrong. Maybe they *were* ready to do better things, even though my gut feeling was to have them do some theatre work, summer shows and a good pantomime, which I could give them.

I pre-empted the TV show with an ad in *The Stage*. After it was broadcast the phone went mad – and I still hadn't got them signed up for me to manage. Dick Condon, who produced the show at the Wellington Pier in Great Yarmouth, wanted them to top the bill for the next summer season, and it was all happening.

But what happened next eventually led to the boys splitting up, proving that I should have gone with my initial instinct and held them back from the start, or at least until I could gain some control of the situation.

About a week before the transmission of *Starburst*, I received a call from Alec Fyne to say they had a six-week slot in the summer for a new comedy show and he asked if the boys would like to be in it. My immediate reaction was, 'No: they are nowhere near ready for that sort of exposure.'

When Alec continued to call me to get a definite reply I tried to weigh things up. I knew how easily TV can kill as well as make careers, but could I stand in the way of this chance for the boys? I figured if I had some control of the material they were to use and could rehearse with them then maybe, just maybe, it might work, and I was excited for them.

I decided to put it to them face to face and arranged a meeting at their agent's house in Doncaster. After they'd signed a management agreement with me, I told them about the series. I told them the truth – that it was a risk and that they would have to work very hard to make it work, but I would be with them every step of the way. The excitement of seeing them so elated at this opportunity overshadowed all doubts at the time.

From the start I had a feeling that the format of the show wasn't right. The boys were joined by a Birmingham folk-type comedy act called Malc Stent, Sonny Hayes and Co, a comedy magic and mime act, and Nina Finburgh, who did comic monologues. It was produced and directed by Colin Clews, a top director at ATV responsible for Morecambe and Wise's early success; I knew him and had worked with him many times. Scripts were written for the boys and John Junkin was the script editor. Every evening after rehearsals I would do extra work with them to try and improve the material – which was, in the main, fairly weak to say the least. But we had to make it work, so we did. The show was duly recorded on Thursday evenings in a small studio at Elstree with a correspondingly small audience.

During Week Three I was collared by producer Colin Clews who told me I was interfering with the production: I was either to stop rehearsing with the boys or, if I wasn't happy, pull them out of the show.

I can't believe I didn't do this at the time. I think it was because the boys were well into the routine of rehearsals, and before transmission it is always hard to tell what the vast viewing public might make of a show. So I decided to keep schtum and say I was busy with other things, but have a look at the show before the dress run, and help them on the quiet.

I never told the boys what had happened then, because I knew they would walk out of the show. Some time later, when I did tell them, Barry said: 'No shadow of a doubt, if you'd told us we would have walked, we were 100 per cent with you.' And I thought: 'Christ, I should have bloody told them!'

They finished the series and almost immediately started rehearsals for a summer show in Great Yarmouth, where Dick Condon's show was being directed by Yvonne Marsh. The summer season, which opened in mid-June, was a disaster. The television series came out late June and ran to the end of July. I can't even remember the name of it, but it was a resounding flop and the Wellington Pier became emptier as the series progressed.

Alec Fyne called me to say that the option of a second series would not be taken up as contracted, although the fee would be paid. The boys were naturally deflated, and although I had a pantomime lined up for them at Blackpool it was still very disappointing. They split up not long after that and Barry started doing an act on his own. He was still working around the clubs until recently, though I understand he has now retired.

To this day, I really don't know why Colin Clews went off on one. I wasn't trying to usurp his authority, just trying to protect an act which had skyhigh potential – and he knew I was part of the package. He told me I was interfering too much but I tried to make it clear that the boys were relying on me, and the material just wasn't that great as it stood.

Actually, the writing side of it may have been a bit of a pet project for him, so that could have been part of the problem. All the other performers on the show were coming with ready-made material; it was only Cheese and Onion who were having stuff written for them, and Colin had made a very public announcement about avoiding established writers and using this as an opportunity to discover new talent, telling *The Stage* in December 1981:

> What I want is someone with a fresh approach to come and evolve a relationship between these two comedians out of their own personalities.

This, in effect, was what had happened with his previous charges, Morecambe and Wise, shortly after they were poached by the BBC: Bill Cotton put them together with Eddie Braben, creating the team which made television history. But Eddie Brabens don't grow on trees and the writer whom Colin selected – 'a travelling salesman for a car seat cover firm in the West Midlands' according to *The Stage* – was not of that calibre.

It would have been wonderful if it had all come

together, but looked at another way Colin had opted to double the risk – untried performers and an untried writer – in a very public arena.

Sadly, I was proven correct in my prediction that they needed work and that it had all come too far too fast. My fault, as I could – and should – have stopped it. It still haunts me a bit even now. It's like one of those Thomas Hardy short stories where some tiny event starts the dominoes toppling: if Alec Fyne hadn't seen that photograph on my desk that day …

It also highlights how fickle this business can be and how much success is dependent on chance: when television opportunity knocked for me, I happened to be ready; Cheese and Onion were not.

BY the end of my second year with Lisa Baron I had virtually taken over BJB Productions and set up concerts and tours never explored with Bunny.

The most memorable of these was an extraordinary hypnosis act which came about after I had been summoned over to Canada to see a spectacular magic show. This had been recommended by a very dear friend of mine, Harry Stanley, an advisor to David Nixon, Paul Daniels and all those great magicians. One of magic's great prop builders, Harry had become mentor and manager to Johnny Hart, another exceptional magician whose act consisted of producing budgies from thin air, followed by a huge cockatoo and then a big white cat; I worked with Johnny a lot and would often follow him with my act, which was great with my budgie jokes.

Harry had told me about Peter Reveen – 'The Great Reveen'– who was touring the biggest magic show in the world, currently playing at the O'Keefe Centre in Toronto. Reveen was willing to pay for me to go over to see the show and bring it to Great Britain; he had already sent his manager and we had toured all the theatres in Britain where this huge show might play. Reveen was actually an Australian who lived in Las Vegas, and his huge magic show had big animals, tigers and others – a fabulous, spectacular evening, not seen in the UK for years … and at the end of the week I was there, he went skint, and so did the show.

Was this the end of my plan to bring The Great Reveen to Britain? Not quite. I just loved this man's showmanship and although he was a magic nut – that's really what he wanted to do – what he made his money with was a sensational hypnosis show like you have never seen: it played in stadiums.

You see, the trick with a hypnosis show isn't about the hypnosis as such: it's about the presentation. The more people you pack in, the more likely you are to have a lot of subjects that you are able to control. If you only have a small audience, say a hundred people, it's quite likely you might only get one or two people who are susceptible; with five thousand in a stadium, you're going to get two or three hundred – *bingo*!

He sent me videotapes and I could see it was a fabulous show. You couldn't acquire a license to do it in England but you could in Scotland, so I booked him into the Playhouse in Edinburgh.

He had a unique selling pattern, where he would give out complimentary tickets and fill the theatre for the first three days: it was absolutely jam-packed. He did the show with his four sons, and his stunning wife Coral, and would ask over a hundred people up onto the stage, dismiss the ones that were no good, and finish up with about twenty. He didn't do all that eating an onion and making it taste like an apple stuff; he got them to do things like blocking up imaginary water coming in from the proscenium arch, and then he'd tell them: 'Go back in the audience, and when you hear this music you will run back on the stage.' After the interval the music would play – and sure enough, all these people would rush back on stage.

Now, with a place the size of the Playhouse in Edinburgh – 3,500 – over the last three days you could really take money. He'd tell the audience, 'It will be a totally different show on Thursday, a brand new show – come back and tell your friends!' He packed it for the last three nights, and did that for eight weeks, breaking house records.

NOT all my shows with Lisa were on that sort of level, but I thoroughly enjoyed whatever came along. We put out a tour of *The Pyramid Game*, a TV quiz show with a well-known presenter, Steve Jones. It didn't do terribly well – we had a problem getting the prizes together – but he was very good in it. I also put quite a few concerts into the Fort, in Jersey, as well as a tour with Frankie Vaughan and lots of nice variety weeks in different places.

I had also insisted on a proper electric typewriter in the office to do better business letters: word processing was not yet upon us in the early 'eighties, but I knew we had to make our office look more efficient. I was still performing my own act, meanwhile, combining my office schedule with one-nighters and concerts in Llandudno for dear Clive Stock, so I really was getting the best of both worlds.

I was happy to be there, and would have stayed, but Lisa suddenly said: 'Fred, I really can't afford you.'

I knew it was nothing to do with that. Since Bunny's death, she had begun a relationship with the repertory producer Charles Vance, who had advised her to get rid of me: the plan was for him to amalgamate his office with hers.

I was on an annual contract and we'd come to the end of my second year; I could see that he was worming his way in there and I knew what was going to happen.

Forced to consider my options, I decided that, as I had made some good contacts over the last two years, I would try to have a go on my own as a producer. There had already been several phone calls from theatre managements to say they didn't really want the Bunny Baron Organisation to present their shows; this had put me in a very difficult situation while I was working for Lisa, but now things were different. Not that I wanted to steal any of Lisa's theatres, but the truth of the matter was they didn't want her – they wanted me. I had already set up the 1982 season with Jack Tripp at the Hippodrome, Eastbourne, which I also did the lighting for, and Lena's show with me at Hastings.

I hadn't actually thought about going into management for myself, but when it came to the crunch I found I wasn't averse to the idea as I'd established my credentials a bit by then. I wasn't overly enamoured with the prospect of being in an office on my own but I was forced into it, so I did it. This was the real big turning point for me, rather than when I started to work for Lisa. I knew I'd really have to commit to this new career; I couldn't go on trying to run it alongside my other work.

I never actively said I was never going to do stand-up again, but I let it take a back step because I really wanted to give management and production a go. Over the next six years I did the odd after-dinner, but as far as performing went that was more or less it: no pantos, no summer shows, no clubs even – and as I'd always enjoyed doing my stand-up act, it was a bit of a sacrifice.

But I knew this career change had to work. I could explain away the 1978 White Rock season as a blip: a lousy venue, a bad season. But it wasn't the only sign that things were starting to change for me.

Fame may come overnight, but it doesn't disappear the same way. There's no sudden draining away: it ebbs, and you don't realise it immediately.

I remember when I first started to notice that I wasn't 'exciting' anymore. Let me explain what I mean by that. Exciting was the reaction when walking on in the Bradford pantomime, when they were really, really waiting for me to come on. Exciting was coming out at the Palladium, and the Blackpool shows, when you felt that the audience was really going: 'Wow!'

Around the time Lisa and I parted as business partners, I was doing odd episodes of a TV series with Lennie Bennett called *Punchlines*. We were introduced one by one, all the celebs sitting in the boxes, and when my turn came I could sense that there was no excitement from the audience anymore. A TV audience will always give you a bigger cheer than in a theatre anyway, because they're told to, but I thought it wasn't as big a cheer as some of the others got. That's when I felt it was waning. It wasn't hostile, wasn't a groan or anything, but it wasn't 'Wow!' More sort of a cheerfully resigned: 'Oh – him again.' That's the first time I thought: 'Hey up! That's not as good as it used to be.'

When my Baron contract wasn't renewed, I could have gone back to performing full-time. But did I really want to spend the rest of my career watching my name slipping slowly down the bill, in fear of the day when it might drop off altogether? Or did I want to take a shot at something which would help my long-term survival in the only business I knew? (I made a lousy undertaker, remember.)

It wasn't without risks. Working for Lisa, in what now seemed like my apprenticeship, there had been the safety net of a salary. Now I would have to generate my own income, rise – or fall – by my own efforts. But it was a new venture. An *ad*venture. As early as 1972 I had told an interviewer: 'A man without a challenge in life might just as well stop living.'

As it happens I did eventually return to stand-up, only without the parrot, when circumstances forced me to reinvent myself yet again ... but that's another chapter.

16: Freddie Davies Productions

I NEEDED an office in London, so I rented a small room on the ground floor of the Regent Palace Hotel. It was almost at the rear entrance and very cheap, one of several which could not be let as guest rooms and which mainly housed the admin for the hotel group. Along the corridor were a corporate travel agent and a ticket tout, but the address was one of the best in London: Freddie Davies Entertainments Ltd, The Regent Palace Hotel, Piccadilly Circus, London Wl.

I furnished it from an auction house in Frith Street, just behind the Prince Edward Theatre, where I bought some good stuff – and some crap – over the years. I won the bid on a pair of Bose theatre speakers worth over £2,000 from a bankrupt nightclub – I got them for £225. I also bid for a wonderful office chair in luxurious leather, swivel and hydraulic lift, which must have cost at least £1,000 when new. I got it for about £25 and pushed it back along Brewer Street to the rear of the Regent Palace ... knackering the wheels.

Several acts asked and some pestered me to represent them and I took on Adam Daye, Dave Butler and Frances Van Dyke, a great speciality violin act from Denmark. There was also an Arab tumbling act, all sixteen of them – I never got them work – Ken Wood, a ventriloquist I had worked with as a Redcoat, and Cheese and Onion.

I seemed to attract quite a few casting directors who were looking for the sort of faces you couldn't find in *Spotlight*. I knew many great characters from my club days in Manchester and was always getting them up to London for castings for films, television and commercials.

It started with a casting agent called Patsy Pollock, who was also a casting director for Alan Parker: she had an office just round the back of the Regent Palace, and she had called me out of the blue, saying, 'I need a craggy kind of character.' This led to other things and I was always ringing up the old comics. She used to say: 'Oh, Alan loves your work, you know.' I said: 'But he never puts me in anything, does he?'

Anyway, I became quite well known for booking odd characters, and when I accompanied some of them to the auditions I'd often be asked in to see the director and occasionally get offered a job myself.

One of these was for a film with Bob Geldof in his pre-*Live Aid* days called *Number One*; I had fixed one of the major parts as a snooker manager for a comedian friend called Tony ('Silly Thing!') Scott. Tony was a really old-fashioned variety comic who was not in a good way at the time – he was living on a caravan site on the Isle of Wight. He had just finished one of my pantomimes playing Dame when Patsy rang me and said, 'I want a cigar-smoking Lew Grade type'. I immediately thought of Tony as I knew he smoked big cigars and was always a bit flamboyant.

I rang him: 'Tony, how was the panto?'

'Oh, it was marvellous, dear boy – marvellous!'

'Have you got any cigars left?'

A sudden change of tone: 'I can't afford bloody cigars anymore!'

'Well, you'd better go and buy one and get up here sharpish – there's a job going.'

I told him to go in with a cigar and be his normal, flash self, and he got the part as soon as he walked in: four weeks' work at Wembley, which was set up for the World Snooker Final, and I found myself cast as the referee. I fetched him a bloody good deal for it as well, actually – better than I got.

Geldof certainly looked the part: a snooker hustler pressured into going pro by a bookie (Mel Smith) who wants him to throw the championship.

There were some very good names in the cast, including the great Alison Steadman as Bob's girlfriend, but I can't say I have very fond memories of making the film. I found Geldof quite arrogant and there was some not very nice banter between Mel Smith and me. There was quite a big crowd of extras as the audience at Wembley and I used to do things to keep them entertained between shots. When Mel asked why, I could only say: 'Well, rather than sit talking to you, I thought I'd amuse the crowd.' Anytime I did try to speak, he would do all that: 'Oh, hang on a minute – *another* anecdote!' Bet he'd have loved this book.

The film was not very good – in fact I don't think Geldof did another.

I HELPED to cast several other films and commercials which had unusual requirements for craggy faces, and through Clive Stock I acquired several West End hotel banqueting and corporate bookings for comedy acts of all types. So it was all go for Freddie Davies Entertainments.

But much as I enjoyed being an agent and getting work for all the old comics, my main focus was production: that was where the creativity and the challenge were. Exploring my new surroundings I would wander round Soho and Wardour Street thinking up new ideas, looking forward to the day a show would appear under the banner of Freddie Davies Productions.

That opportunity came in 1983, when I was asked to produce the summer show at the Hippodrome, Eastbourne, as Lisa Baron had lost the date. It is true that the powers of the Entertainments department at Eastbourne had intimated that they would engage my services if I ever set up on my own. Lisa was not pleased, but I hired her costumes and scenery for the show, so she did not lose out.

I was very fond of Lisa and we became good friends over the years – and, as I had predicted, Charles Vance dumped her when he realised her business was failing. She was still directing pantos up until the late 'eighties and used to ring me often. One day she rang to say: 'I've had a stroke. It's affecting my sight and I've to be very careful because I'm likely to have another one.' She had a series of them before going blind. We got her into Brinsworth House, the theatrical home for the variety artists' charity the Entertainment Artistes' Benevolent Fund, which receives the proceeds from the Royal Variety Show each year. It's for poor and distressed variety artists and Lisa qualified, bless her. It was a very sad end, especially as she'd already been through a lot with Bunny's illness. She died in 2012.

THAT first summer show at Eastbourne was a blessing and, in many ways, a curse. It established me as a producer and enabled me to join the TMA – *Theatrical Management Association* – the governing body for provincial theatre.

The TMA, which admits both theatres and producers as members, sets minimum salaries and rules of engagement, issuing contracts, etc. There is a two year probationary period before you can become a full member, the rules being stringently upheld. It's meant to stop dodgy producers from setting up or staging shows without proper financial back-up and is, in essence, a very honourable organisation. It doesn't stop unscrupulous non-TMA producers from putting on shows and ignoring the rules, though they usually come unstuck when the showbiz union, Equity, demands that two weeks' salary is deposited by the management to pay the artists, in case the show fails and they try to do a runner. TMA members don't have to put up a deposit.

Unfortunately the system falls down if you're foolish enough to go into business with a producer who is not in the organisation. That's what I did years later – and paid the price.

But more immediately pressing on the 'curse' side of things was the error I made in misreading my star for the 1983 summer show in Eastbourne: Russ Conway, the pianist with a huge following in the late 'fifties and 'sixties. Russ remained a box office draw in the right situation – Eastbourne, which attracted an older audience, fitted the bill. I also engaged Billy Dainty, Dave Butler, a West Country comic who had had some success on the TV show *The Comedians*, along with Adam Daye, a very good comedy impressionist, and Sandy and Derick Warren, a classy and attractive musical act.

Derick came from South Africa and Sandy, a stunning redhead with a voice to die for, was English. They were introduced to me by Clive Stock who asked if I could handle them as their agent. Derick and I had professional differences and soon parted company on a business level, but we remained in contact; later he would throw me a lifeline when my fortunes took another turn for the worse.

My experience presenting the show was not a problem: I had bank backing and the finance in place to produce a very good show. I had heard on the grapevine about Conway's tantrums and intransigence, but I felt sure that I would be able to handle him. Being a performer myself, I really thought I knew how to deal with most situations but, as I have said on many occasions, you cannot deal with stupidity.

The trouble started just after Conway signed the contract to do the season, insisting contractually, on a Steinway Grand Piano for his act. Okay. Eastbourne had one, a full concert Grand, which was kept at the Congress theatre and mainly used for classical concerts – and yes, I could use it at the Hippodrome. Next question: what was the model number of the said piano? Okay. We got that for him. He checked the piano's history and condition with Steinway then in March '83, he suggested we should go to Eastbourne to try it.

We met at Victoria Station and I purchased two first class tickets (production expenses, in those days about £10 each) and off we went. I had set up a nice lunch with the entertainment boss for Eastbourne Theatres, who was delighted to meet Russ – after all, he was coming for the season, so would be drumming, or rather tinkling, up business for the town.

We were met at the station and taken backstage to the Congress to try the piano. Russ opened the lid and, with one finger, pressed on three or four keys, then said, 'Why have you brought me all the way down here? This piano is very good.'

Then we went for lunch at a very nice restaurant with the theatre boss and his assistant, in a private dining room. We ordered, and just before service Russ suddenly decided he had to go back to London, saying to me, 'You obviously have business to discuss and I am in the way.' Then he got up and left. Two days later he sent me a cheque for £10 to cover his fare, as if to suggest that the entire expedition – his idea, remember – had been a waste of his time.

A ten-day rehearsal period started in the middle of April and the show, which I had dubbed *Showtime,* was to open on a Friday for twenty-two weeks, with a change of show every Thursday so audiences could see two shows in one week if on holiday. It was decided that Russ would just do his act at the end of the show, about thirty-five minutes.

The press office at the council arranged an interview with Russ for a local paper but, on the morning in question, he failed to turn up. We didn't have mobile phones in those days, so had no way of contacting him. The reporter was quite put out as they had the slot to fill for the next week's edition, so he asked if he could interview me instead and did a piece about my transition from performer to producer. When the newspaper came out Russ was furious and accused me of being jealous and trying to steal his thunder!

It gets better. His first appearance at rehearsals was on Thursday afternoon, the day before we opened. I had sent the cast off whilst I staged and lit his act: he was to play through his repertoire and I would set the lighting and the cues. He sat at the piano and found fault with just about everything: the light was in his eyes – yes, the spotlight, which was on him – so we put a soft gel into the spotlight. Then another light was bothering him. Then the pit band (of three) were playing too loud ...

In the end I almost lost my cool and my son Kent, who was operating the follow spot, came down and just about held me back from slapping him just as the rest of the cast came back to rehearse the finale. They had not seen what had been happening, only that I was busting a gut, shouting for them to leave, saying I would set the finale after the dress run that evening.

The Royal Hippodrome was celebrating its 100th anniversary in 1983, and there was an extensive exhibition of memorabilia on display in the foyer. I thought using this as a pre-show opening might work, and it did: the house curtain went up to reveal a screen on which was projected a list of the many stars who had appeared there over the years, ending with the current season and a lifesize picture of Billy Dainty in a pose. The screen was then flown out to reveal the real Billy, and the show started with the dancers and cast, except Russ, doing the opening routine.

At the start of the dress rehearsal I was centre stalls on row five and Russ came to sit on the end of the row; as he had not been at rehearsals before the debacle of the previous day, he had never seen any of the show. The band struck up the opening number, *Thanks for the Memory*, as the house tabs were taken out and the 100-year nostalgic screening started. Russ jumped up from his seat, shouting to me: 'You never told me it was a *Thanks for the Memory* show – I'm off!' and stormed out of the theatre.

The dress run continued without a hiccup and Conway was back in place for his spot at the end. He went through his act, albeit with tetchy annoyance; we did the finale, had a drink with the company and left the theatre.

The opening night went well and, at the after show party in the circle bar, Russ made a sort of apology for his behaviour, saying: 'I know I have given you some stress'– but that was all he said. I stayed to put on the second show for the following week and really tried to engage Russ in conversation, but we were like oil and water: he just did not like me. I could live with that, but three days after the opening night I was backstage when he came over and said in a loud voice: 'How much did you have to bung the council to get this date?' Now that was a step too far. Furious, I called a meeting with the entertainment supremo as it was also a slur on him.

It's not easy to sack the top of the bill because so many factors come into play: the cost of reprinting the posters alone would be expensive and of course the resulting publicity would not be good. I had a word with his agent, Tony Lewis, who told me Russ would continue to perform as per contract – which he did.

I went back to London and only visited the show on Thursdays to pay the salary cheques and see the change of programme was okay. I barely spoke to Russ for twelve weeks, even though I was paying him £1,000 per week, which amounted to approximately 20 per cent of the show's gross takings. We were civil, just about, by the end of the season, but little did I know that he was really going to screw me up the following year.

At the start of the 1983 season I had, as producer, invited entertainment managers from the various resorts to see my show. Several responded, asking me to make proposals for future years. Torquay, in particular, had really liked the Russ Conway show and asked if I could put this on for them at the small Babbacombe theatre, also famous for older audiences, for their 1984 season. Much to my surprise, Tony Lewis said Russ would do it, subject to the piano being a Steinway. So putting personal feelings aside and with my business hat on, I proceeded to put a show together with Russ as top of the bill.

All was well until I sent the contract to Tony for Russ to sign in late December of '83. Tony rang to say that Russ was away at his retreat in Spain, but would sign it on his return in March. I carried on but did not get any posters printed. Why? I must have had a premonition.

March came and I was badgering Tony to get the

contract signed. Eventually he called me and said: 'Russ has refused to sign the contract.' When I asked why, he said he didn't know, no reason – just refused to sign. Tony was in his office at the top of Regent House, the agent's office block near Oxford Circus; I went to see him but he could do nothing.

My next move was to try and rescue the season at Babbacombe. I had a contract to supply Russ Conway and a summer show; I was to get a percentage of the box office takings but supply all the staffing. I arranged a meeting with the entertainment department of the Torquay council, who turned out to be about ten very nice, old and wise gentlemen. We met in the council chamber and I told them I could not supply Conway, and why, but assured them I could still put on a show for the season – and they agreed that I could.

I then proceeded to engage The Bachelors for two weeks, along with fortnightly runs of other artists such as the Beverley Sisters, John Hanson and Moira Anderson under the banner *Season of Stars*; I did a week myself with the resident company which consisted of solo comedian Barry Cheese (they had split up by now), Adam Daye, a lovely double song and dance act called Taxi and another act I cannot recall. My son Kent was the theatre and company manager.

The season was a business disaster. My friends the Bachelors came direct from their court case which basically was an act to get rid of John Stokes on the pretence that he could not sing; they had split the act up and had some very damaging press. They cost me over £10,000 and emptied the theatre. When I had to take special measures to pay them and payment was delayed by a day, their manager, Philip Solomon – he of the clever accounting skills where my records were concerned – decided to blacken my name in all the venues I was presenting shows. Lovely man.

To make matters worse, John Hanson had to pull out

halfway through his run with throat trouble, forcing Renée and Renato to cover, and the council were becoming restive about the poor attendances. Moira Anderson agreed to bow out and I changed the format to a revue-style show without any top names so that ticket prices could be lowered. It didn't help.

THINGS were much better round the coast at Eastbourne, where the show at the Royal Hippodrome with Dickie Henderson and Peter Goodwright was a resounding success – and, indeed, a very good production. Dickie, a consummate professional, became a good friend. He used to make me laugh. We had this magician on, a girl called Julie Llusion – such a clever name. She was a gorgeous blonde who could have passed for Swedish until she spoke, revealing a rich Stoke on Trent / Potteries accent. So I suggested, 'Well, Julie, I don't want you to speak, I just want you to do a silent, sophisticated, magical act.' She said, 'Awh, Mr Davies, I'll do whatever you want.'

This worked well – until one fateful night.

I'd go on the Thursday to do the change of programme and one night Dickie said: 'Bob, come in the dressing room.' He always used to call me Bob because, on the first day of rehearsal for the opening routine, he walked down the stairway, which lit up as he descended, and he was supposed to do a dance with the girl on his right but kept going to his left. So I said, 'Look, Dick, if you're gonna go to the girl on the left you need to rehearse the routine you're gonna do with her, 'cause you're supposed to be doing it with the one who is on the right.' To which he replied: 'Hold it everybody – Bob Fosse's in town!'

So he always called me Bob: 'Bob, come in the dressing room.' So I said, 'What's up?' He said, 'Have you heard about Tuesday night?' I said, 'No, what happened?''Well, I did the warm-up, Julie was next on, doing eight minutes, no talking. I announced her in the blackout: "Ladies and gentlemen, international illusionist Julie ..."' – and as he said the word 'Julie', the cloth went out, catching the props, knocking them all over the stage. 'Ladies and gentlemen, international illusionist, Julie ... ' – and when he heard the props going, he said: 'THE THIRD WORLD WARRRR!'

So they bring the front cloth in and Dickie goes on again and does a few more gags – he can hear Julie behind him, crying, with the stagehands going: 'Come on, of course you can do it – push the dove back up!' and she's saying, 'Awwww, I can't do it now, it's all gone off!' 'No no, put the bloody silks back in the box!'

Eventually the cry went up: 'She's ready! She's ready!' And Dickie said: 'Ladies and gentlemen ... for the second time this evening ... Julie Lluuu– ' and behind him he can hear her cry out: 'OH SHHHITTTT!'

The cloth went up and she went into her act, all her mascara running, tears streaming down her face, looking like Alice Cooper. Every time she got a trick right, every time something worked, like the dove jumped out of the box, she cried and went, 'Ohhhhhhhh ....' I only wish she could have done this every night.

Dickie did manage to avert, or at least deflect, another disaster during the run – though it says more for his judgement than mine. I had a call from journalist Jonathan Meades, who wanted to do a piece for *The Sunday Times Magazine* on the Eastbourne show as it was the longest running summer show in Britain. Could he interview its star? 'No problem,' I said, 'I'll ask him on Thursday when I do the changeover.'

I told Dickie about the prospect of a nice colour supplement piece. And he said, quite simply: 'No.' 'Oh,' I said, nonplussed. 'Think it might be good for the show.' 'No,' he said more firmly, 'it wouldn't.' I asked whether he would mind if I asked Peter Goodwright, who was second top, to do the piece and he said, 'Go ahead.'

So I went up to Peter and explained how they'd like to do an interview, pictures and everything, and asked if he would do it. He looked at me: 'Why won't Dickie do it?' I was forced to admit that he'd said it wouldn't be a sympathetic piece. 'Well, if he won't do it, I won't do it.'

So with my tail between my legs I got back to *The Sunday Times* and told Jonathan Meades they'd said no, and why. 'Unless ... could we have final approval of what goes in?'

'No, we never do that.'

He did a piece instead about the summer show at Cromer Pavilion, which was directed by Robert Marlowe, who had directed my panto in Torquay in 1972. It was exactly what Dickie had said it would be, opening up with:

> 'The director of this end of the pier show is the toupeed Robert Marlowe.'

I read the first two lines and rang Meades up; it was a Sunday morning, I'll never forget it. He picked up the phone and I said, 'Hello, Freddie Davies here, I've just read your piece about the summer show.' He tried to interrupt, but I told him exactly what I thought of him and his smarmy stitch-up of some decent, hardworking performers, swore at him a few times for good measure and slammed the phone down.

Ten years later he was doing a piece about a new restaurant that had opened in the Regent Palace, and in between having a pop at the waiters for their 'sullen ineptitude' and complaining about the foie gras and his overdone duck confit, I was touched to see that he'd taken the time to recall me 'in full fulmination, ranting and screeching, all psittacine dander.' (That's 'parrot-related' if you don't have a dictionary to hand.)

I WAS also producing pantos during this time, of course. In fact, one of the main things which had appealed to me about setting up on my own was getting the chance to stage more ambitious shows. Working for Lisa had been an invaluable apprenticeship but Bunny Baron was very much on the outer reaches of the panto world: they only really did the dates nobody else wanted, without any real names, just very good pantos. The biggest date they had was Lewisham Concert Hall, where they had to put a star name in. I had seen that and knew there was a wider world that I really wanted to get into, presenting shows on a grand scale in big theatres with all-star casts – I'd even been in a few of them myself.

I produced two pantomimes at the Grand Theatre, Blackpool, the first they'd had since changing back from a bingo hall. *Cinderella* was the first year, 1982/83, starring a very popular local Lancashire folk group called the Houghton Weavers, with the glamorous Caravelles as Prince and Dandini and Blackpool-based John Comer (who played the cafe owner in *Last of the Summer Wine* forever). *Aladdin* followed in 1983/84 with Stan Boardman as Wishie Washie, Cheese and Onion, still together then, as the Pekin Police and Cheryl Murray, who had just come out of *Coronation Street*, as Principal Boy.

The pantomimes were a moderate success but not good enough to continue the contract. I took the management to see Doddy with a view to having him the following year, but the salary he wanted was far too restrictive and impossible for such a small capacity venue, although he did do it for another management some years later. Obviously, they could afford him!

During that second Blackpool season, I also put another panto on, which took me a bit closer to my Palladium-sized ambitions. I had been asked to quote for the Congress, Eastbourne, and had secured the services of Norman Wisdom to star in *Robinson Crusoe* – his usual choice of panto, as it provided the maximum number of comedy scenes to display his talents. I put the proposal in writing to the powers at Eastbourne Theatres department, who seemed keen, and awaited their response.

After about two weeks I still hadn't had a reply but had heard, on the showbiz grapevine, that the New Theatre, Oxford were in the market for offers. I called Sam Shrouder, who I knew, at Apollo Leisure, and fixed up a meeting. The New Theatre, Oxford was a much better proposition than Eastbourne Congress, so that was all to the good.

The deal was agreed with Apollo immediately and all I had to do was talk Norman Wisdom into the change of venue. Not necessarily an easy task: it had taken me ages to get him to agree to Eastbourne.

I flew over to the Isle of Man and Norman met me in the Rolls, admitting that he never got it out normally, so I must have been important. The afternoon was taken up with Norman enacting the whole *Robinson Crusoe* pantomime in his large lounge with grand piano accompaniment, to an audience of one – me. It took about three hours and he played all the parts – Principal Girl, Boy, Dame, etc and, of course, his part of Billy Crusoe, ending with his self-penned theme song *Don't Laugh at Me ('Cause I'm a Fool)*. Did he want to impress me or just need an audience? Both, probably.

It was at this stage that I told him I had to change the venue to Oxford; he agreed, but only if I would provide accommodation on top of a salary of £10,000 per week. I asked John Redgrave to direct Norman's pantomime, as he had worked with Norman on several occasions and Norman trusted him.

A few days before Christmas, I sat in the auditorium with Sam Shrouder from Apollo and watched the opening night show. One of Norman's comedy items with his straight man, Tony Fayne, was to pick Tony's nose and do some elastic business with the supposed snot, which received a 'yuck' reaction from the audience. This was always an awful gag, but seeing it with the general manager of the theatre sitting next to me and people around us retching made it seem far worse.

Sam asked me to take it out, so I asked John Redgrave, the director, to speak to Norman – who refused, saying that he had done it for forty years and no one had complained before, so it stayed or he walked. I knew he wouldn't take it out but I had to show willing for Sam. The problem was no one had ever challenged Norman in the past: promoters are afraid of upsetting their stars and would rather suffer the complaints than be faced with an ultimatum.

On the other hand, I had been in similar situations as a performer, and could understand Norman's attitude: it was part of his regular routine. Not that I had ever refused to go on myself – well I did once, though I was only joking. At the Gaumont in Ipswich, the freezing cold backstage dressing rooms had stone floors and I asked for a bit of cheap carpet to keep the costumes clean and to change on. I was ignored until I threatened to go – when a bit of cheap carpet miraculously appeared. I have a feeling my manager, Paul Kacharia, paid for it.

At the New Theatre, Oxford, the dressing rooms were fine. Norman did his awful snot gag and the show went on to do record breaking business and we all made money. During the run he suggested he take me out for a meal after the show one night, which he did – to the cheapest Indian restaurant in Oxford. He died a multimillionaire. But we were always very friendly, even if he was a mean old bugger. There's no doubt he was one of Britain's best loved, most popular and impersonated entertainers: he never stopped being big business until he stopped working. Barry Cheese did a great impersonation of him, and when I took him down to meet Norman in Oxford, Barry was crying – in awe of him, he was.

Incidentally, the first time I ever saw Norman on stage was in *Aladdin* at the Palladium in 1956/57. I don't know whether it was written for him or whether it was his idea, but he had a way of getting into his act that was pure brilliance. I tried to do it myself but it never quite worked for me.

When Norman, playing Aladdin, rubbed the lamp and a genie appeared, he said to the genie, 'Can you tell me what's going to happen in the future?' The genie said, 'Yes master.' A screen dropped in and he said, 'There will be a magic thing called television, and there will be things called aeroplanes,'– and suddenly there was a plane flying on the television. He mentioned some other things then said, 'And in the future there will be a famous comedian called Norman Wisdom.' An image of Norman appeared on the screen and Norman, as Aladdin, said, 'Bring him here!' And the genie said, 'Master, it is done.'

Blackout, flash – and in that flash, Norman appeared in the familiar too-tight suit and cap, and got a huge round of applause. But then, to a gasp from the audience, Aladdin came on from the wings again: 'Hello.' The 'Norman' in the suit was actually a lookalike called Ken Wilson. 'Who are you?' Aladdin asked. 'I'm Norman,' Ken said. 'And you're on this thing called television?' the real Norman asked. 'I want to be you!' Turning to the genie, he demanded: 'Make me like him.' Blackout, quick change – and that's how he got into his act. Just brilliant.

Oh, and I'm still waiting for a reply from Eastbourne.

AFTER the success of Norman at Oxford, I decided to set my sights higher for the following season. I wanted to put a show into the Dominion, Tottenham Court Road, because there wasn't another panto in the West End – the Palladium was occupied with Tommy Steele and *Singin' in the Rain*. I was going to put in George Cole and Dennis Waterman, who were very big with *Minder* at the time, as Baron and Buttons in *Cinderella*. It would have been a great combination, along with a star cast.

I'd got it all ready to go and needed some financial backing. My bank manager took me to lunch and asked how much I wanted. I hesitated a bit, then said I'd probably need about a hundred thousand over the first two weeks until I could get the box office money. He said: 'Well, I can authorise that now, but if you want more than that I'll have to go to a higher authority.' So I could have got what I wanted.

In the end, however, it didn't materialise. George Cole didn't want to do it and I just couldn't find a big enough name to replace him. Keith Harris put in his own production of *Humpty Dumpty* that year, complete with Cuddles and Orville.

Meanwhile, I still had to find a panto for the season, even if it couldn't be on the scale I envisaged. The Gaumont, Doncaster, seemed a good venue to stage a pantomime and as I hadn't secured a date, I decided to have a go with a rental. The show was *Aladdin*: I was to top the bill, with Ronnie Hilton as Emperor, Jimmy Marshall as Genie of the Lamp and several artists I had known over the years, who were tried and tested: Mair and Des Owen from Blackpool, local juveniles and a great pit band led by Don Shearman with my son, Kent, on drums.

The show was good but business was appalling, mainly due to the miners' strike, which went on for some time over the Christmas period. Based around Doncaster, it totally killed the business and I suffered a big loss. The only person who made any money in the area was the feller who did the catering for the police – he became a multimillionaire.

The following year I finally achieved my dream of staging that Palladium-sized panto. It was a spectacular success: everything I could have wished for.

What I didn't know was that it was also to be the beginning of a series of events which would lead to disaster and send my life spinning in a very different direction.

17: A Webb of Lies

THE year 1985 was to see the beginning of some major changes in my life, personal and professional.

Just after the Doncaster pantomime came to an end I decided it was finally time to split from Jackie and move in with Vanessa. It was my decision and I was entirely to blame for the break-up of my marriage. Jackie was heartbroken, I know, and naturally very bitter for many years.

Over the years I had drifted from her and, being away for weeks on end, it was easy for me to stray from the fold. My status had once been like that of a pop star and there had been one night stands. But I didn't parade my indiscretions in front of Jackie and, though I think she had suspicions, she didn't actually know; we never spoke about them.

It took fully five years before I left, absolutely certain by then that Vanessa was not in that casual category: she was just too important to me. During that time our relationship had been continually on-and-off, as we both tried to fight our feelings; Vanessa even went to Hong Kong at one stage in an effort to escape the situation, but then she came back and everything was rekindled again.

So what made me eventually make the huge decision to walk out of my marriage? All I can say for certain is that sometime after Vanessa came back from Hong Kong it just became impossible to keep it hidden: the build-up of guilt about my deceit and lies was too great. It was unfair to Vanessa and it was unfair to Jackie that I should be so dishonest, and I decided that it was time. And I think Jackie realised it was time because she never asked me to go back when I left. I think in some ways it must have been a release for her too.

Vanessa was someone I had been searching for without knowing it. Apart from being beautiful and attractive and all those things, there was something about her businesswise as well: I felt we were on the same wavelength with her being in show business, but not being a performer, so there was no rivalry or jealousy there, just the knowledge of what I did. There was definitely more compatibility.

Jackie did help me with my work a lot and, particularly when we did panto, she helped me with costumes and stuff and was very useful, there's no doubt about it. She's probably more compatible with showbiz now, as she joined the Lady Ratlings after we parted and has become one of their stalwarts, enjoying the meetings and the women there.

Kent was twenty-two at the time this happened and already going his own way. He had worked on the shows I was associated with and had a good grounding in all aspects of show business backstage, from making props for Charlie Drake to running the Babbacombe Theatre, but he chose to be his own man and became a very good rock drummer; he now teaches drums and percussion. I am very proud of his achievements. He has a lovely wife, Nikki, and I have two gorgeous grandchildren, Ella and Farren, who are very pro-me: 'Grandad's famous!'– they like all that.

Kent has just turned fifty at the time of writing, which brings to mind just how long ago all this was. I said to him: 'How old are you?' He said: 'Fifty.' I said: 'You can't be fifty.' He said: 'I *am* fifty.' He was born in 1963, so he would be. I shudder to think what that makes me.

I SET up home with Vanessa in her flat in Richmond but it was obvious that we needed something a bit bigger, so we moved into a two bedroomed bijou cottage, just behind the station in Eastbourne. We rented a warehouse opposite the house for the scenery we had accumulated for the various shows. I continued to commute to Piccadilly Circus and set about producing the shows for 1985, which consisted of the Hippodrome, Eastbourne and the Arcadia, Llandudno; Clive Stock had asked me to present the season's shows and we booked several big names for the season and concerts.

The show at the Hippodrome starred Ken Goodwin, Susan Maughan, Adam Daye and a duelling piano act, Anckorn & Dolovich, plus a team of dancers from the Bush Davies theatre school in East Grinstead, supervised by the principal, Sue Passmore. Sue was a very strict dance captain, but the show was fun and Ken was, as usual, a great top of the bill for this venue.

I had known Ken for years as we had shared the same agent in Mike Hughes. Ken was the star of the TV show *The Comedians* for Johnnie Hamp at Granada Television; Johnnie made many Northern comedians popular in the early 'seventies with his new show and, with clever editing, only the best gags were shown. He made stars of Charlie Williams, Bernard Manning, Mike Reid, Dave Butler and, of course, Ken, whose obvious delight in the childish jokes he told was irresistible. Some of the gags the other comics told could seem interchangeable but Ken's were his alone, wedded to his unique delivery – not that anyone else would want such *Beano*-level material. 'It's all in the character,' as he told one journalist.

Ken lived in Spain until 2008 with his second wife Vicky, but sadly contracted that dreadful disease Alzheimer's and over a period of five years went steadily downhill. Vicky managed to get him back to the UK, where he was cared for in a nursing home in Llandudno; I saw him occasionally and it broke my heart to see a man once adored by millions in that condition. He died on the 18th of February, 2012. At his funeral I gave a eulogy in the form of a letter to the man that I had known:

> *My dear pal Ken,*
> *When we met in the mid 'sixties, we could not have envisaged what our lives would become – nor that we were at the start of a friendship which would endure for the rest of our lives.*
>
> *We were both struggling comedians from working class backgrounds, performing in the clubs in and around Manchester. You had the talent of being able to play the uke and looked and sounded like your idol, George Formby.*
>
> *We found the same agent who brought us the type of work which gave both of us the kind of lifestyle we could only have dreamed of in those early years.*
>
> *In the early 'seventies, you found your niche in a television show called* The Comedians *and went on to become its star, following all the other comics to close the show during the subsequent tour and at the London Palladium, which led to your appearing in* The Royal Variety Show.
>
> *I recall in 1972 our agent Mike Hughes said you*

were experiencing some difficulties in the Comedians *stage show and asked whether I would travel to Birmingham to see if I could help. I watched the show and saw how well you did in closing the bill; you needed absolutely no help whatsoever. It was just jealousy from the other comedians you were experiencing, nothing more: you were the star of the show.*

Over the years we had similar careers – so much so that I stood in for you on occasion when you were indisposed. Once in a pantomime in Nottingham when I was taking a few weeks' rest, I was called in to play your part of Idle Jack at the Theatre Royal for a few performances, and once for a week in Eastbourne.

In the 'eighties you became a firm favourite at the Hippodrome, Eastbourne, where I had the pleasure of producing you as the top of the bill in several summer seasons. Your dog, Crosby, would bark when I came into your dressing room and on every occasion you would fall about with laughter at my apparent fear. I also had the distinct and proud pleasure of producing your last singing album, which has some of your best work on it.

Over the fifty-odd years I have known you we have had many holidays together, both here and in Spain, and always had fun. Your very sad illness was an enormous blow to us all – and now that amazing smile, the silly jokes, the cowboy movies and continual George Formby films are all sadly missing from our lives, as are you. You were a one-off, Ken, a very good mate, and even though we lost you several years ago we will remember you as you were: a star comedian who was funny and who made us laugh.

Love you and miss you,
Your friend
Fred.

THE year 1985 was also when I finally staged the panto of my dreams. It wasn't at the Dominion, but it was a spectacular show and an undoubted success. Thanks to a costly misjudgment about my business partner, however, it was also the beginning of the end of my career in management.

I was approached by an outdoor show promoter called Joe Weston-Webb, who fancied himself as a promoter of pantomimes. I had been supplying star artists for his steam fair rallies in the Midlands and we had a friendly relationship even though, like many entrepreneurs, he was a chancer who didn't have the capital to finance any project. But like an idiot I still took the bait when he presented his new venture.

He approached me to produce a pantomime at the huge De Montfort Hall – 2,500 seats – in Leicester. They used to have pantos there in the 'sixties and he had got hold of the scaffolding which formed the proscenium arch and fit-up staging from this period when he used to be a stagehand. When I told him I wouldn't be involved financially in any pantomime production at that venue, he said that was alright: he would pay me to do it and would promote it himself as he lived nearby and was well known in the area.

We signed an agreement and I went about booking Britain's biggest and best production of *Cinderella*: even with a reduced seating capacity of 1,900, a venue as large as the De Montfort Hall was massive by anybody's standards and needed a correspondingly large show and orchestra.

The show turned out to be sensational; even the most sceptical and critical showbiz agents and managers came out of the woodwork to compliment me on the production. It had a dream cast with Bill Maynard as Baron, Christopher Beeny (the footman from *Upstairs, Downstairs*) as Buttons, Patrick Mower as the Prince, Stuart Gillies as Dandini, Peggy Mount as the fairy Godmother with Bob Grant and Adam Daye as the ugly sisters. *Cinderella* was played by up and coming singer/impressionist Jessica Martin, and with a great pit orchestra of ten session musicians, including Kent on percussion, it all came together like magic.

It played, quite deservedly, to very good business but Weston-Webb did not pay me the full fee, as agreed, in time, ending up paying the residue owed sometime during the summer of 1986. I vowed that I wouldn't do it again as I'd had to struggle every week to meet this huge wage bill and eventually got payment from him in a very ad hoc way. In order for the show to work I hadn't allowed for much of a profit margin in the hope that the future might prove more rewarding when the venue was established.

After he had delivered the final payment he cheekily asked me to produce a pantomime for the forthcoming season. When I turned it down, he said he would adhere to whatever payment schedule I wanted ... and I eventually succumbed. An agreement was drawn up whereby he would have to pay all advance box office monies into a joint account which only we could draw on, at a schedule to coincide with the respective paydays for the cast.

The cast was duly contracted by me and, once again, the line-up was star-studded. This time the show was to be *Snow White and the Seven Dwarves* with Larry Grayson (King), Rusty Lee (Dame) and Ian Lavender (Stupid Boy, appropriately enough), plus a large supporting cast and orchestra as before.

I was persuaded to do this against my better judgement, and was proved right. A contractual payment system I thought was foolproof was not, as Weston-Webb did not put the box office money into the joint account as agreed. Instead, he used it to pay off his debts, and when he couldn't come up with the payment schedule for the salaries found a feeble excuse to knock me, claiming I had not been honest about the contractual salaries to be paid. So I gave him the contracts, and all the weekly salaries were then paid to the cast direct by him, under the supervision of my financial manager Bob Parsons, which worked out fine.

What he didn't pay for, however, were any production costs, nor my fee to produce the show, which had taken eight months to put together – not to mention the VAT due on all those payments. He gave me three cheques on the last day for £47,000 – and they all bounced.

As a safeguard I'd had a clause built into the original contract which stipulated that any payments not made on time would be subject to a charge of 1 per cent interest per day. I spent a year in litigation and the sum owed rose with the interest to £150,000. Suing him, however, was a waste of money and effort: virtually all my profits for that year had gone down the pan, and I paid out several thousand pounds in lawyers' fees and got zilch.

The thing is, I knew he was a chancer but didn't think he was actually dishonest. I never thought the money wouldn't be paid.

Eventually we met the judge in chambers with our barristers there to put our cases. Weston-Webb's side denied everything, putting up all sorts of reasons why he shouldn't pay; we put up our reasons why he should, then the judge in effect said: 'Okay, let him put the money up, then we can argue about it, but let's make sure he's got it first.' That's when his case fell apart and that's when his bankruptcy proceedings started.

What happened next beggars belief. He actually tried to produce yet another pantomime at the venue – albeit in his wife's name – and without any backing from actors' union Equity he was forced to pay the first two weeks' salary up front. He had not done this by the day of the opening so Equity turned up and refused to let the show go on.

He then scraped up enough money for the show to start – although the pantomime was not in the same league as the previous two years, which box office takings reflected. But the deposit monies paid up to Christmas Eve only. He could not come up with the salaries from then on and borrowed the life savings of £10,000 from the father of one of the juveniles appearing in the panto with the guaranteed surety that he would pay him back or the lights and seats would be sold to repay the debt. But Weston-Webb did not own the lights or seats and the poor parent lost all his money.

The show was taken off two days later by Equity and Weston-Webb was declared bankrupt on January 12th, 1988. Most of the cast who lost out had telephoned me at various times throughout the year and in the lead-up to the production, to ask whether they should work for him, knowing that I had a financial problem with him – but even though I had told them of the ever-increasing sum he owed me, they still went along with the charade.

Weston-Webb was even interviewed by the local Midlands Television news about the debt to me. Asked how he expected to produce yet another pantomime, he said his wife was producing it and that the case with me was in the hands of his lawyers!

As his bankruptcy loomed my lawyers had tried to get me to accept the £5,000 Weston-Webb had offered so they could snatch it – he was still offering it on the steps of the court – but by that time I'd had enough. I don't think I was even angry anymore, just despondent at this man's deceit. And sick of everything: sick of having to depend on people like that who could defraud me; sick of playing for high stakes and the continual seesawing between big wins and big losses ... sick, in fact, of all the things which had once made the move into management seem so exciting.

I couldn't even console myself that I'd given it my best shot and it was a natural time to move on: you can't walk away with dignity when your legs have been cut out from under you.

Could I have achieved more if I'd had a longer run at management? I don't know, but it was a thought which tormented me a bit – and it didn't help to reflect that my downfall had been brought about entirely by my own stupidity in giving Weston-Webb the benefit of the doubt. That first show at the De Montfort Hall had finally given me the thrill of seeing the great panto in my head brought to glorious life. Once I'd learnt about Weston-Webb's unreliability, why hadn't I been content to leave it at that? Now the memory of both those Leicester pantos had been soured.

It still left the question of what I was going to do next. How was I going to make a living? Especially when I was beginning to feel I'd had it with this country, not just with the management thing.

Then, as if on cue, I was suddenly offered a job which promised to whisk me away from all this, a completely fresh start in a new place. I grabbed at it. As the lawyers continued to pester me I told them I had no more funds and had decided to try and work in the USA in a total change of career.

Coming just as it was needed, it was an offer which seemed almost too good to be true ... and as it turned out, that's exactly what it was.

But before I get on to that, another interlude.

18: Not a Delfont, Exactly

THIS story actually starts when I was still working for Lisa, but you'll soon see why it was on my mind at this time.

I was queuing to see the first production of *A Chorus Line* at Drury Lane, which would make this around 1980, and fell into conversation with an American who wasn't sure he'd bought the right tickets. We happened to meet in the interval in the bar, with our wives – I was still married to Jackie at the time – and started to chat. His name was Irving Hirshman and he'd been on holiday in London for a week and hadn't found a decent restaurant. I said, 'You're obviously going to the wrong places,' and offered to take him to Sheekey's, a very nice fish restaurant in Covent Garden, and we struck up a friendship. I told him that I was in management and used to be a stand-up comic – he turned out to be one of the biggest tax lawyers in New York.

Shortly after that, Jackie and I were flying over to Canada to see Peter Reveen's magic show and Irving said,

'You must come over and stay.' We arrived at a beautiful mansion in New Jersey to find he had a function catered for us – with five New York theatre owners present. I was introduced as this big producer from London, and I'd only been doing it for five minutes! I hadn't even set up on my own then. Anyway, we had a very nice evening, stayed for a couple of days and flew to Toronto to see The Great Reveen in action.

Then Irving and his wife came over here for a holiday with us. We hired a car, took them round the West Country and had a great time together.

During that period we talked about business. He asked me who was the biggest entertainment entrepreneur in Britain; at the time it was Bernard Delfont. 'Well why don't you buy him out? How old is he?' I said, 'Seventy.' 'And how old are you?' I was around forty-five then. He said: 'You really ought to buy him out, you know. If there's somebody in competition, buy them out: take it over, do it yourself.'

I said I didn't have the resources. 'Well, get them!' When I asked how, he said: 'Go and talk to a bank. Talk to somebody with money. Anybody.' 'Well that's the way you do things in the States –' 'That's the way you do things all over the world. Everybody's reliant on going to a bank or to somebody with money, or a venture capitalist, getting the money and putting across your vision of what you would do with it. What you need,' he said, 'is a Business Plan.'

For a moment – for more than a moment – I was dazzled. Hypnotised, even. I said: 'Would you help me with it?' He said: 'I can't help you, it's not my business, it's not what I do. When you've got the business, when you're up and running, I can advise you what to do with the capital.'

I did think long and hard about it; I slept on it for several weeks, in fact. But at the end of the day I didn't think

I could handle that weight of business. Irving had said, 'Do you think you could do it better than him?' and when I hesitated he told me, 'If you can't do it better than him then you really don't want to do it – you need to be in a position where you know you can actually pull it off.'

I eventually lost touch with Irving. I don't suppose he's still alive now; he was twenty years older than me. The last time I saw him I was with Vanessa and, coming from a close Jewish family, he didn't approve of my marriage break-up at all. But every so often I think of the conversation we had, the possibilities he unfolded before me as we drove through the West Country. If I hadn't met Weston-Webb, would you now be reading the smoothly-written memoirs of a Delfont-level impressario?

Alright, no need to take a vote on it: I know it was a pipe dream. I suppose I was tickled by the idea of someone suggesting it – and it *is* the way to do business, more so in the States. When the temptation was put in front of me and I'd had time to think about it, it marked out the limits of just how far I wanted to go. I knew I didn't want to be involved as deeply as that. I'm not even sure Irving quite realised just how big Delfont was, with his theatre company and all that. Of course he was subsequently taken over by Andrew Lloyd Webber, so it was possible, but I never visualised myself as being that involved.

Looking back over my time in management, there's no getting away from the fact that when I was with Lisa I made money – not just with the Reveen show but generally. I don't know whether that was because I had someone to answer to, so it was imperative that I did a better deal and was more cautious as a result, but there's no doubt that when I went on my own I made some silly mistakes, maybe because I didn't have anybody else to satisfy other than me.

But when I look back I think – you know, I did what I did, and most of the things I did I thoroughly enjoyed doing. Whatever I do, whatever situation I'm flung into, I always find something within it that will work for me.

Or I try to, anyway.

It's a rule which was to be severely tested during my time in America ... which sounds like a cue to get back to the end of the last chapter and that job offer I announced with those vulturous lawyers circling round me.

19: The Regency Period

THE offer which seemed like the solution to all my problems came from a young man called Robert Earl Jnr. He had been in the catering trade in London and, through a stroke of luck, had made a killing with an opportunist business venture too complicated to explain. Now a tax exile, he had set up several show rooms in Orlando, Florida, catering for the mass market, such as *King Henry's Feast*, a jousting supper show, a Mardi Gras show and supper, and others. Twice nightly they would bus five hundred tourists in, wine and dine them and give them a one hour show.

Young Robert, twenty-two at the time, met me by chance in London and said he had just the job for me. I was to go over to see him and his set-up, but first he wanted to see me in action, so I arranged a gig in Brighton at a mutually agreed date.

He didn't turn up, and when I called the following day claimed he had no record of it, so I should have heard the warning bells. But he was still so insistent that he had a job for me – and I was so eager for a clean break – that Vanessa and I sold up our little cottage in Eastbourne and headed to Orlando.

We went a few days early to see Sandy and Derick Warren, who were now living in Coral Springs, Florida. I had been their agent in the early 'eighties and they had done several shows of mine including the Norman Wisdom pantomime. Derick had secured a job as a Cruise Director and he and his wife Sandy did their act on board cruise ships sailing the Caribbean for a new company called Regency Cruises.

I presented myself at the appointed time at Robert Earl's office and he arranged for me to see all the shows in one night. When he asked me to report what I thought of them, I told him the truth, as I saw it. Potentially they weren't bad, but without exception the presentation was appalling, with lazy performances which needed a kick up the arse.

His response took me aback. I thought Robert had wanted my expertise in production, but it turned out all he was really after was a cheap MC for the Mardi Gras show to do an hour as the punters came in and had their meal before the main event. He offered me $400 (£250) per week for this task, adding that he did not care that the shows were slack and undisciplined in content; the punters only came in once and he was not looking for repeat trade. I thought this attitude was dreadful. It was the the first time I had ever heard anything like it. I walked away.

Back at the Warrens' house in Coral Springs I was in a dilemma about what to do next. I didn't want to go back to Britain but, being almost unknown in the US, how would I get a job?

This was when Derick offered me a lifeline. He

suggested I might like to do my act on a cruise ship. Derick had an agent in New York who had been booking him on ships for some time, and he called him to suggest me as a possible client.

Then came an enormous stroke of luck – for me, this time. The agent was married to an English girl who had been a fan in Britain when she was a child, and told Don he must book me. End of story: the wife has spoken!

When he got back to me, I said Vanessa was part of the act (which she wasn't) and had to be with me. Vanessa overheard the conversation and went quite pale at the thought, but I told her not to worry and we could do some sketches together – though what they might be I had absolutely no idea.

Nowadays, when entertainment plays such a big part of the cruise experience, shows have got as big as the ships can stage, from Broadway type spectaculars to Cirque du Soleil. In 1988, however, nearly all the cruise lines were similar: old ships that had been rescued from the ships' graveyard in Piraeus, Athens, refitted and put to sea with a Greek crew; the cruise explosion with huge 5,000 passenger ships had not yet begun. The Regency Cruises group had three of these older type ships: the Regent Star, the Regent Sun - and the Regent Sea, which we would be on.

The salary we were offered was a thousand dollars a week, along with free food, accommodation and medical costs. We both had to have an extensive medical before we could get a contract and I was almost proved unfit when it threw up the irregular heartbeat which had once threatened to keep me out of National Service. I had to pay for a Holter (heart) monitor which I wore for twenty-four hours - a little device about the size of a mobile phone which monitors your heartbeat via wires stuck to your chest. This proved once again that, although I had an irregular heartbeat, it was regular-irregular, and I was given the all-clear to perform on board the Regent Sea, sailing from Tampa, Florida on April 20th, 1988.

We were engaged for a four-week trial period, which is a misnomer. If they don't like you, you can be dismissed and put off at the next port of call – and many are, believe me: cruise ships don't conform to any employment laws but their own. So I knew we only had one chance to succeed in the first week.

WE arrived at the ship at 12 noon on the day, feeling a mix of apprehension and excitement. I had cruised before, but Vanessa was new to the experience. After formalities with the crew purser, we were allotted our cabin. We were told it had been a passenger cabin in days gone by, before being designated as 'crew'; it was in the bowels of the ship just above the water line, and as soon as the ship moved the waves swooshed by our sealed portholes, which also needed bolted iron covers when rough weather was expected. There were two bunk beds on either side of the cabin with a thick post in the middle and the cabin was about 10m square, but we managed.

In the days that followed, I quickly got to see how the ship was run. Head of the chain of command on board ships is, of course, the Captain, who is in overall charge of the sailing of the vessel but, in the main, just a figurehead for the passengers. The real work is done by the Hotel Department, led by a Hotel Manager who virtually runs the ship: catering, housekeeping and concessionaires (shops). Even entertainment, the Cruise Director's domain, is part of the Hotel Department and all these subsidiaries answer to the Hotel Manager. The Cruise Director also plays a very important part in the overall running of the ship as he is the person out front who deals with the guests on a one to one basis, and programmes all the entertainment and activities on board from daybreak to late night; a cruise ship could not function without someone in this position.

The entertainment department when we embarked on the Regent Sea consisted of a Cruise Director, Ivan Kivett, and his partner Danny, who did a puppet act; Jeffrey Bryer, a great lounge pianist and entertainer, and Dan Stapleton, a magic act who was also a Cruise Director for Regency, briefly on board to check out the ship's new itinerary before returning later in the year. The rest of the cruise staff consisted of a five-strong production group – three girls and two boys who did three one-hour production shows on three separate evenings during the cruise – and two guest acts: me and one other, who would be engaged for four weeks at a time with the possibility of a longer stay if they fitted in and were well received.

My new environment became less daunting when I realised there was a definite hint of Butlins-on-Sea about it. During the day, cruise staff were expected to do Redcoat-type duties – run the bingo, competitions, etc. Not much, but enough to upset those acts who, like the discombobulated Tarby, thought they had been engaged just to do their act. Still, the contract had mentioned this, so there was no point in getting uptight once on board; you were called 'cruise staff'. And the extra duties weren't all that strenuous, really: a bingo session here, working the lights for the show there, or gangway duties for the tours when in port.

But there was one major difference from those old days at Skegness. Rationing and austerity weren't so far away then and those Butlins crowds of the late 'fifties and early 'sixties were usually grateful for what they got, still dazzled by the novelty of everything being laid on. Not so with the Americans in our floating holiday camp. They were obsessed with the weekly 'comment cards' which had to be completed in order to assess the standards in all areas of the ship. Nobody was exempt from this critique – and American passengers can be very unforgiving. Many would lie on the cards to try and get something for nothing or some sort of compensation; some passengers even admitted as much. Each department on board received a weekly score based on the comment cards and you could live or die by these assessments.

My first show on board was very nearly a disaster as I told a joke which mocked the black American accent and a table of black people got up and walked out in the middle of my act. I had committed a mortal sin – and I knew I would be out when we got into port. The CD (Cruise Director) Ivan told me not to worry, but I did: I knew the cards would come in bearing the word 'racist' and told Vanessa to start packing for our exit at the weekend.

Oddly enough, nothing happened. The following week top banana Joe McGrath from head office, who booked all the entertainment for Regency, was on board and wanted to see me working for himself. He seemed to like what I did, but warned me to be squeaky clean: no black jokes. We were up and running.

Vanessa did not have to do anything on stage as yet, but she was given a job in the shore excursion office working alongside Danny, the Cruise Director's partner, and they got on like a house on fire. Ivan Kivett, the CD himself, was a very nice man. Sadly, he had a very weak act, and knew it, so he would always do his act before me, and was easy to follow. What Ivan was very good at was film trivia and would give several talks showing off his compendious knowledge during the cruise. He was a wealthy man in his own right and owned property in Miami including a theatre/cinema. We became very good friends, although I kept quiet about my past, as I had been advised by Dan Stapleton: many CDs, especially the less talented ones, think they are God's gift and can be very sensitive about their positions.

It was obvious from day one that the only job for me in the entertainment department on board was that of Cruise Director. You were in charge: you could choose what you did and when, and you could dictate what other people did; all your bar bills were paid, you had much better accommodation *and* you got $2,000 per week into the bargain. So when Dan Stapleton advised me not to mention all that experience which more than qualified me for the job, I didn't. I just watched – and waited.

I didn't have to wait long.

IVAN and Danny's tour of duty finished and another CD, Bernard Reed, came on board. Bernard was a great comedy magician and probably one of the best known acts working on cruise ships on a continuous basis, something he did for over forty years. He was also one of the nicest, most generous men in the world, although he had the foulest offstage manner imaginable. He christened me Freddie 'Effing' Davies (which made a change from 'Parrotface').

Bernard had worked for Regency's owner, William Schance, when he'd owned a company called Pacquet Cruises, and William loved his work – his magic work, that is. But Bernard was chronically unsuited for the job of CD, and knew it. From the off he paid me to do all the admin work; he hated being at the passengers' beck and call when all he wanted was to do his act. He would constantly be asked questions by the passengers and would snap back: 'Are you stupid? I told you all this at the talk this morning!' Some innocent query when we were in the dining room would provoke a savage attack: 'Can't you see I am eating?!' The final straw was slamming the dressing room door in a passenger's face and injuring his foot in the process.

He lasted about six weeks – and that was only because they had no one to replace him with. When the Operations Director, a German American called Hans Hahn, came on board to sort the situation, the Hotel Manager, a young man called Steve Furness, suggested they should give me a try – not that they had much of a choice.

Steve was another English expat who remembered me with affection from his childhood, so when Bernard walked off he had said, 'Well, Freddie can do the job.' Luckily, Mr Hahn, whose wife was also English, had seen me work a few weeks before and agreed to give me a month's trial. He seemed to like what I did, and the fact that I was older, more mature. In theory, anyway.

In fact I was too old for the job, really. The ideal image for a Cruise Director is a thirty-two year old 6ft blond, all-American boy doing a magic act – Dan Stapleton! – and here I was, a small (5'6") Jewish-looking comic who might tell a racist joke! I suppose I was over-qualified, in that I had management experience, which none of the other Cruise Directors did; I'd had my own production company and been a headline act all over the UK ... not that I told anyone.

I didn't see my new role as a comedown. Survival in the business was what mattered; that was what led me from performing to management, and if it now brought me here, so be it. My fame wasn't translating into jobs at home, even though I was still a household name – like Dettol. So here I was, at the age of fifty, with my young partner, lovely Vanessa, embarking on a new career in the colonies.

The Cruise Director's job was well paid and, with everything laid on, it was money that was hard to spend. Also, with Vanessa getting a wage as the Shore Excursion Manager, it was difficult not to see our situation as a progression: if this was about surviving then we were surviving pretty well. And I had never been salaried before; I quite enjoyed the novelty of it.

But there was more to it than that. As I've said, I hate doing things that are a waste of time. As well as a better cabin and a bigger paypacket, the job offered me a challenge I could seize on. Having already worked ten weeks on the vessel before my appointment, I'd had plenty of time to assess the situation, and the day I took over as CD I started on what I'd been aching to do for all those weeks: putting the entertainment on board in order.

Armed with the office keys, I discovered some proper stage lighting in a locked cupboard. I summoned the ship's Greek electrician and asked him to replace the dull stage lighting spots, which had all been adapted to take 150 watt bulbs. They should have been 500 watt and the correct par bulbs from the cupboard. When he said they wouldn't work, as he had already tried, I told him that they should be paired up in twos on each circuit and then they would; he tried it and it worked – *Voilà*!

My next job was to get rid of a double act called Korkis and Korkis who did a kind of musical saw / clown act, running amok in the audience and getting them to do silly things which were totally unfunny. It was all a waste of time, particularly when there were good acts out there crying out for work.

Sacking staff on a cruise ship can be tricky. You have to do it after hours on the last night of a cruise to avoid them creating problems with the passengers, gaining sympathy and perhaps causing trouble. I asked them to come to my office after they had finished their duties and said they would be departing the ship the following day, which was also changeover day. I had already cleared it with head office and another act was being flown out to join the ship the next day.

Korkis and Korkis were not pleased and, once home, went to great lengths to claim compensation for unfair dismissal. Eventually I had to write a letter to US Equity stating the simple truth, which was that they were not suitable for cruise ship entertainment: by the time they were sent home they had been on the ship four weeks and had died at every performance.

I took responsibility for my staff very seriously. I wanted to show them that they were appreciated and always endeavoured to make them feel special when they had to perform. A lot of acts who came on the ship found it very hard to come to terms with me saying that they were the headline act: on many ships, the Cruise Director was usually the headline act. My first question to them would be, 'How long do you need to do on the stage to make it work for you?' 'Well,' they'd say, not sure where this was going, 'my contract says a fifty-minute act.' 'Yes, but how long do you *need* to do well?'

If they finally admitted, 'Well really, I've got a very good twenty-five minutes,' I'd tell them to do twenty-five minutes and reassure them that they weren't going to lose their job on Friday; a lot of them were frightened of going too well in case they overshadowed the Cruise Director – an awful situation on many levels.

Not having an ego about it, I was more interested in getting the very best from them – and I think, in ninety-nine per cent of cases, I did. Quite a lot of the American Cruise Directors are mediocre MCs and non-performers who think they're in showbiz because they know how to schmooze the passengers. It goes back to that phrase I used earlier about being able to see the bigger picture: I'd been observing it for a few months before I took over, so when the opportunity came I just sort of slipped into it.

All the staff showed great improvement when encouraged. I'd give the production group members MC jobs, for example, so they were able to come out on their own, do a song or tell a joke and introduce the evening show. Occasionally, if they had enough material, I'd even feature them on special late night shows as solo artists in their own right.

Not that everyone listened to advice. We had a husband and wife double act who had come from the north of England club circuit; he was on keyboards and computer tracks, and she sang. Steeped in the clubs, they were oblivious to the fact that their music was excruciatingly loud and kept passengers out of the lounge where they were playing; previous CDs had never told them, and they did not seem to understand that they were, in fact, deafening. I asked them to turn it down to less than half volume and that same evening the lounge in question was full to capacity; they stupidly crept it back up and the passengers stopped going in, until I told them to take it down again.

But we had some great acts on board. One in particular, Pat Murray, a very good ventriloquist with a funny Jamaican puppet called Matilda, is still one of the most sought after acts in cruising. He also works on the mainland and comes from Chicago, where many of his friends and family gathered for his fiftieth birthday in 2007. We became firm friends and he also tried his hand at cruise directing but did not really enjoy the extra workload, so he prefers to be the headline act on board, a position he fills with great aplomb.

We also worked with Howie and Bert, a great comedy

juggling act from Las Vegas. Our magic acts came mainly from Los Angeles and were booked by a Scot who resided in LA and was a member of the Magic Castle in Hollywood, famous for its nightly shows by the world's greatest magicians. You have to be invited by a member to attend, but it is a very special evening if you ever get the chance.

MY month's trial was successful and I was then able to give Vanessa a job which she embraced and thoroughly enjoyed, that of Shore Excursion Manager. She took charge of all the shoreside tours, taking up to $150,000 a week in the Caribbean and double in Alaska. She worked mainly with one member of staff but was ultimately responsible for all the cash and the booking of the tours plus paying the shoreside operators, usually in cash. She loved the job and, in particular, Alaska, where she booked helicopter tours to the glacier top and six-seater sea plane trips to hidden lakes and stunning salmon bake trips, along with fishing trips for Alaskan salmon and halibut.

Vanessa didn't escape performing altogether as she also did a couple of songs with me and a short cod mind-reading skit. She was very good at it. She'd be blindfolded on stage and I'd go into the audience, pick someone, and say: 'What is this lady wearing on the third finger of her left hand?' and she would say: 'A fingernail.' 'No,' I'd reply, 'higher than a fingernail.' 'A knuckle.' 'No, it's round, it's brown and it's got a hole in it.' And she'd say: 'A bagel.' So I'd say, with heavy emphasis, 'She got it on her wedding day. Why would she wear a bagel on her wedding finger?' And she'd shout: 'It was a Jewish wedding!'

We were both happy in our jobs and enjoyed some great holidays in Florida for the short periods we were afforded between contracts, which were usually about four or five months in duration with, say, four weeks off. Our first contract, when I was promoted to CD, lasted seven months, and we were exhausted by the end. As soon as I got off they rang me and said, 'Can you come back?' There was some other crisis going on. So I became a bit of a blue-eyed boy, really.

We stayed with the company, enjoying good jobs and great weather in the Caribbean. I used to organise golf junkets for passengers, which meant I could improve my game along the way, playing up to three times a week in exotic locations like St Lucia, St Thomas, St Kitts and Barbados. I am not a very good golfer and at these courses you had to use a golf cart to get round, mainly because of the length of the course but also to optimise the amount of golfers playing and shorten the tee times. The heat played a big part in the golf in those climes: it was just too hot to walk.

Summers were spent cruising from Vancouver to Whittier, Alaska, taking in the majestic and wonderful inside passage through Canada then back into the USA waters of Alaska, with regular visits to Ketchikan, Juneau (the capital), and Skagway, an old mining and prospecting town which looked like those in the old western films. We also anchored near Sitka and tendered the passengers to the small town for the inevitable shopping sprees to which the Americans are so devoted; the Cruise Director would plug the stores and receive a kick-back.

Cruise Directors were renowned for being very wealthy in the 'seventies and 'eighties, before the industry had a shake-up and decided to put its own 'Port Lecturers' on the ships. What had happened was that, once the shipping companies realised that the CDs were making so much money, they decided to cash in themselves and employed companies who supplied Port Lecturers to do the 'Shopping

Talks', thereby getting a percentage of the kick-backs. These would give port of call talks, highlighting the shops who would pay the company for the plug, so the CDs lost out.

But the situation was self-defeating, as it was only the Cruise Directors who had any real clout on the ships regarding the punters, and that is why the system had worked. The Port Lecturers would attract a relatively small audience for their talks as they were obviously about the money, whereas the CDs were about impartial advice – allegedly. I was just at the end of the kick-back era but still received several back-handers from the shops who felt that the CDs were giving them a service.

IN North America, the Walt Disney operation is second to none as regards attention to detail and showmanship. Unfortunately, not everything is up to Disney standards but the American public expect nothing less, even when they're not paying top dollar – which could make for problems on board cruise ships such as ours that showed their age at times. We came in for some poor comments, mostly unwarranted, as we had a very acceptable product for the price.

People on holiday, or vacation, tend to stop their thought processes and expect to be taken by the hand and led everywhere – 'nobody told me' syndrome. Usually they don't listen properly so you have to repeat everything, but they still don't get it. Being an Englishman abroad, and in charge, I found that I could sound a bit pompous and posh on occasion, so I had to tone my 'Englishness' down a bit to be acceptable.

This also applied to my act. There was something very liberating about performing in front of audiences who, in the main, didn't know me from television or anywhere else, which meant I was free to drop the Parrotface stuff and just go with whatever worked.

Samuel Tweet will always be part of me but I have to admit there have been moments of frustration in Britain when I didn't seem able to get away from him, particularly on television.

Comedy's become the master now and comics are able to dictate their own terms, but this wasn't the case at the height of my fame in the 'sixties and 'seventies, when there were only two or three channels. Often I'd go prepared to do something else and they would say, 'Oh you've got to do the thing with the hat.' When I did TV series with the Bachelors and David Nixon, I would try to do a different sketch, or a different character, every week as well as a bit of Samuel Tweet, but the hat was the staple thing – a bit like that old variety hall stipulation 'act as known' which locked a performer into the same routine year in, year out.

It was difficult to find anything strong enough to follow Tweet, but I suppose, if I'm honest, I didn't try hard enough to change. In fact, if I was to sum up what I think went wrong with my career it's that I didn't pursue other characters soon enough. Really, I should have made an active decision in the early 'seventies to try and move away from that and do other characters; there were one or two things on the David Nixon show that I should have explored more, for example, and as early as 1968 a *Stage* article had praised me as: '...a first rate character comedian, playing parts totally unlike his celebrated Mr P on Ken Dodd's radio show.'

Looking back, I feel even more strongly now that the 1974 Samuel Tweet TV series really didn't do me any favours. I felt it branded me as a children's entertainer which, as far as I was concerned, I wasn't – I mean, I was for that purpose, but I never saw myself as that. It was a sideline: I'd been making the odd appearance on kids' shows in character as Tweet, but it had never overwhelmed the adult act before.

But maybe I'm kidding myself here. There's no doubt kids loved the character and would impersonate Samuel because it was slightly rude to lisp and appear to spit in someone's face, hence the Parrotface fan club and *Buster* comic and panto and all that. He was born in the clubs but it could be he was always destined to be a kid's character. Not that the distinction really matters much nowadays, I suppose: most of the people who come to see my stand-up are adults remembering me from their childhood.

Either way, there was a time when I felt that Tweet had become a bit of a monster: I'd lumbered myself with the character and couldn't really find a way out of it. I mean, I didn't particularly want to finish it as it was still getting big reactions and I was doing well with it, but over time it just fizzled out, became out of favour.

So in many ways it was a relief to go to the States and not have to do it. In England, if I worked somewhere and didn't do it, it would be: 'Oh, why didn't you do that?' but it was easy to imagine people saying: 'Oh, why's he still doing that?' So here was a rare opportunity to reinvent myself and my act for an entirely new audience who came without any expectations.

I resurrected some of my old material to start with but soon saw that anything specifically British would have to go. Over the weeks and months I developed an entirely different act, more relaxed, specifically for the ships. I did a lot of shipboard material: visiting the doctor on board, the food, eating too much and jokes about throwing up. There was even a crack about how some people come on as passengers and leave as cargo.

I also did a routine about stupid passengers – not those in the audience, of course, last week's lot, who had asked questions like: 'Who is steering the ship if the Captain is in the dining room?' 'Do the crew sleep on board?' 'Does the ship generate its own electricity?' 'Why don't you have pool tables on board?' I said that one woman had asked, 'On the last night of the cruise if I put my packed suitcase outside my cabin door, what do I do with my nightie in the morning?' and I'd told her, 'Sleep without it and you might get lucky!'

SHIPBOARD life is very far removed from everyday living on land. The ships are like villages, with staff on board from just about every nation in the world pulling together to make the operation work, from the Captain and his sailors, who get the ship from A to B, down to the galley staff, cleaners and housekeeping dept, chefs, shop staff, hairdressers and casino staff. We were all part of this big ship's family who worked and played together. There would be parties in the crew cabins with lots of drugs around, although I was never offered and never partook. Booze was plentiful and duty free: I never paid a bar bill once I became CD, with an allowance of $150 per week which was hard to spend, so I was always buying the cruise staff drinks to use up the allowance.

A weekly cruise would take on its own personality. There would be a large party of, say, 150 from some organisation or other who would have cocktail parties to which the CD would be invited, in addition to the Captain's cocktail party on the first sailing evening, when the Captain would greet every passenger with a handshake as they entered the lounge. Tedious as it may sound, it generated lots of cash for the photographers who took photos of each passenger as they shook hands with the Captain! (800 passengers, $10 per picture ... do the math.)

The Captain would then be introduced on stage and make a short speech in the show lounge, introducing the ship's officers who would parade in a line before the audience. The Captains were all Greek and would speak in broken English accents which could sometimes be quite humorous. I was once introduced as the 'crewiz' director, 'Danny' Davies. When I told the Captain later that my name was Freddie he got it all screwed up and called me 'Frendy' Davies, and, to many cruising pals, I am still 'Frendy.'

We had many incidents during our four years at sea, some sad, quite a few hilarious – and lots of times when you felt like throwing some passengers over the side of the ship.

During my second stint as a CD in 1989 we had a wonderful Captain called Metaxes, who had huge perfect teeth and was always smiling. During one particular cruise, I had this idiot passenger who pulled me to one side and informed me that we had run aground the night before, just at the mouth of the Panama Canal; he had spoken to a woman who had told him she had seen a tug pulling the ship off the sandbank, or whatever it was.

Running aground is a very serious maritime incident and would not go unnoticed by the Captain and crew, but this feller had started to circulate his fellow passengers with this stupid rumour and got up a petition to have sight of the ship's log. I informed the Captain that a passenger wished to see him and told him what the problem was. A meeting was set up in the Lido Lounge near the rear of the ship.

The passenger, the Hotel Manager, Captain Metaxes and myself were seated round this table in the Lido when the Captain, still with a huge smile, asked to see the petition which the man was clutching. He would not let go, so Metaxes asked the man what his question was. He said: 'I demand to see the ship's log, because a tug was alongside on Wednesday night,' adding that it was his opinion, and that of many others on board, that the ship had run aground and the log would state this.

Still with a big smile, the Captain looked the man in the eyes and said in his broken Greek accent: 'You 'ave accuse me of running this ship aground?' 'Yes,' he replied. That was enough for Metaxes. 'What it is you have accuse me of is a serious error of judgea-ment, and for this I will disembark you and your family at our next port of call which is at 14.30 today in Aruba. I do not wish that you should be passenger on my vessel.' And with that he got up from his seat and walked away.

The man packed his cases and was escorted with his family down the gangway by security guards when we docked in Aruba, cheered off the ship by all the other passengers. That was the first and only time I ever saw a passenger getting his comeuppance; usually they would be humoured, but this guy had really been a dickhead.

On another occasion, I was in my office on the ship in Costa Rica when the Captain called me: 'Frendy, I have the Presidentay ofa Costa Rica in my office and I like you to come up to meet 'im.'

I went up to the Captain's cabin and found myself shaking hands with the President, whom he had met that morning at the opening of a pineapple factory near the docks, hence the invite. The Captain asked me to accompany them on a ship's tour, although the ship was pretty empty: as we were in the Port of Limón, on the coast of Costa Rica, for just one day, most passengers were off on tours to the capital city, San Juan, as the only thing in Limón was the grotty docks.

The small entourage of the President, the Captain, the Chief Engineer and myself walked round the ship's open deck with deck chairs and sun loungers, almost deserted apart from one lounger occupied by a little Jewish lady from New York who was asleep and snoring. As we approached the foot of the lounger she woke with a start, looked up at the President and said: 'Who the hell are you?'

'I am the President of Costa Rica,' he said, making to greet her; she refused his hand and turned over to continue her snooze, saying: 'And I'm the President of the United States – get lost!'

I made some excuse like she had a touch of the sun and we rushed him to the bar.

AMONG the special groups often on board were parties of gay and lesbian cruisers, but usually gays; in more recent years a shipboard get-together is organised for these under the banner 'Friends of Dorothy', although we had one party of 140 men who came as an organised group from a travel agency enterprisingly named 'Now Voyager' (it gets worse). They were all on second sitting for dinner at 8.15pm, meaning they would see the second show at 10.30pm, so none of them would be present for the first show at 8pm.

I would do the odd gay joke – nothing offensive, or so I thought, until I did the gags when they were not in the room. All hell broke loose, and all of a sudden I was homophobic – me – after a lifetime in showbiz! They asked me to attend a meeting at midnight in a room they had declared was 'Their Room' – well, it was one of our smaller lounges and I had laid on a bar and a trio to play so they could dance together without disturbing the straight passengers unnecessarily – and they still called me homophobic!

They filmed the meeting with me answering their questions. Their main beef was that they imagined I had done the gay jokes because they were not there; I told them the gags were part of my regular act, and that they were not that special. Later in the week several of them told me there was a faction of the party who were intent on bitching about everything, who had latched on to me in the hope they could get some recompense, as is often the case.

A passenger on his third honeymoon once confided to me that he got upgraded everywhere he went because he always shouted the loudest and demanded to get his own way; the powers that be would rather pacify a belligerent client than argue in front of others.

In the United States, service is God and they are proud of the service they give but do expect to be rewarded, often asking for a tip or saying one has been added to the bill, an attitude in direct opposition to that of the UK. The Brits are known as bad tippers around the world, as we tend to tip for the actual service provided, not as a God-given right.

PEOPLE go on cruise ships for holidays, of course, and Christmas on board an American cruise ship can be the worst time of the year for the staff. Not just because they are away from their homeland, but because of the barrage of demands made by passengers who have chosen to go on a cruise at that time of year.

The passengers are mostly people who have nowhere else to go for Christmas, or Jews, who are not supposed to celebrate Christmas. Grown up kids who can't stand the rows send their parents on a ship as a 'present' for Christmas; there will also be many single people; Christians expecting full Christmas services on board; Catholics expecting full Mass; and Jews expecting to celebrate Hanukkah.

Carols and Christmas music are shunned by the Jews so you have to have a room without Christmas decorations and not playing Christmas music. I had to take a beautifully decorated tree down and de-decorate one lounge because of complaints – and can the New York Jews bitch? You betcha! They have a degree in it. New York has some of the rudest people on earth, as most people know – but most people have not been on a cruise ship with them at Christmas.

At this point let me say that I have nothing at all against Jews. In fact, through most of my life, people have thought I must be Jewish. I look Jewish; I sound Jewish; I love all my Jewish friends, of whom I have many, but I am not Jewish – or, as I would often joke: 'I'm not Jewish but my mother and father are,' or 'I'm not Jewish but I'm saving up.' Both of which remarks were complained about on board ship. Once after I'd made this confession a lady took me aside: 'Oh my God, Freddie, you're *not* Jewish?! How do you manage?'

You could even say I've been the victim of reverse prejudice. I was up for a very good part in Jack Rosenthal's *Bar Mitzvah Boy*. Until, that is, I told the director I wasn't Jewish. I said: 'Well, what's the matter? I look Jewish enough.' But no.

Another time I was being interviewed by *The Jewish Chronicle*; he got halfway through the interview, looked at me and said, 'You *are* Jewish, aren't you?' 'Er, no.'

His muttered 'Shit!' synchronised exactly with the snapping shut of his notebook.

The worst Christmas I ever experienced on board ship was at the end of 1990 – and in the interests of balance I have to say that a little Jewish lady from New York was my salvation on that occasion. I mentioned earlier that a weekly cruise could take on its own personality and this was one of the most bizarre examples. It was Saturday 24th December, the ship was the Regent Star, and we were scheduled to do our usual seven day cruise out of Montego Bay, Jamaica, calling at Ocho Rios, Jamaica, Costa Rica, The Panama Canal, Cartagena, Columbia and Aruba. But Manuel Noriega had been ousted from Panama and the US Government had closed the Panama Canal for safety reasons, so that, in effect, screwed the cruise up before we got into the other problems.

At the end of each seven day cruise we would

normally dock at around 7.00am, disembark the passengers from 9.00am onwards, and they would be flown home. The ship would then be cleaned and dressed to look spick and span for the new lot, who would be allowed to embark from 1.00pm.

As we were coming into Montego Bay, however, the sea swells reached twenty-five feet and the ship just could not berth; we went round in circles. At around 1.00pm we managed to dock and disembark the passengers, who all had to be found accommodation or a rearranged flight back to the US – a mammoth task in itself. The embarking passengers, approximately 800, had been well looked after and bussed to nearby hotels by our shore staff, who came down from Head Office each week as usual, to see the operation ran smoothly.

Now here's where it gets really silly. All the new passengers knew of our problem – they could see the ship bobbing about in the bay; they knew full well it was not our fault – and yet they embarked the ship from 6.00pm like wild beasts who'd just been uncaged.

Everything was wrong, wrong, wrong: the wrong cabin, the wrong luggage, the wrong staff. My office adjoined the purser's and the baying crowd was ten deep at their desk; the girls were in tears at the abuse. I tried to help as a puce-faced, yelling woman grabbed my arm, having been turned down for a cabin upgrade as the ship was full. Vanessa had to drag me away from her as she screamed: 'You people are all horrible!'... and this was before we had sailed an inch.

I rapidly tried to start some kind of entertainment at 10.00pm, but no one turned up. The dining room succeeded in trying to fit everyone in and feed them all. Then they found out that we were not going up the Panama Canal and all hell broke loose. Nobody knew where we were actually going because we could not contact anyone on any of the Islands to make alternative arrangements – Christmas!

December 25th dawned and I was up and about early, still trying to do some kind of programme for the week, without knowing where we were going. The ship had a weird kind of atmosphere, unlike anything I had ever experienced on board. We had a Christmas present Santa event scheduled in the main showroom lounge, and that went down fine – well, apart from Pat Murray, the ventriloquist, making a very drunken appearance in a Santa costume four sizes too small for him; some of the mums weren't too thrilled.

The Captain's cocktail party and show did not go down well at all: they hated us. We should have sailed at 4.00pm but were delayed yet again by a family suddenly deciding to disembark and go home, so we didn't sail until 6.00pm. It was mooted that we should go to the ABC Islands: Aruba, Bonaire and Curaco.

About an hour before we sailed I was in my office when a 4ft 10in tubby sixty-five year old New York Jewish woman wandered into my office and asked who I was. I told her I was the Cruise Director. 'Waddya do, buddy?' she yelled. 'I see to all the entertainment,' I said. 'Well, get me another pillow, I need another pillow!' 'Of course, Madam,' I said, and went with her to her cabin, collecting a pillow from the housekeeping office on the way. 'Anything more, Madam?' 'Yeah, sure is, I need a bax [*box*] to ship my foir [*fur*] coat home – it's too friggin' hot and I need to ship my foir home!' 'I will see you get one,' I said – and did. I never saw her again until the end of the cruise, when she came to my rescue.

The week got worse and the passengers continued to hate us to such an extent that two lawyers opened their cabins as a law office with a sign on the door, taking names to present a 'Class Action' against the company. But for what? None of the events which unfolded were any fault of the company; they were a *force majeure*.

The week ended on the Friday night with the show lounge being taken over by the passengers, and the two lawyers holding a meeting where they were actually taking money from the passengers who wished to prosecute the company; I think it was $10 per head. The hotel manager, a cowardly Frenchman who had removed his epaulettes from his shirt at the start of the week in order to avoid being recognised, actually allowed this meeting to take place on our property against us! Twat!

The saga was brought to a close when a passenger stood up and read from the small print in our brochure and terms of contract which clearly stated that the Captain could, and would, decide where the ship should go if he so decreed.

End of story? Not quite.

One of my many duties on board was to give lectures and talks about our ports of call: every Friday I would give a talk at 11.00am, advising passengers on how to disembark the following Sunday morning. I usually made this talk quite light-hearted and amusing and, in any normal cruise, would have had them eating out of my hand. Not this time: they just glared at me throughout the forty minutes.

At the end I asked, as I always did, whether it was all clear to them about what to do with the luggage etc, and whether anyone had any questions. The room was deathly quiet, then one person shouted: 'NO, you are very unclear!' 'AND YOU'RE OBNOXIOUS!' shouted another. The little Jewish momma, whom I had provided with the extra pillow and box to send her fur home in on day one of the cruise, was sitting right in the front of the stage. She jumped up to her full 4ft 10in height, stood on her chair and shouted: 'Listen up everybody, the ship's shit but he's a doll!'

Within a few hours the dreadful nightmare was over – and the following week's cruise, which started on New Year's Eve, was a much needed breath of fresh air.

I DID deserve the blame occasionally. I had several bad experiences when I lost my patience instead of just walking away, but as the Cruise Director I felt it was my responsibility to protect the other members of staff by insisting they refer all pain-in-the-arse punters to me, so I could deal with them personally. I could handle most occurrences, like the gay party, but there were times when I know I probably overstepped the mark.

The last straw was on the New Year Cruise just before we left, 31st December 1991. I had programmed all the smaller lounges to finish their music at 11.45 pm so all the passengers and staff could be in the main showroom for the midnight celebration and champagne, which was flowing freely.

I was in full flow myself, with novelty dances, party games, singalongs, etc in the main lounge, when the Hotel Manager, Deiter, a kind German man whom I respected, called me to one side and informed me that a travel agent with a party of nineteen was complaining in the Panorama lounge at the front of the ship. Apparently, he could not understand why the Polish trio was due to stop at 11.45pm, and had complained to them. They explained that they were scheduled to finish then and that only their boss, the Cruise Director, could change the time. I asked Dieter to tell the boys to continue to play until midnight, so all was sorted. Or so I thought.

I conducted the midnight festivities and once 700-odd passengers were really rockin' and rollin' I grabbed a bottle of champagne and four glasses and made my way to the front of the ship and the Panorama Lounge to give the Polish trio, who were also many miles away from home, a celebratory drink.

As I approached the lounge I could see an altercation happening in the middle of the small dance floor. The leader of the trio was talking to an irate, red-faced man who was the worse for drink. I came up behind him and heard him say to the bandleader: 'I told you I would get you to shtay on – I told that Cruise Director I would report him! It was me who got you to play until midnight!' The poor lad just repeated what he had been saying all night, that Freddie the Cruise director was the one he needed to speak to.

At this I said, 'Can I help you, sir?' The man veered round, his face bright red. I said 'Sir, you got what you wanted, now what is your problem?' 'You shouldn't have scheduled them to shtop in the first place,' he started. 'Sir, you got what you wanted, so what is the problem?' 'You are gonna lose your job,' he slurred, jabbing me with his finger. I said, 'Would you be so kind as to step out to the corridor with me a moment?' and walked away.

He followed and, when we were one on one, I told him he was a prat and a jumped-up arsehole and that we had been pulling out all the stops to entertain them since 8.00am that morning, even though all he seemed to be able to do was abuse and harass the staff and musicians, then I told him to go fuck himself and walked away. If he reported me, I said, I would deny everything, as he had proved he was an arsehole. (I would have called him a wanker, but that word is not recognised in the US.)

He did complain, of course, but at least I got some satisfaction on disembarkation day. The man was at the purser's office, which faced mine; the Chief Purser called over to me that the man who was standing there had had his flight cancelled and what did I think they should do about it? I suggested they try and get him on a later flight and to treat him in the manner in which we would all like to be treated, and not the way he had treated us. I never heard another word.

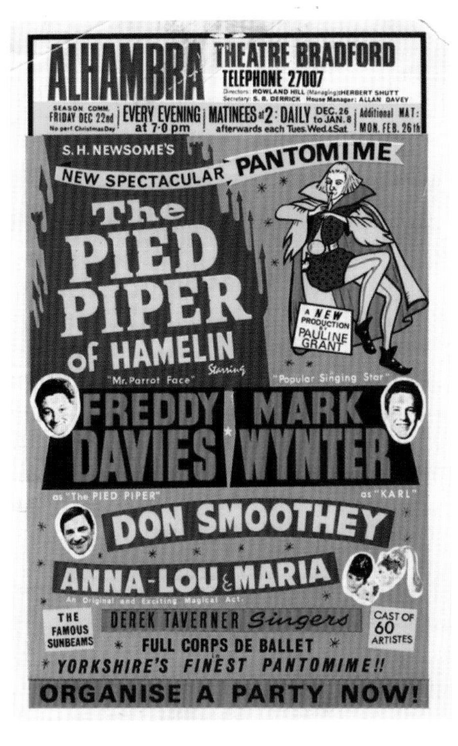

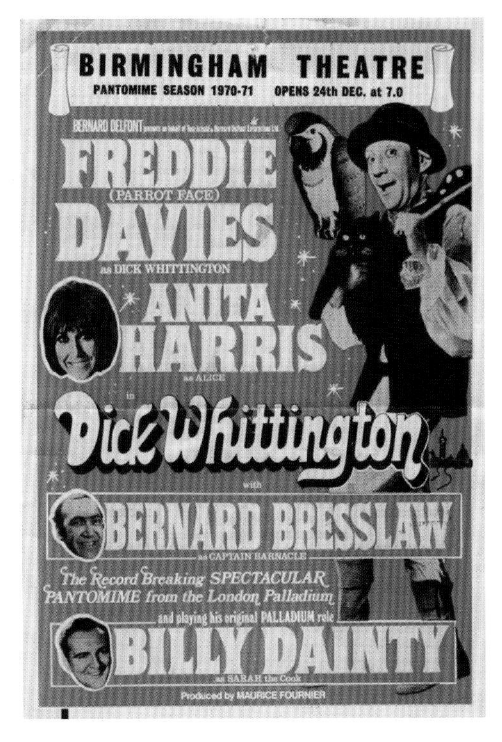

Above left: My very first starring role in panto at the Bradford Alhambra, 1967-68. It ran for 12 weeks. *Above right*: Another great pantomime with a fantastic line-up in Birmingham, 1970-71. *Below*: Various shows over the years, all with a memory or two.

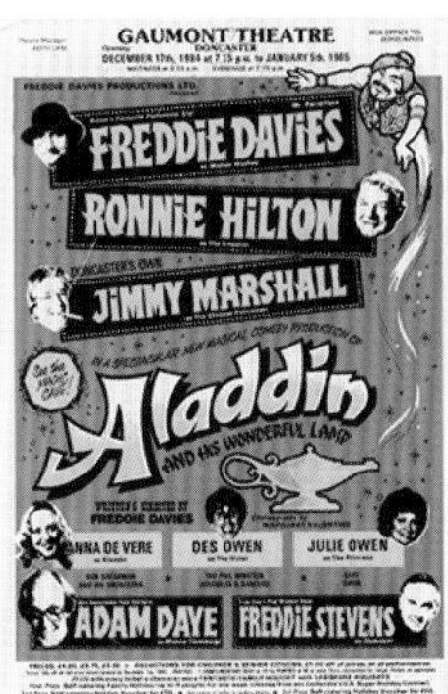

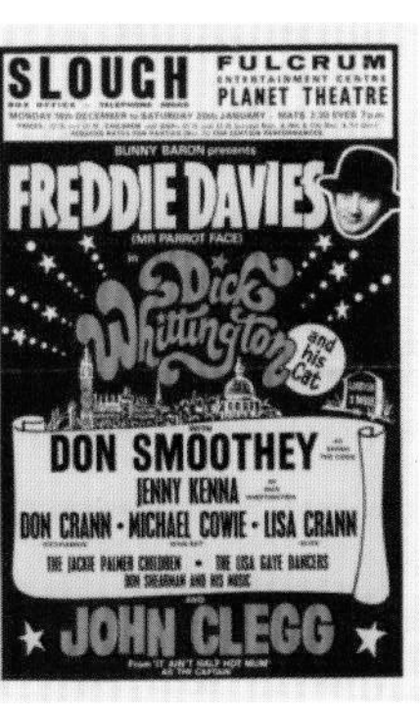

Left: Panto at Birmingham Hippodrome, 1970-71. Me as a right Dick, Anita Harris as Alice, Billy Dainty as Dame and my dear pal, 6ft 6in Bernard Bresslaw, as the Captain - a great foil for 5ft 6in me.

Above: With Henry Cooper at the Water Rats Ball, 1974.

Below: The Pied Piper at the Coventry Theatre, 1966. Norman Vaughan, Frankie Vaughan and me with the chorus at the dress rehearsal.

THE STAGE and TELEVISION TODAY, March 5, 197

IE DAVIES is one of the few comedians who can claim to have done a double act with an international
ddie is currently starring in "Aladdin" which has done such fantastic business at the Bristol Hippod
run, which was due to end on March 7, has had to be extended for a further week and will now f
h 14. Of the many people who have packed the Hippodrome, none enjoyed it more than the Bristol born
RY GRANT, who was in the city to see his mother. So much so, in fact, that not only did he go round
ddie after the show and congratulate him, but also had a go at doing a "MR. PARROTFACE" act hims

THROUGH UNFORESEEN CIRCUMSTANCES

Above: Someone else trying to cash on my fame. Cary Grant in Bristol, 1970.

The Stage Archive

Right: ABC Blackpool, 1966. This show ran at total capacity business for 16 weeks, twice nightly.

Left: Me and my son Kent learn how to tweet.

Below: Playing the Pied Piper at probably the best pantomime theatre in the UK - the Alhambra, Bradford - with the famous Sunbeams, 1967-8.

Above: The Comedy Band sketch with Don Crann, always a panto favourite.

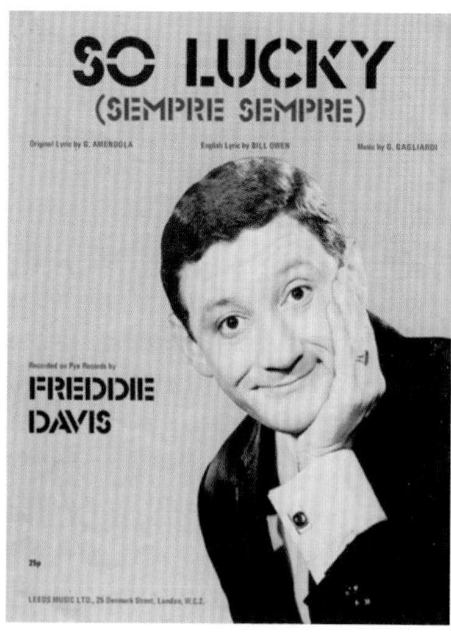

Above and below: On record with my one-hit Brazilian wonder and an album for children.

Above and right: Immortalised in cartoon strip form for four years courtesy of *Buster* comic.

Above: At the Victoria Palace, 1969, in The Bachelors' show.
Left: With dear Frank Mansell, my greatest mentor.

Above: Introduced to HRH, the Duke of Edinburgh, at a Water Rats lunch. Henry Cooper, Phil Hindin, David Berglas and Al French look on.

Left: Among King Rats at the top table in 1973 sit David Nixon, Cyril Dowler and Ted Ray.

Right: With my dear pal Frankie Vaughan.

Above left, centre and right: My two grandchildren, Ella and Farren. My brother Peter, sisters June (on my left) and Shirley. My favourite picture of Vanessa.

Above: Ship officers dine on the Panama Canal aboard the Regent Sun, 1989. I only went once and this was it!

Left: Of all the ships in all the world... why this one?

Left: Vanessa and me doing our turn on board. *Above*: Don't shoot the actors, just the variety turns...

Above: Cast and crew of *Harbour Lights*, which lasted two BBC TV series. See if you can spot Nick Berry and me.

Above: My first straight acting job in *Loves a Luxury* - but the digs were crap!

Above: With Sarah Moffett, John Junkin and Mina Anwar - the cast of Victoria Wood's play, *Talent*.

Left: Put that light out! *Harry Potter and the Prisoner of Azkaban*. Thirty seconds took two days to shoot.

Right: At home in North Yorkshire with Vanessa and our three King Charles spaniels, Dottie, Dora and Daisy.

Scenes from Funny Bones: A victory shuffle as the Parker Brothers learn of a final chance to shine, in the cult classic film of 1995. *Centre left:* Watching the man on the swaying lamp post. *Centre right:* Working with Jerry Lewis was a delight. *Bottom left:* Helpless as a tragedy unfolds. *Bottom right:* It always ends in feathers.

MY cruising days lasted approximately four years, on and off. We eventually left the company because they decided to cut the shore excursion budget, and Vanessa's pay, by 50 per cent, and she decided that a stand had to be made. I stuck it for a week then left as well.

This wasn't just about showing solidarity: we had had some great times and experiences travelling the world and meeting and working alongside just about every nationality, but I was fast approaching fifty-four and, as I have stated, the job of CD required a younger man. But I really got a lot out of my years at sea. Apart from anything else, it was good to know I could survive when taken out of my comfort zone as a performer. I'd developed a whole new act which still felt true to me and proved I could reach audiences without any help from Parrotface – almost as though I'd taken a different turning in those old club days and no one had called out for the budgie joke which had determined the course of my career.

Being away from England had made the reinvention easier, too, knowing my efforts weren't about to be picked apart by some snide Jonathan Meades-type doing one of those 'how the mighty have fallen' pieces. As I've said, I didn't see it that way, and on the rare occasions when there were English passengers in the audience, quite a few said: 'Oh, it's nice seeing you doing this – we wondered what had happened to you.'

In fact, I'm inclined to think I was pretty lucky to end up where I did, especially as I fell into it by chance. When I left England in the late 'eighties, summer shows were already in decline; now it's more obvious than ever that cruise ships really are the last bastion of variety.

One final memory to conclude this brief history of the

Regency period. As I've said, there was a definite air of Butlins-on-Sea when you were working the cruise ships, and it wasn't restricted to the occasional Redcoat-type duty. Most of the operations at Butlins were geared to getting as much money out of the campers as possible, and the same applied here. One of the perks of being on the cruise staff in those halcyon days was the taking of money from the passengers for ship's events like bingo, at which I was an expert, horse racing, which was a particularly strong pull, and guessing the mileage covered from noon to noon.

We would take the money for these events and pay only half back in actual prize money, which could be quite substantial. We would laughingly have a 'big' bingo prize at the end of the cruise for, say, $1,500, which would have been accumulating on a daily basis. The ship's cut could be anything from $10,000 to $15,000 per week, and this paid part of the wages for the cruise staff. It would be divided into twelve equal parts, called 'points': I would receive two, the Hotel Manager one, the Chief Purser, who was also the ship's accountant or cashier, would get one, some points would go to shoreside staff and some would be used to pay onboard cruise staff.

If you're wondering why I'm telling you all this, it's because of a remark made by one Chief Purser as we were counting the spoils in my locked office at the end of a cruise. Her name was Gabriella Hammerdinger and she was, of course, German. As we were counting the money I pointed out that we were no different from the pirates of old, as we stole the money from the passengers and shared it out amongst ourselves at the end of the journey.

Gabriella was a vivacious, raven-haired, sexy lady with an air of superiority about her, and she never took any prisoners where the passengers were concerned. Her full lips were bright crimson and, as she took a drag of her cigarette, she leaned back in her chair and said, in her heavy German accent: 'Frendy, we are *not* like pirates.'

'Oh,' I said, 'why?'

With a deep sigh which seemed to encompass every last stupid passenger request and complaint, she replied: 'Pirates never took dis shit.'

20: Red Light Time

WHEN Vanessa and I left cruising it was a blessing, really. Quite apart from anything else, we'd been out of the country for four years and needed to get a home together.

In 1989 we had purchased a small cottage in a tiny Scottish village called Fearnan in Perthshire, overlooking Loch Tay, which we called Minstrel's Cottage, after a favourite black and white cat of Vanessa's. It was in a poor state of repair, so we had extensive work done whilst we were cruising.

We'd been homeless when we went to the USA and had stayed with Jean, an old schoolfriend of Vanessa's, and her family, during our first break from the cruise ships; Jean, a Scot, had settled with her husband Alastair in the nearby village of Aberfeldy, and the beauty of the area appealed to us. Within a short time of actually living there, however, we realised that although Minstrel's Cottage was warm and cosy, the weather in this part of Scotland was dreadful: it rained most of the time and there was thick snow in the winter. Our hideaway began to feel a long way from civilisation.

Meanwhile there was still a living to make. After the Weston-Webb fiasco I had absolutely no wish to get back into management, so I contacted an agent who booked the QE2, Garry Brown, who immediately got me ten weeks' stand-up work on the UK to New York run. I didn't enjoy this much, apart from the last trip which took in the 4th of July in New York Harbour with the international Parade of Tall Ships; Vanessa came with me and it was simply great.

I did a commercial for Prudential Insurance, courtesy of Peter Chelsom, and several after-dinner engagements, but work was fairly thin on the ground otherwise. I think we even considered going back to the cruise ships but my main concern was being in the UK for the filming of Peter's *Funny Bones,* which I felt was about to happen. I had already missed the chance of playing Josef Locke's musical director in Peter's first feature film, *Hear My Song,* as I couldn't get time off from cruising, and I didn't want to make the same mistake again with a film I had so much more invested in.

After a year, however, with *Funny Bones* no closer to a start date, I decided that I really needed to get myself an agent. I wrote to several and received a reply from ATS, a Leeds-based agency which I'd had some dealings with in the past. Stanley and Michael Joseph had owned and run the famous Leeds City Varieties for many years but had sold it to the council and moved into offices.

I was expecting to be offered stand-up and panto, but they also had an acting department, run very efficiently by Sharron Ashcroft, an ex-casting director for Yorkshire Television. She suggested I might like to try and get some work as an actor, so I made the fourteen hour round trip from Pitlochry to Leeds for a meeting with her. She agreed to give it a go and very quickly got to work: within days she was contacting me with offers.

We decided to move down to Yorkshire so we rented a cottage in Boroughbridge, situated between York and Harrogate and a great centre for getting to London, Manchester and all points east and west ... and so began what I suppose must count as my fourth career to date, as a straight actor.

Well, straight-*ish*. I did *Last of the Summer Wine* and several episodes of *All Quiet on the Preston Front*, about a group of lads in the Territorial Army. Colin Buchanan's character, Hodge, worked in a garden centre and I was an angry customer who kept coming back to complain that the decoy heron he'd sold him was useless, as it didn't frighten the other herons away and kept toppling over into the pond and killing the goldfish. It was odd, because they had a lot of new young people in the show, like Alistair McGowan and Caroline Catz, but the producer really wanted me to be in it and kept bringing my character back to visit further mishaps on him.

I also did *Lost Empires*, a radio adaptation by Bert Coules of JB Priestley's novel about a music hall troupe set just before the First World War. I played Harry Burrard, a comedian whose act is out of date and who has become paranoid, convinced he's being spied on by management and that the word has gone out to a claque in the audience to 'Give Burrard the bird' and scupper his career. If you saw an earlier TV adaptation you will know I was playing Laurence Olivier's part; I was thrilled about that. Now I just need Archie Rice and Hamlet for the hat-trick.

The drama, made for broadcast during Priestley's centenary in 1994, was in three one hour episodes recorded over a full week in Manchester, with a day at the Oldham

Coliseum for audience reaction during theatre scenes. Tom Baker, playing the lead, would keep interrupting the recording to tell us what he thought the script ought to be doing. And he got on everybody's nerves with it.

On the last day of the studio recording, we were all on the floor for the scene where my character shoots himself, the idea being they're all onstage being rehearsed when they hear a gunshot. The producer said 'okay,' and we let out a sort of general gasp: 'What's that?' and there was the sound of someone running to Harry Burrard's dressing room.

Suddenly Tom Baker boomed: 'No, no, no, that wouldn't happen like that. I was on Clapham Junction station once and a man threw himself in front of a train...' – and I said, 'Why, was he talking to you?' I couldn't resist it. The company roared – I mean, talk about a corpse, everybody collapsed. And Tom Baker looked at me and gravely intoned: 'Davies, I owe you one.'

The following day, we did the scene onstage at the Oldham Rep and Brigit Forsyth told me, 'I've started to dine out on the story about you and Tom Baker' – so my apologies if this story is already familiar to some readers.

But we became good friends, Tom and I, and I later did an episode of *Medics* with him. He was definitely a great character and still has one of the most distinctive voices on radio and television. We'd go in the pub: 'What do you want, Tom?' 'Two pints of bitter.' During the recording of *Medics* I also met a man who was to become a dear pal, Don Henderson; we later did an episode of *Casualty* together.

I also really enjoyed filming a children's drama series, *Elidor*, during this period. This was an adaptation of a novel by Alan Garner about four children who discover a gateway to a dangerous world. I played a mysterious shop keeper. The fantasy element was balanced by its being set in modern-day

Manchester, so I felt at home. The original novel is even grittier, as it's set in the early 'sixties, in a city still visibly ravaged by the war.

Enjoyable as these jobs were, however, they still felt like a curtain-raiser for the main event. And finally, in 1993, the call came: 'It's Peter: I've got the money from Disney – we're going to make *Funny Bones*.'

21: Funny Bones

'YOU'RE awfully strange bedfellows, you and Peter.'

The speaker was Lionel Jeffries as we drove to the station after Peter Chelsom's wedding. 'Not really,' I told him, 'I gave him his first job.'

'Good God, did you really?'

As I said earlier, *Funny Bones* was really conceived backstage at the Gaumont, Ipswich, where I was directing my first panto, way back in 1974. This, if you remember, was the production of *Cinderella* that featured the non-talking donkey – and gave an eighteen year old aspiring actor his start in showbiz.

Peter's mother, Kay, was an old friend from my Blackpool days: she and her husband Reg rented a lovely antique and Italian marble shop called The Golden Age in the Butlins Metropole building. I'd often bump into them on my visits back to the town, and one day Kay asked if I could do anything for her son, who was just finishing school and was mad to become an actor. I interviewed Peter and gave him the job as an ASM (assistant stage manager) and small parts in the panto at Ipswich.

One of his tasks was to sweep the Shetland ponies' shit up after Cinderella had been whisked off to the ball in her glittering coach – what you might call learning from the ground up. But the show got him his Equity card, and during the season he had a whale of a time keeping the girl dancers happy and listening to the backstage chat from the old pros. He really picked up the feel of the business that I grew up in and always said he would try and recapture this era in his future work.

Peter became a very successful stage and television actor, working with the Royal Shakespeare Company and the National Theatre; he played Lionel Jeffries' younger self in a Dennis Potter TV drama. After about ten years, however, he set his mind on becoming a film director. He got experience with television commercials then wrote and made his first film for Channel 4 in 1986.

This was an eleven minute epic named *Treacle*, after the old Harry Champion song *Put a Bit of Treacle on My Puddin' Mary Ann*. Set in Blackpool, it's the story of three generations of comics. I played the grandad, who appears in flashback, and the grandson was played by Stephen Tompkinson, superb in his first film.

The idea came from telling Peter about my experience of being placed on a chair and telling jokes at my cousin's pub when I was ten, but there is one crucial difference. Encouraged by Jack, I was eager to perform, but the little boy in the film isn't.

The film opens with my character's funeral, then we see his son, played by Ken Goodwin, on a tram in Blackpool, thinking back to his experience in my dressing room, being put up on a chair to do a turn with everyone stood around waiting (actually friends from Peter's am dram days in Blackpool). He tries, and fails – and that's the moment which has become the grown-up Ken's abiding memory of his father.

At the end of the film, Ken watches his own son (Tompkinson) doing a turn in front of a large audience. Although it's a savage, modern reworking of his grandfather's song it captures the bawdy spirit of music hall and scores with young and old alike: the more mobile pensioners are on their feet and cheering by the end. Ken doesn't have that many lines in the film, but his face speaks volumes as he takes in his son's triumph: we know that, for him, this confirms that the talent in the family missed his own generation.

That's the essence of the story, although it doesn't begin to convey the wealth of incidental detail which Peter manages to pack into those eleven minutes: poignant but comic glimpses of the hand-to-mouth existence of Ken's character, Alfie Duffell, and strange, dreamlike moments evoking the town's faded grandeur.

I particularly like a short scene where Ken is giving a singing lesson to a young lady. He does the 'as the actress said to the bishop' line, but it's lost on her: 'Not actress, Mr Duffell – musical comedy, perhaps.' Ken sighs to himself and you just know that's only the latest in a long line of misfires with audiences over the years.

Peter's next foray into film-making was the feature-length *Hear My Song* about Josef Locke and his tax evasion problems in Blackpool, as written about earlier. Peter really wanted me to be in the film, which was made in 1990, but I was still working for Regency Cruises and just could not commit, so he put Harold Berens in the role of Joe's MD for his comeback concert. It was a nice little part, actually; I'd like to have done it.

Funny Bones

The film came out in 1992 just as we finished working for Regency and we were invited to the premiere at which Princess Di was guest of honour, making her first speech. Josef Locke himself attended, and sang *Hear My Song*, after which he was surprised by Michael Aspel with the Big Red Book and we were all whisked away by coach to Teddington studios for his *This is Your Life* in which I talked about my time with him in Blackpool.

FUNNY BONES was made after *Hear My Song* but the screenplay had been written much earlier. Shortly after *Treacle* was made, Peter Chelsom arranged for a meeting with the dramatist Peter Flannery and myself to discuss a treatment for a script about comedy and the idea of going to the extreme to obtain that extra laugh.

During the meeting, which took place in the sedate setting of the library of the Masonic Hall, I illustrated the different types of comedy which might be explored – and not just by talking about them. I did funny walks to demonstrate physical comedy, which must have been quite a sight for several old men looking over the tops of their newspapers.

As we talked about changes in comedy, Peter FIannery asked me about the difference between stand-up and physical comedy. I explained that at the turn of the century, before amplification, comics had to be physically funny and couldn't just rely on their voices. They had to look absurd, which is why a lot of them were eccentric dancers or grotesques: they needed to have funny bones, really.

Peter Flannery said, 'That's a great title!' and that was the name of the script from that day forward, surviving all its many rewrites. It's explained in a key speech by Jerry Lewis to his son in the final film:

> I think there are two types of comedian – there's a funny bones comedian and a non-funny bones comedian. They're both funny: one *is* funny, the other *tells* funny.

Not that I'm claiming credit for the term. I don't know whether he coined it, but it was something I first heard used by Ronnie Corbett in 1971, when we were both doing summer season in Yarmouth; he was at the Britannia Pier and I was at the Wellington. He came to see the show one night and told me afterwards: 'You know the difference between you and me, don't you? You've got funny bones and I haven't.'

That's the first time I consciously remember hearing the phrase, anyway. It stuck with me – and not just because it was such a generous compliment from a fellow comic (thanks, Ronnie). Those two words seemed the perfect shorthand for the qualities I'd seen in my grandad and some of the other comedians I'd watched in my early days, men who could walk on stage and have the audience falling about before they'd said a word. It wasn't just about craft: however much they'd honed their talent, it seemed to be something innate.

All the ideas about comedy in the film came from me, but I had nothing to do with the storyline. I don't know how the two Peters divided up writing duties, but Peter (Chelsom) had appeared in the original 1982 RSC stage version of *Our Friends in the North*, which Peter (Flannery) had written.

I mentioned earlier that my grandad's 'paper slap' routine is used in the film for dramatic effect, but I didn't explain how. If you remember, in Jack's double act there's a silly argument between him and Ruth ('A wire's a telegram!') which ends with her whacking him over the head with a rolled-up newspaper, at which point he shouts out: 'Take the iron bar out of it!'

Now, that last line is just a throwaway gag. The routine is pure slapstick and the assault is with nothing deadlier than newsprint – though it can make for a satisfyingly loud cracking sound when handled correctly.

But one of the two Peters seized on the suggestion in Jack's line, and in the final film, when Lee Evans is rehearsing the routine with Oliver Platt and shakes the newspaper out, we see an actual metal bar clang to the floor. Lee shows Oliver that it was safely strapped to his arm during the assault and only fed out through the rolled-up paper afterwards ... but this is intercut with a flashback where we see that Lee's character did lose it once during a performance and actually killed a man with the bar.

IT'S easier to say what *Funny Bones* isn't than what it is. As you've probably guessed from the above, it's not a comedy, even though it's about comedy. I once lent the DVD to a young actor I was working with and asked him the next day whether he'd enjoyed it. 'Oh yes,' he replied, 'we were rolling on the floor laughing.' So I knew he hadn't seen it.

It has several interwoven plots, so it's hard to sum up. At its simplest you could say it's a rites-of-passage story: a failed comic goes back to the scene of his childhood in search of renewal and inspiration – which he finds, though not quite in the way he expected. But it's also a drama about a family steeped in comedy who have been forced into the situation where they can't work anymore until they are redeemed at the end of the film. Not to mention a sort of crime caper: the tale of a hunt for a mysterious egg with life-giving properties.

But a bare outline of the plot strands doesn't begin to do justice to the richness of the film. Like *Treacle*, it is, above all, a love letter to Blackpool, beautifully shot, evoking a vanished era of entertainment.

Peter Chelsom initially sold the script to Working Title Films, but they sat on it for about five years. After the success of *Hear My Song*, however, Peter pitched and sold the film to Jeffrey Katzenberg at Walt Disney Productions, having to buy it back from Working Title, which he eventually managed to do in 1993. I believe I was one of the first people Peter rang to say, 'I've got the money for *Funny Bones*.'

I was in almost daily contact with Peter during this process as I was the only person cast from the very beginning and had quite a large part in the film. Peter's co-producer was Simon Fields and together they assembled a great cast including Jerry Lewis, Leslie Caron, Oliver Platt and, in his first film, Lee Evans. George Carl and I played a famous comedy double act, the Parker Brothers, who starred regularly in Blackpool at the Tower Circus, not unlike the real-life Charlie Cairoli. Bruno, my character, is divorced from his wife (Leslie Caron), and has a son (Lee Evans) who has funny bones: 'greater, funnier than any of us.'

Making the film wasn't all plain sailing, however. I wouldn't be true to my experience if I didn't mention that my friendship with Peter was put under tremendous strain before and during filming, and I came close to walking away. *Funny Bones* was a huge project compared to *Hear My Song* – Hollywood money and a great responsibility for him – and he had a crisis of confidence.

One morning during rehearsals at Ealing I was rehearsing a scene with George Carl and Peter seemed to be getting a bit tetchy. Then he said, 'I just don't think I can make this work at all.' I asked him what he meant. 'Nah,' he said, 'I just don't think it's going to work with you at all; I just don't think it will work.' I didn't quite understand, but then the penny dropped: *He actually wants to get rid of me. We've come this far. And I've put all this effort into it.*

This wasn't just about being rejected for a part. Peter and I had been very close from him being eighteen, and it was a friendship that had continued through his acting years. He said, initially, that I was the person he wanted in all his films; he was totally beholden to me and I embodied something of the spirit of Blackpool. And my thoughts on comedy hadn't been restricted to that meeting at the Masonic Hall; they had been shared in countless conversations and phone calls, and I'd even laid them out on paper for him.

Comedically, nearly everything in the film had come from my input, in fact, though when the film was being financed and I asked about some kind of credit or acknowledgement he wouldn't give me any and was really quite arrogant about it. He claimed he had spoken to dozens of people about the orgins of comedy and that the ideas in the film had stemmed from talking to all of them. 'Oh?' I said. 'Why did you use all my ideas, then? Where did the paper slap come from, and all the items in the circus, the swing doors and the ship routine with the fish? Even the title!'

I didn't pursue it, even though I'd had to explain to the designer how all the comedy props worked and even sourced a proper old ghost train owned by a feller who collects old fairground items. So there had already been a certain amount of tension between us before rehearsals had started, but Peter's words in the rehearsal room that day revealed a hardness in him which I hadn't seen before.

I didn't yet have a contract, but I did have a letter of intent which stated clearly the amount I was to be paid, so when the producer, Simon Fields, started to say that they would try to make sure I got as much severance money as possible I made it clear, in no uncertain terms, that I wanted it all, and I wanted it today. I was furious at this turn of events, but it was more than that: I was deeply upset and disillusioned.

I went back to the hotel and fumed: when Peter tried to call me during the afternoon I put the phone down on him.

Simon rang later, saying that it really had to be sorted and that they were both coming to see me. Vanessa, who was caught in the middle of all this, had a go at Peter like you wouldn't believe, and she hit the nail on the head: 'You've always known what you're getting with Fred. How dare you treat him like this! I think it's absolutely disgraceful!'

I think what had got to Peter was that I wasn't really a trained actor and hadn't come through the drama school route, as he had, and he thought I'd have difficulty doing the part – even though I knew the character backwards and had virtually told him who the character was. Comedians do find rehearsing difficult, as I said earlier: gags can only be tested with an audience, so the process is alien to us. I've seen actors in panto go spare when the comic says: 'Here I do a funny walk, slide down the stairs and finish up in the orchestra pit.' They want to see it in rehearsal so they know what to expect. I can understand that it must be very frustrating for directors too, but Peter knew me well enough to trust that I would deliver the goods: that was what hurt.

Over the years I have got better at going all out in the rehearsal room, though never to the extent of trained actors – and yet they all seem to admire stand-ups, saying: 'Oh, I could never talk to the audience.' And maybe this is just the comic in me talking, but I do believe a case can be made for holding something back until the actual performance.

Working with some young actors recently, I watched them rehearse and do it perfectly, as they'd been trained to do, while I was just stumbling through, getting the words out for the kids. But when they went out on the night there was a slight nervousness, an edge to them; their performances were down when mine was up.

It's just a different approach. I recall Peter telling me at the first readthrough that because he was a proper film actor Oliver Platt could have shot the film there and then, that he was ready. I'm not sure I would have agreed.

Peter would give me notes that were actors' notes, but I didn't need them to make me do it differently. Also, I think the producer Simon Fields may have helped plant a seed of doubt in his mind: when Peter first introduced me to him, Simon's response was: 'He's nothing like the character.'

They had even got as far as enquiring about other actors. I know Trevor Peacock was in the frame, though I don't think he was available for all the days required. It's such a specialised part that I still really don't know where Peter was coming from, other than the fact that I wasn't a drama school actor.

But we sort of patched it up, and when I went in the following day, he greeted me at the door, put his arms around me and started to cry; I was in tears, too, still very emotional about it all. After that we went up to the rehearsal room and carried on. It was never mentioned again.

I CAN'T pretend that this didn't affect my experience of making the film. Even though we'd made up Peter could still be very tense on set, but I do have happy memories of working with such a wonderful cast.

I found Jerry Lewis a delight from the moment I tentatively tapped on his shoulder. He had just arrived and was sitting a few rows down from me in the middle of an empty circus, so I thought I'd better go and welcome him. He was immediately very warm – 'Oh Freddie, I've been dying to meet you, I've heard all about you!'– and he remained that way all through filming.

Jerry had his own troubles. I remember the day he

had to make his big speech, really one hell of a speech, in which he has to tell his son that he's not funny. We were in trailers next to one another and Jerry had just been walked down by the second AD (assistant director) or somebody to the beach to do the scene ... and nobody was there. They hadn't set up or anything. There are all these lines of communication on a film set, from the first AD to the second to the third to the runner, so wires get crossed and then there's a bloody panic when they start running around like chickens with no heads on. I used to say, 'Are you sure they're ready for me? Am I gonna stand there for two hours while they set up?' Though I knew the answer would always be: 'Oh yes, they sent for you, they want you there right now.'

Anyway, he came back and he was in a filthy temper, screaming and shouting. So I went in: 'What's up, Jerry?' 'Those bastards,' he said, 'they sent me down there and they're not fuckin' ready, there's no cameras there, there's nobody there, in the middle of a bloody beach they've got taped off.' I said, 'Are you alright with the speech?' His wife said, 'No he's not.'

I asked if he wanted me to go over it with him. 'You wouldn't, would you? I'd love you to hear it.' He handed me his script and was absolutely word perfect:

> It kills me that I got lazy, using writers, not using me. We were funny people! We didn't have to tell funny stories. We were funny. We had funny bones! And the thing that kills me the most is watching my own son flop time after time. What kills me is however much I spent on writers and coaches, it hasn't worked for you, Tommy. Godammit, it's like you're too educated to be funny. All this analysis. I did that! Tommy, I think there are two types of

> comedians. There's a funny bones comedian, and a non-funny bones comedian. They're both funny. One *is* funny, the other *tells* funny. And Tommy ... It's time you knew ... and this kills me the most, but you're neither. You're not funny. Know it now. They're not gonna stand and cheer for you, no matter what you do.

I said to him: 'Don't do it again. Do not. Do that. Again. Forget about it now – just go out and do it.' He did it in one take and came back to his trailer.

There were times when Peter's continuing tension during filming led to multiple takes. Jerry and I had a scene together where I tell him that I know about his affair with my wife and he asks about Jack, the son he has never seen until now:

BRUNO

> I believe he's greater, funnier than any of us. It's like ... If we'd all wanted to have the funniest child at the expense of everything else, then our prayers were answered. Too loudly. You know you've heard people say they've had a love child?

GEORGE

> Yes, in the 'sixties. Go on.

BRUNO

> Well, I know you and Katie were in love and all that. Look, I don't mind. Honest, I don't. But it's like he's – a laugh child. And we've all paid for it.

Peter shot eight takes and Jerry said to me,'What the fuck is he doing with the takes? There's nothing wrong with the first one.' I could only say, 'He's the boss – he wants us to keep doing it.' He never got a better take: the first one was great.

Little George Carl was sat there and, bless him, he didn't know what was happening. Peter would say, 'Let's have a shot of George now – look at Freddie,' but he never took any notice of him; I don't know why. Peter would say to me, 'Don't keep telling him what to do,' but he only took any notice of me. At the end of the film Peter admitted that I'd dragged George through it, but what else could I do?

Peter did apologise about his behaviour afterwards. There were long, personal letters telling me about the way he was feeling at the time, saying he had never worked like that since, and explaining the pressure he was under from Disney. But during all the tension on set, he would have moments with the producer, Simon Fields, sending one another up. One day Simon suggested, 'Say you're not coming in tomorrow. That you're walking out on the film.' 'What for?' I asked. 'To wind him up!' After everything that had happened I could only reply that I wasn't in the right frame of mind.

And Lee loathed him. I don't know how it came up, but I remember saying to Peter, 'He hates you, you know.' Peter said, 'I want him to hate me, because at the end I really want to see viciousness.' And there's no denying he got a brilliant performance out of him; I think it's the best thing Lee's ever done. I can't imagine anybody else playing the role.

I wasn't in on the day Lee was on the sway pole for the film's climactic scene, as we'd already done all the reaction shots. This was a prop police lamp post, fifty feet up in the air – and flexible, as the name suggests. It was something Peter remembered seeing as a kid at the Tower

Circus in Blackpool: it was gaslit, and a 'drunk' shinned up the pole to light his cigarette.

For the film a platform had to be built, with an expensive contraption to twirl the pole round, but it made for a spectacular climax (which I won't spoil here in case you haven't seen the film). Lee could easily have climbed to the top but they wouldn't let him; he got halfway up then one of the stunt doubles took over.

The stunt double was also one of the pair who did the cartwheels which George Carl and I supposedly perform when we finally get the chance to revive our act, though as George was seventy-four and I was fifty-seven at the time, I think we can be forgiven. It's actually a very funny moment in the film: we've accidentally inhaled powder from the mysterious egg that everyone is searching for and bound into the ring, rejuvenated, as though no time at all has passed since we last performed. I could do with some of that on prescription now. Note, by the way, that I'm wearing the homburg in that scene. I didn't particularly want to use it in the film, but Peter kept putting me into it. George always wore his hat anyway.

In the film there's a quick montage of some famous comedy routines with George and me, but a lot more was shot which didn't make the final edit: we did a paper-hanging scene, for example. The waiter sketch, which you do see, was jollied up with lots of business invented on the day because the props department, dozens of them, were having difficulty making the custard pies.

I had a 'splosh' recipe which I'd remembered from my Butlins and pantomime days. I believe it was a Charlie Cairoli recipe, done with actual shaving soap sticks, not shaving foam, and you have to shred them down and mix with water then blend it all into a thick paste which makes the proper 'splosh'custard pies. The prop people were using foam out of a canister which would go flat after five minutes, so I got them to send somebody to Cusson's Imperial Leather soapworks in Manchester and bring the shaving sticks back. We decided to do something which was messy that we could get some comedic value out of in the meantime, and that's how the splosh and spaghetti scene came about.

I remember Leslie Caron was sat very close to me, on the edge of the circus ring, watching it, and she said to me afterwards, 'You do remind me of Cary Grant, because he started out as a circus clown, you know. I was in a film with him called *Father Goose*.' Like the world didn't know. She was a sweetheart: I remember once saying, 'I must dance with the lovely Gigi,' and we had a little waltz around the studio floor.

Sadly, George was suffering from Alzheimer's by the time the film was made, but he did everything he was told – with a little help from his friends – and his wonderful mime routines were captured for posterity. When we were filming at the famous Ealing studios, George, along with his son and daughter in law, who were looking after him, and myself were accommodated at the Dolphin Square Hotel and picked up by car every morning at 6.00am. Every morning en route to Ealing George would say to me, 'Freddie, why are all the shops closed?' and I would reply, 'Well George, they don't open until nine o'clock.' Every day the same question.

On the final day of the shoot we got in the car, and as we set off I said, 'The shops are closed until 9.00am, George,' and he said, 'Yes I know, you have been telling me for three fucking months.'

I last saw him when I went to Las Vegas the following year, 1995, when *Funny Bones* was released; even in the depths of his Alzheimer's he remembered me and hugged me. George sadly passed away in 1999. During our many scenes together he told me how he had started in show business as a bareback rider, then an acrobat and dancer, before he devised the act which would last him for the rest of his life as an eccentric mime getting tangled up in the microphone lead etc, which was a surefire hit all over the world, as he never spoke a word. He was booked to appear at the Crazy Horse cabaret venue in Paris, a contract which continued for twenty-two years.

I liked the first cut of the film I saw, which was shown at the Curzon; Peter later told me he spent the entire film watching me, more interested in my reaction than anything else. In particular I liked the relationship the family had and the fact that Bruno felt no animosity towards his ex-wife Katie: he was still fond of her, and the backstory was that she had moved on because of the tragedy which we see in flashback in the film. I don't think by any stretch of the imagination that Jack, Lee Evans' character, was mad: I think he was thick as opposed to mad, but knew all the tricks of the trade; I quite liked that aspect of it.

I'm proud of the film. It was very well done – and very well shot, by Eduardo Serra. I didn't watch the rushes myself but Peter would ring me every night to enthuse about some close-up he'd just seen: 'Your face is unbelievable.' It's a bit mixed up because several of the stories got dodged about a bit because of time, but Peter has never been asked to do a director's cut or supply any extras for any subsequent video or DVD releases. A great pity, as there's a film in the comedy routines alone.

I don't know how he decided what and what not to cut, although some things just became redundant, like a scene with Joanna Lumley's character. She flew into Blackpool Airport to switch on the illuminations but the Head of Tourism, Minty (Richard Griffiths) had already agreed to let

Jerry Lewis do it. There was a shot of her behind glass, arguing with Minty, before she got back into the plane and flew out again. It wasn't necessary, so it had to go, even though it meant we lost a nice moment when Minty's assistant gallantly wallops a randy reporter on her behalf.

Other cuts did affect clarity a bit. If you've seen the film you will know that George and I, as the Parker Brothers, sell our act to Oliver Platt against the advice of Leslie Caron. I tell her 'We really need the money, Katie,' but as there isn't any further explanation, you'd be forgiven for assuming it's just a general need for funds – especially as we're living next door to the constant rumbling of the ghost train.

Actually, a scene was cut out with Minty, George and me where Dolly, Oliver Reed's character, says, 'I want £5,000 off each of you!' to pay for the missing egg. Minty protests that it's not his fault, but the powerful and dangerous Dolly won't be swayed –and that's why we were so desperate to sell the act.

This was followed by a huge reception scene, also cut, which was filmed over several days in the garden of Knebworth House, near London, with hundreds of extras and guards at the gate. George and I had come to give the five grand to Oliver Reed but when Jerry Lewis's character saw us and declared that George and I were two of his oldest friends, Dolly tried to stop us handing over the money because he didn't want him to know he was blackmailing the two old fellers. This was also the scene where Dolly persuades Minty to have Jerry's character switch on the Illuminations, so once it went, Joanna Lumley's scene no longer made sense.

Peter got some very good people around him. John Altman did the incidental music which had some very nice moments in it. And the decision to use American blues and jazz recordings was inspired: instead of sounding alien, those old records seemed to capture the spirit of Blackpool in a way which seemed fresh rather than simply nostalgic. Actually, it's not all that surprising: a lot of those performers were showmen who came from a vaudeville background and knew how to entertain, which is what Blackpool is all about.

The cameraman, Eduardo, was a top guy who had done many major films including *Girl With a Pearl Earring*, which did a wonderful job of recreating the scenes in Vermeer paintings. I always like to know about the technical side of things and Eduardo really took an interest in telling me why he wanted certain looks in *Funny Bones* and how he achieved them. It would take him hours to get the effects he wanted but it really paid off. I'm especially fond of the early sequence where Oliver Platt is driving down in the car, looking out at what is somehow both a modern day scene and a dreamlike vision of Blackpool as it used to be: the two old biddies on the beach, the woman in the booth, looking out at him.

In all, Peter took out about forty-five minutes from what he'd filmed. A lot of it was the drugs subplot involving Oliver Reed's character and those mysterious eggs, though he had to leave some of it in to justify using him. It's a pity, because it means the significance of the eggs is almost totally lost. But a bare-bones *Funny Bones* is still an experience a lot richer than many films, and it does capture something of the essence of comedy, so that's not too bad a memorial.

Peter and I are on good terms these days, and if he phoned me tomorrow about an exciting new project, of course I'd do it. But I don't think he ever will. He has called *Treacle*, *Hear My Song* and *Funny Bones* his 'Blackpool trilogy', so I think he reckons he's paid his dues now.

22: ...And After

FUNNY Bones was due for release in September 1995. I was convinced it would give my career a lift and generate some work, but before that I still had to earn a living.

I took a pantomime for the 1994/95 season at the Mansfield Civic with Bob Carolgees and Spit the dog; it was *Dick Whittington* and it was a fun show. Bob was Idle Jack and I played the Captain of the ship – not that everyone appreciated my efforts. I remember one night Vanessa and I were having supper with Roy Brandon, who played Dame. His wife, who was sat opposite me at the table, said, 'We had a great Captain last year in Colin Baker.' Thinking that perhaps she didn't realise I was playing that role in the current show, I said, 'I'm really enjoying playing the Captain.' But she only repeated, 'Oh yes, he was definitely the best we have ever had.' What I think she meant was that he played it straight – I played it for laughs.

The following summer season I suggested to the producer of the Clacton summer show, Francis Golightly, that

I might be an addition for his *Cascade Revue* and could be a special guest to Bernie Clifton, who was a mate, as we wouldn't clash. He told me he couldn't afford to have me but if he cut out a boy dancer he was going to employ, there would be enough money in the kitty. So, to get the deal straight, he would be paying me just a bit more than a boy dancer.

I did the show as it was a short season. This bread and butter work made a bit of a change from being on a film set and being in the UK, rather than cruising the Caribbean, meant I had to dust down my old act, but it turned out to be pleasant enough.

Unfortunately Mr Golightly was not: getting me cheaper was just another nasty tale for him to tell his cronies around the business. What really annoyed me was that I had, on many occasions, helped him out with artists in the past and never asked for any favours in return; now, when I was in need of a little help myself, he turned into a bitchy queen. He would regale us with the news that the show was taking more money than ever before but refused to offer me a small bonus on top of the minimum rate he was getting me for. He knew I was hard up and behaved appallingly, and then lied to others that I owed him money. The *Stage* review began:

> Yet again, Francis Golightly defies the economic odds to present a summer season of top talent and dazzling colour at the West Cliff Theatre.

So now you know how he managed it. Still, with a major film about to come out I was able to keep positive by thinking of all the work which would be winging my way.

Vanessa and I decided to tie the knot and married in Harrogate the day before the London premiere of *Funny Bones*, 25th September 1995.

IT became clear very early on that *Funny Bones* wasn't going to become a blockbuster. It did get some very good reviews but fell by the wayside quickly, as many films do. It only lasted a week in the cinemas here; after that they didn't want it.

I seemed to be the only actor in the film who did any real publicity for it in the UK. They flew Oliver Platt over on Concorde, and Leslie Caron, but neither Jerry Lewis nor Lee Evans came to the premieres in London and Blackpool.

The reception in America was even worse: it hardly got released over there. They put it out in New York, and I know it was on in LA, but nobody saw it. They put it into the San Francisco Film Festival as the last film – it wasn't in the competition – and they just about paid for my fare to go from LA to San Francisco to attend it, putting me up in a hotel. George was there and we went up on the stage together; they needed somebody from the film and nobody else was there, except Peter Chelsom and Simon Fields.

The Americans didn't know how to sell it because they didn't know quite what it was: 'rolling-on-the-floor' comedy it is not, despite the claims of my young actor friend. And quite apart from the odd premise – a drama about comedy which is not very funny, even though it's about being funny – it had no Hollywood A-listers, so it really needed careful attention and support from Disney's publicity machine in order to build the audience it deserved.

In the event, it all felt a little downgraded: Jeffrey Katzenberg had left Disney and no one really wanted to know. I know Peter was disappointed: it was his life's work.

The film has acquired a cult following over the years. It's occasionally shown on TV and I still get asked about it. It's currently available on DVD, but the description on the packaging might lead you to expect a different sort of film:

Funny Bones

A ZANY LOOK AT TWO COMEDIANS WHO'LL DO ANYTHING FOR A LAUGH!

I think I prefer the description in an article by the novelist AL Kennedy:

> *Funny Bones* fits into no known genre and makes no compromises about its many, many peculiarities. It nods fondly in the direction of vaudeville pieces such as *Duck Soup* and has the humanity, imagination and emotional range of a good screwball comedy. The plot is a law unto itself. We begin all at sea and stay there – encountering violent death, magical powder, corrupt policemen, adultery, flashbacks, theft, comedy turns, despair, classic patter and *commedia dell'arte*.

Though I admit it's a bit long for a strapline.

I had the chance to go to Los Angeles when the film came out and went to stay with my dear friend Joe Baker, a British comedian who had made his way in the show business of Hollywood and appeared in several movies and US TV shows. I usually stayed with Joe and his wife, Ann, a British TV actress from the 'fifties and 'sixties TV soap *Emergency Ward Ten*.

I had also been invited to the Hollywood home of Ruta Lee, who had appeared in *Funny Bones* as Jerry Lewis's wife. Ruta, a seasoned pro, had been one of the original brides in the movie *Seven Brides for Seven Brothers*, and lived in a real Hollywood mansion on Laurel Canyon Drive which had belonged to Rita Hayworth and Orson Welles. We first met on the catering bus in Blackpool, and I remember warning Ruta that if Vanessa called during lunch she was to keep schtum, as I was having chips, which she had strictly forbidden. My mobile rang and Ruta heard me say I was eating lunch – at which she shouted: 'He's having a fucking apple!'

Ruta had a very good and prestigious agent in LA, Sid Craig, and offered to arrange a meeting for me. He needed to see me in action and arranged a private showing of *Funny Bones* at Walt Disney Studios. I was allowed to have some friends along, so I asked Tony Hawes, a comedy writer who had settled in LA. His new wife, who was much older than him, happened to be Stan Laurel's daughter, Lola, which swayed him as he was a huge Laurel and Hardy fan. They came to the showing along with several magical pals from the famous Magic Castle in Hollywood. Viewing the film in a private cinema within the Disney studio walls was a wonderful experience.

Sid Craig hated the film but liked me in it, and offered to become my representative in LA. Now here's the rub! I was due to fly back to the UK the following day and my ticket was non-transferable. Either I could stay and pay another fare or come home to little work.

I was so short of money at the time that I reluctantly decided to go back, even though Sid called on the morning of my departure to say he had a casting for me at Paramount. He did say he would put me up for parts and that if the studios wanted me to come back to LA they would find a way, but I never went back. In hindsight I suppose I should have stayed or at least said, 'I'll be back in a couple of months,' and gone back and had a go, but who knows?

I ALREADY had a new agent in the UK. My pal Don Henderson had introduced me to his agent, Derek Webster, who had a very successful agency called AIM with some big hitters like John Thaw, Brian Blessed and Richard Attenborough, and I had decided to leave ATS in Leeds for this London-based agent, who I felt would be a better bet with the film coming out pretty soon.

But now that *Funny Bones* had been released work was still thin on the ground, and I just wasn't getting anywhere, despite having two agents. As I ruefully remarked to Martin Kelner, who interviewed me around this time, 'I'm out of work all over the world.'

As the terrible lull continued I finally admitted to myself that I needed a back-up … and that's when Vanessa and I decided to take on a pub.

23: Last Orders

NOW – assuming you've been following the story and aren't just leafing through this book at random in a charity shop – you'll appreciate that this was a pretty major move, though I can't quite remember what was going through my head at the time. Did I see it as a short term measure? Or after the disappointment over *Funny Bones* was I finally admitting that I might have to make my living another way?

Actually, I think I felt that I wasn't earning, and that was my primary thing. I'd been advised by a very good friend that celebrity pubs worked, and I knew Thwaites Brewery in Burnley because I'd done that advert for 'Thwaites Thtout' in 1966, my year of media saturation. So I rang up the managing director and said, 'What's the possibility of getting a pub?' 'I don't think you'll have any problems, Freddie – we're closing them by the minute.'

This didn't put me off, though maybe it should have done. He sent me to see a few, which were awful, but then, in the little village of Burscough in Lancashire, I saw a place called the Lathom Slipway. It was in a picturesque setting by the side of the Leeds Liverpool Canal, complete with a huge garden.

That garden decided it for me, because I could put a marquee on the side and have entertainment. We sold our house and moved into the pub, thinking that once we'd got everything sorted we could put a manager and a chef in; we didn't intend to run it ourselves.

I was not naive to business in any way and although people were trying to rip me off they only did it once. I was up to all the wheezes, all the stealing, as soon as I moved in. I knew the place was being robbed. I took the existing staff over and one of them only lasted about three days. I could tell that they were handing money out over the bar.

I called this person over and we went into a kind of unfunny crosstalk act:

'There's money missing out the till, do you know what's happened to it?'

'Are you accusing me of stealing?'

'No, there's money missing out the till and you're the only one behind the bar, so tell me, have you any idea where it's gone? Did you see somebody go behind the bar and take the money out the till?'

'Nobody's allowed behind the bar.'

'No, you're the only person there. Can you tell me, have you any idea where the money's gone that's missing out the till?'

'Are you accusing me of stealing?'

And so on. They never came back to work but got away with about seventy quid on the night. There had even been a cheeky offer to check their bag, knowing I wouldn't find anything: 'No,' I'd said, worn down by then, 'I don't want to check anything, I'm just asking you a question.'

Our big opening weekend was planned for three weeks' time. We advertised it and had a great jazz band from the QE2 in the garden and Jim Bowen came down. We were so successful that there were people standing ten deep at the bar: the pub couldn't cope with the business. It took me two days to count the takings and I thought, 'Wow, this is the way it's going to go.'

And so it did – at first. We had a rival publican up the road and were caning him. It was very sad – we ruined him, in actual fact. But I have to say he didn't do himself any favours. He came down for a drink once and offered to give me a bucket of ice as my machine had packed up, so I walked back with him to his pub, about three hundred yards up the canal. I'd just sacked a guy for stealing and had told him all about it, so when I walked in I was gobsmacked to see that he was now my rival's head barman!

The miscreant didn't see me immediately as I was behind his new boss. His first words were: 'Well, are we doing better than them tonight or what?' I spluttered: 'What are you doing with this feller?' only to be told: 'Oh well, you know, you've got to give everybody a second chance.' What an idiot! He was a sometime writer who finished up being carted away by the police and the brewery for unpaid bills.

But then the police stopped me having entertainment on that scale without a licence as the pub couldn't cope with the toilet facilities and parking and so on. You had to have a meal if you went into the marquee, and that sort of covered the fact that there was entertainment on, but we were only allowed a maximum of two people on stage and couldn't have karaoke – there were all sorts of rules and restrictions.

Without proper entertainment I knew this wouldn't work. The pub was just an ordinary pub: it had a local clientele, but not enough to make it viable. So the only way to go was to apply for an entertainment licence, which was in the local council's power to grant.

Eventually I got building plans together which satisfied the council's criteria. I listened to the fire brigade telling me I had to have this escape here and that ladder coming down there and so on but, providing I did all that, I should be able to apply for a licence. It seemed to be a done deal. Or so I thought.

But when we applied the entire village, virtually, got a petition up to say why I shouldn't get it – they even hired a barrister to represent them at the council meeting. Although I had a huge car park, they didn't want the cars going through the village and said it would cause disruption; the people in the lane that led up to the pub didn't like the fact that there was already a lot of traffic passing. I'd had no warning about this and was totally unprepared, so I was on the back foot from the start.

I came away from the meeting having been turned down. I knew that if I badgered them and employed legal services I'd probably get it eventually, but thought if they didn't want me I might as well go. I handed the pub back to the landlords, Thwaites, within four weeks, put the company into liquidation and moved on. And so ends the saga of the pub. We lasted two summers and two Christmases with it; we were actually there for twenty months altogether. We did have some very nice regulars and locals who had a special dinner for us when we left, but we were glad to get away.

It hadn't been fair on Vanessa either. I was going away doing stuff when it came up – a variety tour for Johnny Mans, for example – which left her having to organise a very busy kitchen on her own. We did get agency staff but they were generally useless and it was just a disaster.

TOWARDS the end of our time at the pub I did a stage show for Jimmy Perry. This counts as a bit of a disaster, too, but at least it was more fun to be involved with.

Jimmy rang me because Brian Murphy (of *George and Mildred* fame) had pulled out of a long-cherished project of his and he wanted to know if I could step in. I was booked for a week with Danny La Rue in Billingham, but the producer, Duggie Chapman, agreed to release me.

The show, which Jimmy was producing himself, was a lightly disguised musical play about the life of Sid Field, the comic who had once been my grandad's feed. It was supposed to have been toured with David Suchet, who had rejected it once he'd seen the script and gone on to do another play about Field, without Perry's involvement, which had already had a West End run.

Refusing to admit defeat, Jimmy reworked his play, originally called *Dirty Old Comics*, and retitled it *That's Showbiz!* But it was still basically the Sid Field story, the only difference being that this Sid didn't die prematurely but went on to become a TV gameshow host.

Anyway, Jimmy decided to mount this production and called all his markers in: Su Pollard and Carmen Silvera were in the cast, and Ted Rogers played the Sid Field part. I'm afraid it wasn't very good: badly directed by John B Hobbs and under-rehearsed. It went on for one week only at the Wimbledon Theatre in the hope that Jimmy would be able to bring managements in and maybe sell it as a tour.

The funniest thing that happened in the show was on the opening night. As well as being under-rehearsed it was under-teched, as Hobbs had tried to do it all in a day, and the sound man didn't know who was on and off with the radio mics – I had to get my son Kent up to help. During the final scene, the Sid character's funeral, Su Pollard could be heard in the dressing room through her radio mic, effing and blinding – 'I'm not wearing that fucking costume!' – and it was all going out over the front of house. The place was in hysterics; it was terrible – funny, but terrible. June Whitfield said to me in the bar afterwards: 'For God's sake leave that in – it's the only thing that's any good in the show!'

But we had a great time doing it, as with all these things; everybody had a lot of laughs. I played two parts: one half of a double act with my dear pal Bryan Burdon and a character based on the Jewish agent Mannie Jay – who represented my grandad, as it happens – and I had the best song in the show, a Durante-style number called *They Don't Get Applause*.

Jimmy certainly caught the flavour of touring in variety and, properly staged, it might well have worked. But we'd only had two weeks' rehearsal, which just wasn't enough. And the fact that Jimmy hadn't really done enough to cover his tracks also left the play open to attack. John Thaxter commented in *The Stage*:

> Comparisons with the recent Sid Field bio-play are inevitable ... but where David Suchet had Field's famous comedy routines Rogers was too often sidelined as the narrator, with only well-worn gags and one-line sketches to round off his comic pedigree.

By the way, that review also notes that:

> The versatile Bryan Burdon and Freddie Davies as Kenny and Bernie ... literally came into their own when their lines unravelled and they could fall back on ribbing and improvisation.

I will be putting my hands up to a few choice examples of unprofessional behaviour in the next chapter, but as a matter of historical accuracy I have to say that on this occasion I am totally blameless. And so is Bryan.

What happened was that Su Pollard, who played the Sid character's mistress, cut three scenes accidentally: she missed five pages then suddenly Bryan and I were on in the next scene, so we had to try and turn the story round, with lots of frantic: 'Yeah, but what happened last year was when he was …' and 'Yeah, but then he was touring with the …'

Normally these things recede in the memory – you pick up the threads and move on – but of all the stage shows in which I've appeared over fifty-plus years of developing my art, this had to be one of the few preserved for posterity: Bryan's son, a video technician for Sky Sports, recorded it.

ONCE the pub was over and done with, Vanessa and I bought a house and moved back to Eastbourne in January 1998, not sure how we were going to support ourselves on the stray bits and pieces of work which seemed to be all that was coming my way. After the first night at Wimbledon I knew we'd never see *That's Showbiz!* again, so there were no illusions from that quarter.

And another dream was starting to look threadbare. It was now over two years since *Funny Bones*, once the focus of all my hopes, had been released to massive indifference on both sides of the pond. Yes, some critics had said nice things, but it was getting a bit too late to pretend that their words would ever translate into offers of work.

So what was next? Some other venture doomed to failure which would only drag us down further? I was beginning to wonder what there was left to try.

Little did I know that our luck was about to change.

24: Up in the World

IMMEDIATELY after we got rid of the pub I started getting work again, funnily enough. I don't think there was any connection: it wasn't generally known in the business that I had the pub and it had never stopped me doing the odd thing which did come my way during this period. As well as the play for Jimmy Perry and the tour for Johnny Mans, I had done *HettyWainthrop Investigates, Last of the Summer Wine* and a few one-nighters. So there had been work – just not enough to sustain me.

Whatever the reason, almost immediately after we left the Lathom Slipway I found myself being offered the first in what was to become a string of jobs, on stage and screen, which would occupy me almost continually over the next five years, culminating in a three month run in the West End with one of the most prestigious theatre companies in Britain – which isn't too bad for a tatty music hall comic.

ALMOST immediately after going back to Eastbourne, I went on a sixteen-week tour with *Talent,* a Victoria Wood play which saw John Junkin and me as the funniest double cod magicians in the business. Vanessa was the Company Manager, so things were looking up for both of us.

There was a trick in the play called the six card repeat, where you have six cards, take three away, count them out again and you're still magically left with six. Now I was the conjuror's pal, not his proper assistant – I was just helping him out because his wife was at a beetle drive. I'd go through the trick, find I still had the six cards, but wouldn't know why, and I'd keep looking at them as if it was a bought trick which I hadn't quite grasped yet and thinking: 'Hang on a minute, if you've got one, two, three and you throw them away and you've still got one ... ' and then, as I counted them out again, I'd end up with seven cards.

It used to get such a roar, such a round of applause. When Victoria Wood came to see it she brought her magician husband Geoffrey Durham, otherwise known as the Great Soprendo, who said to me: 'I've never seen that done before.' I told him about my own background in magic and admitted I'd originally done it as a deliberate mistake one night to make them laugh onstage.

Talent hadn't been staged a lot; this was its first major tour. Although it had started life as a stage play in 1978, it had been adapted early on as a TV show, which maybe suited it better. Julie Walters and Victoria Wood had the lead roles and rubber-necked Nat Jackley played my part. I don't think he could do the trick properly – then again, I don't have his legs.

The play doesn't quite work on the stage. At least, they didn't get it quite right, though they tried to – poor direction again. It was too short to start with, and they had to put one of Victoria's *Kitty* monologues in front of it.

Talent is about a girl, Julie (played by Walters on TV), who's waiting to take part in a talent contest in a nightclub, and it all takes place in the dressing room. She's got a friend with her, Maureen, originally played by Victoria Wood and, as she's getting ready, she does a whole lot of dialogue about *New Faces*, the TV talent show that was big when the play was written.

Which handed me the best line in the entire play. After about half an hour of the girls, these two old buggers just walk into the dressing room: John Junkin, who's supposed to be this magician – and me as his assistant for the night, in this awful dinner suit that I've borrowed, with a flat cap on. John introduces himself ('Ello!'), explains he's in the competition too ('I'm doin' me magic act!') and asks Julie, 'Haven't I seen you before?' She says: 'I've been for an audition for *New Faces*,' but he says he hasn't seen that. Then I pipe up, in a doleful Yorkshire accent: 'We can't get *New Faces* on our telly.' 'Oh,' she says, 'why not?' 'It's got no plug!'

There were nights when it would get a huge reaction, because it's such a ludicrous line. And some nights it would get nothing, of course, as ever was. Anyway, that's the premise: two acts in the dressing room getting ready.

John Junkin was just marvellous. I knew him from before: we had done a cruise together, years ago, when he compered all the shows and did quiz programmes. He'd also been the script editor on that ill-fated Cheese and Onion show (though I didn't hold that against him: no one could have rescued those scripts).

John had terrible emphysema and had to have a breathing apparatus with him, poor love. He'd given up by the time of the play, but had been a very heavy smoker – he used to have a lighter around his neck in the old days. I can even remember him swimming in the sea with a fag on the go.

We shared dressing rooms and played cards all the time, having many wonderful conversations. He was a very erudite, clever man, who used to buy every newspaper every morning and do all the crosswords before lunchtime. He had started off as a teacher before getting fed up with the bureaucracy and moving into the wider madness of scriptwriting and acting, working with talents as diverse as Joan Littlewood, Marty Feldman and Morecambe and Wise – he wrote a lot of their later shows with Barry Cryer. If you ever get the chance to see the recording of *The Blackpool Show* in which I appeared with Bob Monkhouse, John played Tony Hancock's feed, the rather fey Evelyn.

But as far as I'm concerned John Junkin's greatest role was that of barrack room lawyer. It was for one night only, and I had the best seat in the house … the only one, in fact.

There was a bit of tension between us and the two girls in the show. The actress playing Maureen was supposed to be a little fat girl – that was the character, as the Victoria Wood part – but she copped the needle because she said we were referring to her as if she was actually fat. It was ridiculous.

Things got more heated after we played a matinee at the Ashcroft Theatre, Croydon. There were about twenty people in the audience and there was a scene where John and I had to walk out off the set through a door and then right across the front downstage and off the other side. An old agent friend called Keith Salberg was sat in the front row and I heard him say: 'Better than working for me – you get more money.' I quietly muttered, 'Anything's better than working for you,' and walked off.

Well, the girls complained that I was talking to the audience, and the producer who was putting the show on came to sort it out. And John Junkin wouldn't let me speak! We were having a meeting in the green room at the next town, Cheltenham, and the producer listened to the girls' comments about how I was undisciplined, and all that crap.

John broke in: 'What are you talking about? It doesn't matter what he says on the stage because it's all bollocks anyway – in any case, he's not from the acting profession, he's a variety artist – leave him alone!'

John may have looked a bit like a Bassett hound, bless him, but he was a terrier that day: he just wouldn't let go – he wouldn't even let the poor accused get a word in edgeways. Eventually I just had to sit back, put my hands behind my head and bask in the reflected glow of a masterly, if somewhat overlong, performance. The producer's ears must have been ringing by the end; I seem to remember him backing out the door as though fearful of starting John off again.

But despite episodes like that – or maybe because of them – *Talent* was fun to do. I enjoyed it, particularly working with John. It was a pretty extensive tour – didn't do great business, though it did alright in some places.

Victoria Wood loved it. She wanted me to do an episode of *dinnerladies* and asked to let me off, but we didn't have any understudies. The part was the husband of Thelma Barlow's character, Dolly; Jack Smethurst played it in the end.

When John died in 2006, I thought back to our time together in *Talent*. We covered a lot of ground over those sixteen weeks; every night we would chat about something. He was quite bitter about a lot of stuff, in particular a game show format he'd devised which he believed had been stolen. I remember talking to Barry Cryer about it, and he shook his head: 'Poor John – you've really got to let these things go.' There was even a court case, which may not have helped his later television career. But John Junkin made an indelible mark as an actor and writer on more than four decades of British comedy.

TOWARDS the end of *Talent* I got an offer out of the blue for a new TV series called *Harbour Lights*, starring Nick Berry. I knew Nick, having worked with him on *Heartbeat*, and I think he put my name forward for the role of George Blade, though the producer, Steve Lanning, was already a fan of *Funny Bones*. His nephew had been second AD on it, in fact, until he'd had enough of Peter Chelsom's testiness and handed in his resignation after only three days. But as far as I'm aware nobody else was in the frame for the part.

And certainly not Bill Maynard. I'd done an episode of *Heartbeat* at a time when he was causing quite a lot of problems on the show. He would take the script away and alter it, bringing it back the next day. I remember the trailers in a circle on the shoot and Bill shouting out of his caravan at Nick: 'I see they've shown another clip with me in it. That'll mean the bloody ratings'll be up!' But saying it for real. Nick just went, 'Yeah, yeah, of course, yeah.'

Harbour Lights was set in the fictitious town of Bridehaven, in reality, West Bay in Bridport, Dorset. It was where Nick's character had grown up and he was coming back to take over the job of Harbour Master. Steve Lanning had an apartment in West Bay, which is why he did it, featuring a lot of people who lived there.

It had quite a big budget and hopes were high, but it wasn't a huge ratings success. Unfortunately the scripts weren't very well written – they'd got individuals to write them – though one or two of them weren't bad. We all thought that it was a perfect Sunday night series, because it was quite gentle; in fact we were told it was for Sunday night. But the BBC put it out on a Thursday with a repeat late on Monday night.

They decided to go for a second series, though they

did a big cull of the characters and only about five of us went back; this was explained away by the idea that a group of racketeers had driven half the town away. Because there were fewer characters, the regulars were given more to do – I featured in every episode. In the first series I'd had a wife and kids – there was a storyline about my wife being done for shoplifting and going to prison – but, for the second series, I'd become the café owner. How I'd managed this was never explained, as I'd worked at sea all my life and had a tattoo on my arm and stuff, but never mind; it was enjoyable to be playing a straight role which allowed for comic moments.

I WISH I could say the same for my next job, a rather straight play produced and directed by a feller called Ian Dickens. I met him via my pal Jack Smethurst, who was appearing in one of Ian's productions and was very eager that I should meet him: 'I'm sure you'll be able to do one of these plays.'

I went to meet him and, sure enough, Ian said: 'Oh, I'm a big fan of yours, do you fancy doing a play?' 'Yeah,' I said, casually, 'I don't mind.' He came up with Agatha Christie's *Murder at the Vicarage*, sent me the script and said: 'Can you inject any comedy into the inspector?' 'Well,' I said, 'it's a bit straight, but I'll have a wee look.'

I got to the first day of rehearsals in Lowestoft, where we were opening. The play had a big cast: Susan Penhaligon, Barbara Murray as Miss Marple, and quite a few television faces. After the first day, Susan said to me, 'You know, if you need any help playing this role, I'm quite willing to help you.' She then looked at me and said: 'You only have to ask. You do know that, don't you?' I said, 'Of course I do, Susan.' She was very sweet, but I thought, 'What am I getting into here?'

I tried to concentrate on the fact that I was top left on the bill, and was being paid good money. And it went on to do very good business, there's no doubt about it. But Agatha Christie is very wordy, and there was no humour in the part at all: any time I tried to do anything it was wrong. I was a variety artist in the middle of all these actors who were terrified that I would ad lib and throw them, and I soon got the impression that they didn't think I was any good in the part. I know I was terribly miscast. Once I tried to lighten things up by squinting at Barbara but she yelled at me not to do that when she was concentrating – and that was during rehearsals!

Harbour Lights was being shown at the time, and I recall Ian Dickens, the Agatha Christie producer/director, came in once or twice and said, 'I'm loving *Harbour Lights*, haven't you got anything better to do?' I said, 'What do you mean?' 'Can't you get another job?' he asked. I said, 'Well, I'm doing this one.' It was all very jokey, but there was a definite undercurrent: he really wanted to get me to leave.

But Dickens shot himself in the foot and actually helped to bring the other actors round to my side. On the last week of the run, and we did about sixteen to twenty weeks, Susan Penhaligon said to me, 'I'm going to tell you something now. On the second week in Blackpool, Dickens came to me and said, "Is there any way you can fuck him up on the stage? Because I wanna get rid of him." We were all appalled by this.' I said, 'Why didn't you tell me?' and she said, 'We didn't want you to walk.'

I remember he'd phoned my agent up to say I was messing about or something: I was missing the finale or I was late on one night. It was all bollocks. Derek came to see it at the Churchill in Bromley, and I asked him what he thought. 'Well,' he said, 'you're not great in the part but you're certainly not the worst person on the stage – there are people a lot worse than you.' So I took great comfort from that and carried on.

I remember one night Susan Penhaligon and I were sat in the wings waiting to go on, keeping very quiet, because we were always getting 'shushed'. Ian Dickens' girlfriend was running the prompt corner and he was with her, taking an aspirin or something, and I said, 'Look at him over there, taking a tablet. No matter how many tablets he takes, when he wakes up in the morning he's still gonna be a cunt!' Susan almost corpsed on stage after she went back on. Anytime I see her now I say, 'Do you remember?' and she says, 'I certainly do.'

We survived it, though there were many, many nights when poor Miss Marple, Barbara Murray, lost the script and didn't know where she was, and I'd have to bring her back because she'd usually be having some conversation with me.

She got all ballsed up one night and I said, 'Yes, but what I think you mean is that if the murderer had come in through the French doors instead, that would have meant that the gun would have been left lying on the ...' and it brought her back. She came to me after the show and said, 'Oh thank you, Freddie, what I would have done without you?' I thought: 'Well, trust me a bit more, then.'

But she was alright in the end – in fact, they nearly all came round in the end. Barbara and I were both dog lovers, which helped us form a bond. She had two tiny doggies touring with her, and one of them got very sick and had to be put to sleep; I went out, as I had an hour's break in the show, and got a little syringe so she could put some water in its mouth.

Despite the legit actors' fears, during the whole twenty-week run there was only one comic ad lib which I will admit to – though I reckon I can put up a pretty good case in my defence, even without John Junkin to fight my corner. It happened towards the end of a Saturday full house performance at the Devonshire Park Theatre in Eastbourne, just as we were getting near the denouement; I was waiting in the wings, ready to come back in as the inspector. There was a coffee table downstage and the vicar's wife had made tea for the doctor, but as she was pouring it out she spilt it, and the tea had gone all over the table and was pouring over the edge like a waterfall.

She completely ignored the fact that it had happened, never thought to say: 'Oh I must go and get a cloth,' or something – anything to cover the obvious; she just kept to the script as though nothing had happened. Meanwhile the tea was still dribbling over the side of this coffee table in full view of the audience when I entered.

Her first line to me was, 'Would you like a cup of tea, Inspector?' Well, it was like a red rag to a bull: 'No thank you,' I said, looking at the mess, 'I don't think you've got enough.' It got a roar of laughter and a huge round of applause, because the audience were just waiting for some sort of acknowledgement.

After the show, the silly man who was playing the doctor, an older rep actor who played my part after I'd gone, screeched: 'How dare you do that!' I said, 'How dare I do what?' 'Ad lib like that!' I said, 'Somebody had to say something! You can't just carry on when something happens like that, you've got to say something. It may not be in your discipline but it is in mine!'

'Oh,' he said, unconvinced, 'well, you made me look a fool!' I said, 'No, I never interfere with nature!' or words to that effect. I could feel myself getting angry because I knew, instinctively, I was right ... though I will admit it might have been a bit more dignified to stop once I'd made my point.

That was the only time anyone ever got a laugh in twenty weeks of that entirely humourless play, and I was only responding to circumstances. It's like a relief to an audience, that sort of thing, like lancing a boil.

I don't know if it's true or not, but there is a story about Rex Harrison farting onstage during *My Fair Lady*. There's a hush, as though the audience can't quite bring themselves to believe what they've just heard. The play continues, unimpeded, but there's something hanging in the air ... so to speak. Then Harrison has a fairly innocuous line, something like: 'I assure you that my manners are every bit as good as Colonel Pickering's.' Now that isn't a ribtickler normally, but it's enough to serve as an acknowledgement of what has just happened, and the audience erupts.

MY next job also involved working with 'real' actors but, in complete contrast, this proved to be an absolute, unalloyed delight from start to finish.

Towards the end of the run of *Murder at the Vicarage,* I had a call from my agent Derek to say that the RSC were asking about my availability from September for six months. I said I didn't do roadside calls anymore (geddit?) but it came to pass that a musical version of the children's classic *The Secret Garden* was about to be produced at Stratford Upon Avon, with Adrian Noble directing, and they wanted to see me for the role of Ben Weatherstaff, the gardener.

This came as a complete surprise. Derek hadn't put me up for the part and I couldn't understand how they'd come by me because of my background. I felt slightly unworthy at the prospect of mingling with genuine thespians (as Samuel might spray) in the hallowed Royal Shakespeare Company. I remember saying to the casting director down at Stratford, 'Why me?' and she looked at me and she said, 'Why not?' But even if it was odd that they would look in my direction, I was very happy to do it – and what pleased me more than anything was being given the opportunity. I went down to meet the musical director and the choreographer at the RSC's London rehearsal rooms in Clapham. Gillian Lynne showed me the few steps that I was expected to do in the dance and the MD taught me the song:

> For an old man knows how a year it goes,
> How the cold hard ground in the spring comes
> round ...

As I sang and stamped around it was difficult not to feel that something might be about to come round for me too, after the disappointments of recent years. But I knew I was getting ahead of myself – I hadn't even met the director yet. Once I'd been put through my paces I went home and waited for a call.

It came, and a couple of days later Adrian Noble, a most friendly and nice man, was sitting me down and putting me entirely at my ease. He said, 'I've been reading about you, and I think you've had just an amazing career.' I thought, 'For a man of his stature to know about me – well, he's done his homework.' He asked me to read, and I asked, 'Can I make it more Yorkshire? It's not really written in a Yorkshire dialect.' 'Oh please, put your stamp on it – do it as you would do it.'

That was all I needed. So I did it and he said, 'That's fine, now I just need to get my head round everything, so I'll let you know...' he almost said yes there and then. And the following day it came back that they would love me to do it.

We rehearsed for four weeks at Sadlers Wells in Islington. The first day began with cakes and biscuits and tea, and everyone meeting one another or renewing old acquaintances; I was delighted to see Peter Polycarpou, who reminded me that I'd got him his first job (he never paid his commission!). Then, after about half an hour, the actors assembled round the table with all the RSC people sat behind in rows. My understudy, Ray C Davies, had introduced himself and was sat next to me; he's actually a very good dancer, Ray, and has done some major musicals including *Chitty Chitty Bang Bang*.

Adrian started out by telling a story about producing Shakespeare in Japan, and how he was taken aback when all the actors brought their agents with them for the first rehearsal. He tactfully indicated that this was less than ideal and, after some negotiation, the agents left.

The ice broken, Adrian then went round the room: 'I want you all to introduce yourself and tell us what part you're playing.' He did all the RSC people first, then got to the actors and when it came to me, I said, 'I'm Freddie Davies, playing the part of Ben Weatherstaff, and this'– I pointed at Ray – 'is my agent.'

It cracked up the room. Adrian looked at me, wagged his finger, and said: 'I'm going to have to watch you, I can tell.'

After Sadlers Wells we moved on to Stratford. There were ten weeks of rehearsals in all, a luxury I'd never known before. We all had one day with a Shakespearean voice tutor and did sonnets individually, as part of the process; there was also a visit from the famous voice coach Cicely Berry, and time with the director on our own, when he would analyse the parts and talk about the historical period and everything. It was just an amazing and wonderful experience. Coming from an environment where rehearsal time is usually cut to the bone, I did wonder at first what we would find to do. But then I could see that they spent time getting it genuinely right, so that when the show opened, it would be as good as it could be.

The whole process was lovely. They did the dance routine everyday – the gardeners' dance – and watching

Gillian Lynne inventing it on the hoof, so to speak, singling out members of the company she wanted as the dancers, impatiently dismissing all the others, was a joy. Because of her great age – she was seventy-four or five then – she had an assistant, Alex, with her, and she would describe the step that she wanted to do. I remember saying to her: 'You never do anything twice, do you? You never do a count of four and then a count of four.' 'No,' she said, 'I never do.' 'Why?' 'Because it's boring. Never repeat anything. Everything has to be original. New.'

The Secret Garden is about Mary Lennox, a little girl who has been orphaned and goes to live with her widowed uncle in a house on the Yorkshire moors. She's spoilt and arrogant, as she grew up pampered by servants in India – but now she's isolated and rather lonely, as her uncle, a very unhappy and depressed man, leaves her to her own devices.

Over time she makes friends with a housemaid, Martha, and my character Ben, not to mention the little robin he calls the 'real gardener,' who leads her to a hidden garden which becomes her own little world.

I had some business with the robin in the show which came about during rehearsals. Mary has a line like: 'I saw that robin again today.' I said to Adrian, 'Would you like me to magically produce it?' 'Ah,' he said. 'Can you do that?'

The props department made a little robin and I did the trick, which they loved, so they invented this whole thing about the robin appearing all over the place, then disappearing into thin air. When it disappeared there was a sound effect with the wings fluttering and a tweet as if it was going up into the sky; it was a lovely effect.

But one night I accidentally dropped the bird. As I went to throw the little robin away, it fell out of my hand and lay there on the stage.

Dead.

The girl playing Mary Lennox looked at the bird, looked at the audience, and then looked at the bird again. Luckily my variety training kicked in, and I said: 'I don't think he wants to go anywhere tonight.' I picked him up and eventually disappeared him. But that was all part of the learning process, which I just loved.

Mary finds a little boy hidden away in the house, an invalid who supposedly cannot walk. It turns out that this is her cousin Colin, and his father has been avoiding him because he is a painful reminder of his late mother. With help from Martha's brother, Dickon, Mary takes him into the garden, which was his mother's and tended by Ben, and its magical properties allow him to walk again.

A poignant moment in the piece is when Colin walks and he asks Ben how his mother died. For the first time, as he's never told anybody before, Ben tells him. Ben is the only one who was in contact with the garden physically when Colin's mother was alive and knows its secrets: he tells Colin how his mother died, he was there, he witnessed it all, and he knows why his father is depressed. It's a wonderful scene to play.

In fact, everything about the experience of working on the show just seemed to fall into place. When we got to Stratford I rented these amazing digs in the centre of town. It had been a corporate let, a flat owned by two gay gentlemen who had retired to Malta because they had bad arthritis. It was a fabulous apartment, with three luxurious bedrooms and a big lounge, worth a lot of money, and it was empty. The estate agent said, 'We'll have a word with the owner and see if he'll let it to you for what you can afford to pay.'

I went back to the theatre that night and the lovely man who was dressing us said, 'My friend rang me today from Malta and he said, "What's Freddie Davies like?"' 'Oh? What did you say?' 'I told him you were a very, very nice man – so he's going to let you have his flat.'

So I had this amazing apartment and this wonderful, unexpected job. Once, when we were walking around the open air market at Stratford, a woman jumped out and said: 'Ey! Aren't you Parrotface?' I said, 'Yes.' 'What you doin' 'ere?' I told her I was at the RSC. 'Bloody 'ell,' she said, '*You've* come up in the world, haven't you?'

The Secret Garden had already been produced in 1991 on Broadway, with Mandy Pantinkin as Mary's uncle, Archibald Craven, and later in Australia, with a cast which included Philip Quast, who would play Archibald in the RSC production. Philip is somewhat unknown in this country but is a stalwart of the musical theatre whose voice and acting are superb.

The show was thoroughly revised for the UK version. Marsha Norman, writer of the book and lyrics, and Lucy Simon, who composed the music, were present throughout the rehearsal process. The essence of it was the same, however, and it worked in my favour as there was an extended dance routine around my song about the garden.

They edited it again for the West End, and took quite a lot out of it, including a routine that I did with Mrs Medlock, which was a shame, because it was a nice piece. But I still had that dance and the hope-filled song that I'd learnt at the audition:

> For an old man knows how a year it goes,
> How the cold hard ground in the spring comes round,
> How the seeds take hold and the birds unfold,
> How an English garden grows.

And things really had come round for me, there was no denying, after the box office failure of *Funny Bones* and the all-time low of running the pub – not to mention being miscast in that Agatha Christie play. I was now holding my own with legit actors in one of the greatest theatre companies in the land. Ben may not have been the biggest part in the show but his role was crucial, and the luxury of that long rehearsal process had allowed me to give of my best. In fact, we were all – and there's no other way to put it – bedded in, and played for three happy months at the Aldwych Theatre.

BY the time *The Secret Garden* finally came to an end on June 2nd, 2001, I was only a few weeks shy of my sixty-fourth birthday. If I'd wanted to I could have seen it as a fitting end to my career, as it would certainly have provided a neat conclusion for this book, bringing the story full circle: there I was, after all, performing in theatres again, even doing a bit of that old disappearing magic I'd first practised as a teenager.

But whether or not the RSC's production of *The Secret Garden* proves to have been the culmination of my career, I can tell you now that it wasn't the end. I had absolutely no thoughts of retiring – even after my recent heart attack, I still don't, though I'm now in my mid-seventies as I write this.

And quite apart from the further twists and turns of my career, there was a major shock waiting around the corner in my personal life – one which would send my mind racing back to my earliest days and really bring things full circle.

25: Over the Border

THE following year Vanessa and I decided to move back to Scotland. This turned out to be a mistake.

It followed a couple of other moves, as we'd sold our house in Eastbourne during *Harbour Lights*, staying with the film unit in Dorset before buying a house in the delightful Yorkshire village of Marton cum Grafton. This was partly because of an old uncle of Vanessa's who was in dire straits: he had Alzheimer's and his wife had died. Vanessa was his only living relative, so we brought him with us to Yorkshire and he went into a very nice nursing home not far from us.

He passed away about eighteen months later, and it was then that we made the decision to go back to Scotland, where we'd first made a home after our time on the cruise ships. We'd really only left so that I could be more accessible for the acting jobs that Sharron Ashcroft of Leeds-based ATS had been getting for me, but now I had plans to go into business for myself.

I was intending to open several children's academies for acting, dancing and singing, and I started off in Aberfeldy, the Perthshire village where we were living. The school, called Stage One, was well received, and we produced some great little shows at the end of term, but I couldn't get enough students to make it viable. I wasn't allowed to teach, of course, because I'm not qualified, but I did do a few drama sessions when a tutor didn't turn up and thoroughly enjoyed working with the kids, who were thrilled because I'd just got the latest *Harry Potter* film and they were full of it.

If you've seen *Harry Potter and the Prisoner of Askaban* you will know that I have a cameo as a talking portrait – who says I'm no oil painting? I also played Robert Redford in one of several TV appearances I made around this time.

Well, sort of. I was cast in Hugo Blick's quirky series *Sensitive Skin*, and I was supposed to be the embodiment of Joanna Lumley's frustration. I was done up in a white naval uniform, sort of a cross between Redford and Richard Gere in *An Officer and a Gentleman* ... typecasting, of course.

Joanna Lumley was just gorgeous, and very patient, because it was all my dialogue; she only muttered. Though she did point out – in character, I mean – 'You're nothing like Robert Redford,'– which gave me the satisfaction of saying, 'Well, it's your frustration, your imagination that's causing that.' In other words, whether she liked it or not, the figure before her represented the sum of her desires. Ee, lad, it's a tough business sometimes ...

Sorry, where was I? Oh yes. After a couple of years I closed the school, though I intended to reopen it in about six months' time. I had some very bad payers who just would not pay the school fees on time, and it was these five or six fees which would have been the profit margin. It was really annoying me – they were bringing their kids in their £35,000 cars, dropping them off and then skipping out. At the end of the day's classes I'd ask, 'Where's your mum? Is she coming to pick you up?' 'No, I've got to meet her on the corner.' They were really avoiding paying and it wasn't even expensive; we were cheaper than all the other schools. I think they saw it as free babysitting.

This venture wasn't like the pub, because I was still getting acting work; I just fancied the idea of it, and having seen the entertainment business from so many sides, I felt I'd got a lot to pass on. I'd been exploring the possibility of setting up another school in Perth, so after Aberfeldy closed, I concentrated on trying to get that off the ground. However, Stagecoach had opened there, which didn't do me any favours, and I didn't pursue it in the end. Anytime I saw the kids in Aberfeldy after that they would ask about the school, but I never reopened it; think I lost my enthusiasm for it a bit.

After a while it became clear that, despite the bits and bobs of TV work, we could do with another income, and that's when the Sheep Shop came up. This was a little emporium in the nearby town of Pitlochry which specialised in sheep-related goods: woolly hats, socks, little plastic sheep – sheep soap, even. Oh, and wool. It was owned by a neighbour of ours and Vanessa had been working there part-time, so when the owner wanted to sell up, she felt it was something she could do.

About a year later, Vanessa had to have a couple of months off looking after the new puppies our dog, Daisy, had given birth to, and I seemed to end up in the shop most of the time. That second month stretched out into another and another and, in the end, I got used to doing it: 'Oh, I'll get in the car and go.' Actually, I didn't mind – it gave me something to do when I wasn't doing any other work – and, in fact, I rather enjoyed it.

As ever, I tried to make the best of things, playing about on the computer and getting stuck into this book, so it wasn't too bad. There wasn't really any embarrassment about being recognised: most of the customers didn't know who the hell I was as we had a lot of foreign visitors, so it didn't bother me.

More annoying was the fact that most people would walk in, have a wander about and then leave without actually putting their hands in their pockets, as though this was a free art gallery to while away a drizzly afternoon. I went into a sort of low-level Butlins mode, trying to jolly people along into parting with their cash, but it didn't help much.

Still, at least I didn't have to grin and bear it all the time, unlike the real Butlins. I remember one occasion in particular, when we hadn't had the shop long. We'd taken over all the old stock, but as I was kept busy pricing new stock as it came in, there were still a few old price labels knocking around. One feller came in for babies' bootees and held up three pairs with different tags: 'How much are these?'

I quoted the newest (and highest) price and explained that the others were old stock which hadn't been re-priced yet. He didn't look all that pleased, and I didn't want to lose a sale, so I said, 'Tell you what we'll do, I'll do it the middle price.' To which he replied: 'It's people like you that give tourism a bad name.'

'Oh really?' I said. 'Well, piss off – get out of the shop!' 'You can't do that –' 'I own the shop, I can do what I want – get out!' 'But I've come all the way from Edinburgh –' '*Get out!*' I have to admit I quite enjoyed seeing someone else in the role of affronted customer.

There were occasions when somebody would recognise me but, at the end of the day, I was only helping Vanessa out, although it was claimed on the internet that I was running the Sheep Shop and had given the business up. This was never the case, although being in Scotland did eventually lead to me losing my agent Derek Webster because it was difficult for him to handle me with everything happening in London, and I was finding it impossible to get down to London for gigs.

WITH the end of my plans for the stage schools and the difficulty of getting acting work it became clear that we would have to move again. The Sheep Shop was never going to make our fortune, and over the last two years of our time in Scotland it ran at a loss.

We moved back to North Yorkshire and one of the first things I did, appropriately enough, was to reprise my role as Ben in *The Secret Garden*. It was an opportunity I never expected to have again – and almost didn't. I couldn't believe it when I was asked to audition for that role of all roles, particularly for a profit share, so I didn't pursue it.

But they advertised again after they started rehearsing, so I called up and told them, 'I'm coming to London on Friday and if you want me to do it I will – but I won't audition.' They rang and said, 'Of course; come and help us.'

They had cast it well and there were some lovely voices in it. It was billed as a concert version and had a limited amount of staging, although dancing wasn't possible in the cramped confines of the King's Head in Islington.

This was the original 1991 Broadway version of the musical, not the RSC's reworking, so it was a slightly different experience for me. It didn't matter too much from my point of view, however, because the two big dance routines which had been added to the RSC version couldn't have been done at the King's Head anyway, and there were some numbers we didn't do in the West End which had been put back in. I was thrilled to be reunited with Amanda Goldthorpe-Hall from the RSC production, who was playing Mrs Medlock. Also in the cast, playing Colin, was Jason Donovan's son, Zac; Jason was almost in tears as that made it third generation: his dad is the actor Terence Donovan.

But what they didn't tell me was that there was absolutely no money in it. It didn't occur to me that I wouldn't, at least, recover my expenses, but once the producers had taken their expenses, it worked out at about £4.58 a show for everybody. I was annoyed that they hadn't built anything in for the artists. I do understand the concept of profit share, but I didn't think it was to be such a very low sum. Coming from so far away and obviously costing more than being at the end of a tube line, I wondered why it hadn't been spelt out to me.

The deal at the King's Head was only 45 per cent of the net. Most of the cast emailed me saying how upset they were and thanking me for fighting for them as, in the main, they were fresh out of drama school and too frightened to argue with the management, who treated the artists with contempt, exploiting their desperation to be seen, an attitude which leaves me speechless. When I took up the cudgels for the company the producer accused me of bullying her, but how can you put on a show with professional artists and not factor in any money at all for them?

Still, two very positive things came out of it. Before I did the show, I hadn't realised how out of practice with the discipline of performing I had become, thanks to my time in Scotland. After a couple of performances, however, I was fine with it, and the experience proved to me not only that I could still do it, but that I really wanted to go on doing it – in fact I couldn't think why I'd ever stopped. Making my comeback in a role I knew and loved had been an ideal way to test the waters, so in one sense I had been lucky the part came up when it did. I also got a new agent out of it – which made it a bit easier not to dwell on the cost of commuting from Yorkshire to London every week.

By now, you're probably thinking that surely this must be the end of the story. But I've left out a discovery I made when I was still in Scotland – that surprise I referred to in the previous chapter.

It's about Jack, the man I thought of as my grandad.

26: Quaint Songs and Queer Dances

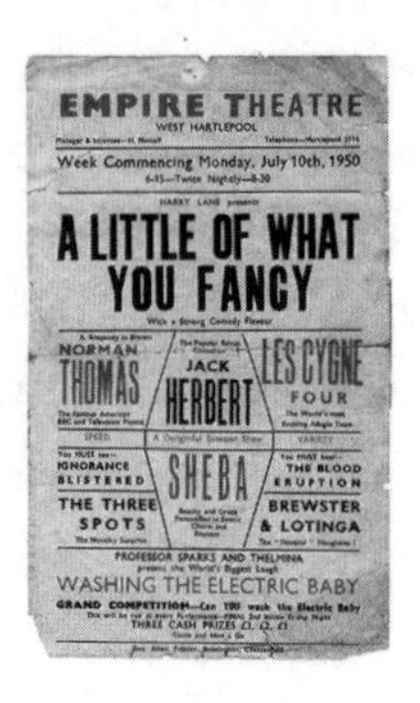

JACK Herbert died in 1969 but had never been far from my thoughts since then: he had an odd way of flicking up into my life. There had been the Jimmy Perry musical about Sid Field in which I had played a character based on Jack's agent, Mannie Jay, and while *Funny Bones* wasn't about Jack as such, it was a world he knew, and it had resurrected his stage routine. My career had followed a different pattern from his – the days of variety and touring revues had gone – but every time I stepped onto a stage I still felt a connection with the man who had led by example, inspiring me to go into the business.

But in Scotland, around 2006, a chance remark brought Jack back to mind more forcefully, in a way which was completely unexpected and which was to change my life, and my idea of who I was, forever.

I had been corresponding with Tim Boyle, a cousin of Jack's whose hobby is researching his family tree – he works for the Forestry Commission, funnily enough – when at one point he hinted that it was believed in the family that Jack was my father.

Which came as a total surprise to me. I had never, ever got any sense that he was my father. It had never been intimated. I couldn't see it at all; I was shocked. It had never manifested itself at all in my childhood or beyond. Ever.

I didn't know quite what I felt, but knew I had to find out more, so I had a couple of conversations with John, Jack's surviving brother, then in his eighties. He told me that their sister Florrie was convinced Jack was my father. But when I thought it over, it didn't add up. I mean, I had always felt that there was a very strong bond between us, particularly a comedy bond, as I've said. But important as Jack had been to my childhood and choice of career, I don't think he ever treated me differently from the way any grandad would. I searched my memory for some significant moment or telltale remark, but there was nothing.

True, Jack and Ruth were around a lot during my childhood, but my mother Joan was Ruth's daughter, so there was nothing unusual in that, especially given Mum's fragile state. Jack did take me out to the theatre a lot, but it was his world: I never saw him mix with anyone outside the business, not really.

What I do remember distinctly is that we were talking about a film with Rita Hayworth or Jane Russell. I was only a kid, and in a very theatrical way he said, out of the blue: 'Yeah, but she's got big tits.' And I was quite shocked that he'd used the word 'tits', a word from the school playground.

But then John went on to tell me that he went to see Jack in 1937 at some theatre where my mother was a dancer in the show, and pregnant with me. Jack told him that the father was a man called Billy Costello, who had been the original voice of Popeye in the cartoon and was now taking a stage act around the halls in Britain.

I asked my dear friend Roy Hudd whether he knew of this man, and Roy obligingly sent a photograph – which, it turned out, looked nothing like me at all. I went through the pages of *The Performer*, the variety artists' trade paper, but as a dancer in a troupe my mother's role wasn't important enough to be singled out for mention in advertisements or reviews, and as Costello appeared on any number of different variety bills around that time, I couldn't even track down the particular theatre where I might (repeat: *might*) have been conceived.

By this point, however, I was fascinated. It hadn't consciously mattered to me as a kid, but now I realised that yes, I really did want to know who my father was. I asked Jack's younger brother John if he would do a DNA test with me and he agreed, providing I paid for it, which I did.

We had the test, a swab from each mouth, and the result came back … inconclusive.

When I chatted it over afterwards with John, he happened to mention: 'Well, you know, Jack and I had the same father but we didn't have the same mother' – which I could have done with knowing a few days earlier.

I got in touch with the laboratory, asking them to explain all the lines and graphs in the printout I'd been sent, but it soon became very clear that there was nothing more definite to be taken from it. Having got so far, I had to ask: 'Is it not possible?' And the analyst said: 'Well, this line here says it could be, but it's so far removed as they had different mothers, so it's not like …'

And as he tailed off, I knew that this was as much as I was ever likely to know. There should have been some snippet there, something to point me towards an answer, but there wasn't. So I still don't know.

Turning it over again in my head now, I still don't know how I feel or what to believe. In some ways I want Jack to be my father; in other ways I don't. It may not have been incestuous, as he wasn't my blood grandfather, but if he had slept with Joan, it would still have been the most terrible betrayal of Ruth.

If it was known in the family, I can't think Ruth would have been forgiving of it. She'd have thrown him out, if she'd known; this was quite a feisty lady – she'd had a career and a business before hooking up with him, remember – but I never saw any animosity towards him. They often stayed with us in Salford, and I never got that impression at all.

Although I do remember that he and Gran used to do this weird doubletalk whenever they wanted to say anything private in front of me. Pig Latin, it's called; it used to be very popular in America. You put the first letter of a word at the end – for example, the word nix, meaning no, would be 'ixnay.' I could never understand it and it used to drive me mad that he would do it. Were there secrets he and Ruth were keeping from me? Anyway, there is no one alive now who knows the truth, and perhaps that's a good thing.

In one sense, it hardly matters. I may not have had a dad when growing up, but there's no doubt that Jack's influence and inspiration have enriched my life and career, from the moment he first took me backstage at the Salford Hippodrome, letting me soak up his and countless other acts from the wings until each gesture, each intonation, each pratfall was bone-deep. If I do have funny bones, as Ronnie Corbett said, I owe that to Jack's encouragement and not to some stranger.

THE test – or at least all the reflection on Jack it provoked – did have one positive outcome. I was already planning this autobiography and knew he would feature in the account of my childhood. But the more I thought about it, the more I saw that wouldn't be enough. One way or another Jack's life was bound up with mine and I began to see that I couldn't tell my own story without also telling his – going beyond personal memories and trying to piece together what I could of his life and career.

I say 'piece' advisedly, because when I got going, it was a bit like trying to put a jigsaw together from the incomplete contents of several boxes. The performances of Danny Kaye and Sid Field, the two other players in that dressing room scene which made such an impression on my ten year old self, were captured for all time by the great theatre critic and essayist Ken Tynan, but there is no equivalent pen-portrait of Jack that I've been able to find. I saw him many times onstage, but it is sobering to reflect that it is now almost sixty years since I last watched his act: the details of seeing him, as recounted in Chapter Two, are now about as much as I can remember.

So I had to become a sort of detective-cum-historian, poring over the pages of *The Stage* and *The Performer* for dates and clues. I hope that what follows will be enough to suggest a picture – even if there is still the odd gap in the sky.

I spoke again to John, who sent me his memories of his brother as well as some autobiographical notes of Jack's, originally written 'on scraps of paper end.' These paint a picture of his earliest days and his introduction to the business. John thinks they were probably written around 1937 or 1938, when he would have been in his early forties.

It's not clear why they were written – could he have been planning to write his autobiography, or had he been approached by a magazine or newspaper for background information on a show? Was it simply that he was becoming wistful and nostalgic as middle-age approached?

There is also the suggestive possibility, if John's estimate is correct, that these words might have been penned around the time of my birth.

He was certainly at the top of the tree as a performer then, with a golden opportunity about to fall into his lap, as I'll discuss later. But the most important thing for the start of his story is that Jack's own words describing his earliest days and his introduction to the business have survived:

> I was born in the year 1896 (don't say 'why?') in that beautiful old town – Scarborough (Yorks), rightly named as the Queen of Watering Places to those who knew it in the old days. When I was quite a toddler my father had a pub almost opposite St Mary's Church, called the Albion Hotel. I was clever enough to fall down the steps to the front entrance, cut my eyebrow and have several stitches put in; a scar I carry to this day.
>
> My father took another pub called The Whitby Arms in Waterhouse Lane; a pub I shall always remember, for it was in that particular pub that I got interested in show business. I was only a little lad, going to St Mary's School, but one of my pals was a boy called George Zalva, whose parents ran the circus in St Thomas's Street, which is now the Opera House, and every Saturday afternoon George would take me into the circus to see the show. Doodles was the clown; a tiny little man who could do anything. When he asked for boys to go into the ring for some comic interlude I was there at the double and got bashed with a bladder.
>
> I used to sit enthralled watching the equestrians, the acrobats, the animal acts and so on. But what thrilled me most was a grand finale – *The British and*

> *the Boers*. It was really spectacular. Bugler Dunne was the boy hero of that time. There was prop shot shell flying about, the brass band was playing popular Boer War melodies like *Goodbye My Bluebell* and *Goodbye Dolly Gray*. I can still smell the smoke of the blank cartridges, the gunpowder, the red fire and all the rest of the sham battle. We youngsters used to cheer ourselves hoarse. I used to go home that excited I couldn't eat my tea and used to jump up at night-time in bed, fighting Kruger and Cronje.

This would be around 1900, when the Relief of Mafeking was being celebrated around the country and the names of the South African president and the general who started the siege were on everybody's lips; Stan Laurel recalled playing the role of Bugler Dunne, the fourteen-year-old hero of the battle of Colenso, in a reenactment staged by his father in North Shields.

There were other influences beyond the clowning and thrills of the circus in Jack's early days. His first professional job aged nineteen, as noted in *The Stage* in 1915, is in a concert party, which is hardly surprising, given that they were so much a part of his childhood:

> Another thing that will remain in my memory was the Pierrots. In those days they used to perform on the sands alfresco; Collins were the main troupe.
>
> They used to make up in the digs and walk down the main street to the pitch from different parts of the town. It was nothing to see a couple of them in their white suits and Black Pom-Poms, skull caps etc, also a full stage makeup on complete with beauty spot. No one ever took any notice; it had gone on for year after year.

> Collins used to perform just below the spa; people would stand on the spa and watch the show. Of course the artists in turn used to come around and 'bottle 'em' with a long stick and a black velvet bag at the end or sometimes the audience would throw coins into a hat held by a bottler.
>
> After a morning show, one or two of them used to come to the Whitby Arms for a quick 'un. My father kept a small back room for them so that they could be on their own; have a quiet drink and a smoke, etc.
>
> My father was born in the theatrical business. His father before him and his father before him; that makes Great Grandad a pro. I can remember Grandad (HT Butler the first). He had long silver hair, a silver moustache and always wore the broad brim of his large black trilby hat turned up – a typical actor laddie. He toured in several plays before my time when drama companies used to tour week by week, like the Musical Comedies, Opera companies and of course Variety Acts. His name was Henry Butler. My grandmother was a vocalist with one of the leading opera companies of that time. Her stage name was Bella Tremayne. I have only a vague recollection of her.

Henry Butler and Bella Tremayne – Jack's grandmother Margaret – can be found in the pages of *The Stage* in the 1880s and 1890s, appearing in melodramas such as *East Lynne* and *The Curse of Drink*. An advertisement in 1887 indicates their specialities:

> Mr Henry Butler … Heavies, Old Men, Mrs B., Character & Singing Parts

It may have been Margaret who passed on the comedy gene, as several reviews praise her playing in the comic scenes of such plays as *The Ticket-of-Leave Man*. But comedy seems to have been passed down in the family generally: Jack's uncle Harry (HT Butler the second), started off as a comic actor, specialising in 'Light or Eccentric Comedy, Dudes.' In fact, one 1898 review of the melodrama *A Woman's Victory* praises his playing in terms which could equally apply to Jack's later act:

> His funny patter, quaint songs and eccentric dancing are very well received.

Jack would only have been two years old at the time, but might he have witnessed his uncle in a later production, or clowning around at home? He writes:

> My father's eldest brother, Harry, was also a pro like his father. He toured in several plays doing comedy parts. He afterwards turned to producing and was one of the early revue producers. He was also a pantomime producer for Francis Laidler. I believe he was to go to Hollywood to produce for a firm of film-makers running Christie Comedies. Whether he did or not I do not know as I have lost touch with him but I have a recollection of him being for a long time with Leon Salberg at the Alexandra Theatre, Birmingham. He was also many years with Francis Laidler at the Theatre Royal, Leeds where a magnificent pantomime was produced every year and ran on, if I remember rightly, almost until Easter, in the old days.

All but forgotten now, in the 1920s Al and Charles Christie's comedies ('stories first and laughs second') were considered a serious threat by no less than Hal Roach, but as far as I can tell Harry didn't make it to Hollywood: Sandra Archer of the Academy of Motion Picture Arts kindly conducted a search for me and found no trace of him anywhere.

From around 1907 onwards, he was certainly kept busy working as stage manager for Francis Laidler at the Prince's Theatre, Bradford, then at the Theatre Royal, Leeds, before producing pantos and revues himself. He doesn't seem to have given up acting entirely, however, as a 1913 panto review notes Harry's readiness to deputise as Dame for an indisposed actor.

He had particular responsibility for the juveniles in pantos – 'Laidler's little sunbeams'– and also managed a juvenile act, Ray and Zack. Jack writes that Harry couldn't get any work for them and was 'on the verge of packing it up' when Frankie Allen of Moss Empires offered them a week's work as a tryout:

> Ray and Zack clicked, and went round the 'Big Time' Theatres for years.

And that's where Jack's notes about himself and his family come to an abrupt end. If he ever committed any doubts to paper about the wisdom of entering show business those particular confessional scraps haven't survived – though that baptism by bladder does suggest that his choice of career was pretty much a foregone conclusion.

His adolescence will have to remain a blank but advertisements and reviews in *The Stage* allow us to pick up the story once Jack's decision has been made, and through those we can trace just about his entire career through the rise and fall of variety. By the age of eighteen, he has become joint leader of a concert party called *The Puppets*. An October 1914 advertisement, soliciting bookings for the following year, proclaims the show 'The 'It of Vaudeville' and *The Stage* certainly reviews it in positive terms. There seems to have been a longish tour, including five weeks in Ireland and dates in Wales which took them up to the end of September 1915. Jack gets his first mention in a review on the 1st of July, 1915 as 'a comedian whose songs and mannerisms are original.'

Remember that, because those mannerisms will feature again later.

Later that month, an article headed 'A New Enterprise' praises the company's courage in launching a new concert party 'at a time like the present', singling Jack out as 'an excellent comedian' who also has 'considerable ability as a dancer.'

Inevitably, 'the present' caught up with Jack and there's no more mention of him in *The Stage* until 1919. I vaguely recall seeing a photo of him in uniform although I can't be certain now whether that would have been a stage act or the real thing. John writes:

> He was in the army but Emmie, his younger brother, who had a tough time as a machine-gunner, seemed envious when he said Jack saw no action as he was always busy on the entertainment side. Emmie spoke with grudging admiration of Jack's progress with the opposite sex! He was known as 'Handsome Jack.' The army was his apprenticeship to showbiz.

Jack reappears in *The Stage* in April 1919, looking for work:

> Wanted Monday next,

Jack Herbert
(the cheerful chap)
in Quaint Songs and Queer Dances
coms. Palace, Retford

He secured at least one booking, although the *Stage*'s critic wasn't impressed: 'The list was completed by Jack Herbert, comedian, with a soldier's song and indifferent patter.'

A few months later, however, he got what appears to have been his first big break, in a musical comedy or revue – in those days the distinction wasn't a hard and fast one – called *Ginger*. Tom Major (aka Major-Ball, father of John) is the principal comedian and the show was written by Kitty Major, his first wife. Jack is billed alongside one Bert Brookes as 'Nature's Own Trench Comedians.'

This show may be the source of the photograph I remember. It was produced by Bernard Mainwaring Dunstan, a GP with enough money to indulge his love of theatre.

Jack must have made a strong impression as two more shows for the same producer follow in quick succession in the next few months, with Jack promoted to principal comedian. *The Stage* starts to look upon him favourably ('funny in the extreme'), but it's not until 1922 and a revue called *Jingles* that Jack seems to attract real attention, playing alongside Hylda Baker, who became a lifelong friend.

However much money the good doctor had to spend on his shows, *Jingles*, produced by Harry Day, was probably several notches higher up in terms of prestige. Day, who had made his name with touring revues, had been approached that year to produce a lavish revue called *Rockets* at the London Palladium, and an advertisement for *Jingles* assures us: 'Same as toured by Harry Day on the Moss Stoll LTV Circuit'.

So it seems fair to say that in 1922, at the age of twenty-six, Jack had arrived as a major force in revue. When he lists his previous shows in an advertisement in 1930 this is the earliest one he mentions, which suggests he knew he'd come into his own. But if you're looking to have his performance conjured up for you, Ken Tynan-style, forget it. The reviews are warm and positive but they don't actually say all that much:

> ... essentially a song-and-dance entertainment but nevertheless Mr Jack Herbert finds many opportunities for the display of his own particular brand of humour, notably in the Battleship and Shipping Office scenes, and as the Judge in the laughable vocal Breach of Promise trial. ... a quaintly effective North Country style which is provocative of laughter ... a talented comedian, kept the audience in a merry mood ... and his burlesque work with Hylda Baker, a clever comedienne, was especially well done.

You had to be there, I suppose. Incidentally, Hylda Baker was a huge friend of my gran's, so it's possible Jack and Ruth may have met around this time. I remember she came round to lunch once when I was staying with them in London in 1947. My grandmother said to her, 'Are you come for some lunch?' She said, 'No, I'm going home for lunch.' Then when Gran was serving it she said: 'Where's mine?' so Gran had to share the plates out so she could have some. Strange woman. She used to travel with this monkey on her shoulder which used to piss down her: horrible little thing it was.

Anyway, Jack played in *Jingles* for ten months, then in a show called *Pick O' the Bunch*, after which, in 1924, there was *Come In*, a 'cleverly written and well-conceived burlesque' which got a rave review:

> More than special attention has been paid to the selection of the cast, and first and foremost is Jack Herbert, a comedian of much ability. If there is any complaint to make it is that this artist has more than his fair share of work, but he accomplishes his task with infinite ease, and is able by his quaint mannerisms to keep his audience throughout in merriment.

And note that there's another reference to the 'mannerisms' which first made an impression in *The Puppets*.

Come In ran for seven months, then he starred in another revue, *British Made*, for fifteen months. This was the beginning of a long professional association with Myrtle Grove, wife of Mannie Jay, a singer and 'useful assistant in the comic scenes' who would work alongside Jack in two more revues.

So what was *British Made* like? *The Stage* tells us rather sniffily: 'It relies, for the most part, on its broad comedy, for which Jack Herbert is mainly responsible, as the leading comedian.'

Which doesn't really get us very far. A 're-production' of *British Made* is announced in February 1926 but this seems to have been shortlived as, four months after this, Jack announces he is once again at liberty: 'Refer anywhere or anyone of importance.'

There is then the bizarre promise (or threat) of a revue to be called *Ratepayers*, with Jack among the cast, requesting dates from 'August Bank Holiday onwards. Production date settled.' But that doesn't seem to have come to anything. Which is just as well, as the next revue he was engaged for was one of his biggest successes: Clara Coverdale's *Spotlights*.

Clara Coverdale, better known for her many juvenile

troupes (Gracie Fields had been one of her 'Nine Dainty Dots'), had branched out into revue in 1924. Her first show, the betting-themed *10 to 1 on*, featured Jimmy James as principal comedian and may be deserving of a footnote in history for another reason: according to Jimmy James' son, James Casey, Max Miller took his costume and persona from the spiv character Jimmy played in the revue.

Ruth Beaumont was also in the company, so it may be that Jack and Gran met through Clara Coverdale rather than Hylda Baker. John isn't sure either way: 'I never heard how he met Ruth. I always thought she put him in one of her shows.' Whatever the answer, they were certainly operating in the same circles.

Jack and *Spotlights* appear to have been a perfect fit: he is, we're told by the *Stage* reviewer, 'the type of comedian necessary to ensure the success of revue.' No longer 'the cheerful chap', a December 1926 ad for *Spotlights* includes this wording:

> Jack Herbert,
> The Yorkshirebite,
> A Leeds Lad Who Leads In Comedy

Which, I have to admit, slightly surprises me: 'Yorkshirebite' suggests shrewdness in business dealings, putting one over on someone – it comes from a folk song in which a ploughboy gets the better of a highwayman – and I don't think Jack was like that onstage or off.

Anyway, Jack seems to have been in demand around this time, as on 13th January 1927 he uses the pages of *The Stage* to announce: 'To the several West-End Managers, Agents and proprietors from whom I have received offers, please accept my best thanks. My arrangements are all complete. Comfortably settled under Miss Coverdale's management for a long period.' Which proved to be true. Clara Coverdale herself died in June 1927 but Jack continued to work for Coverdale productions until July 1929, eventually thanking them for 'three happy years.'

Again, most of the reviews of *Spotlights* are brief, but there is at least a hint of Jack's distinctive character:

> A comedian who knows his business is Jack Herbert, whose pleasant, unforced humour is free from exaggeration, and yet always funny in its results. He can strike a more plaintive note too …
>
> Laughter is kept in the ascendant by Jack Herbert, whose unforced natural method adds to the hilarious effect and his nonsensical rhyming in the tenth scene has a comic appeal of its own ....

Only *The Scotsman* paints a more detailed picture, suggesting that Jack tailored his material according to stories in the news, like the race to be first to fly across the Atlantic – and that plane, if you're wondering, is a dig at the de Havilland-designed 'Moth':

> Revue comedians, whatever else they do in their spare time, must read the newspapers. Only to a revue comedian is given the opportunity of working into his part – with more or less relevancy – topical skits on the latest 'Stop Press' sensations.
>
> Most of the fraternity take their chances fairly regularly, and hence the first scene of *Spotlights* at the Theatre-Royal. Jack Herbert, a young but talented humorist, fails to fly the Atlantic in his 'Myth' machine but he makes a safe landing on the stage, and later on the audience is not sorry that his

> aeronautical attempt ended sadly, for he improves at every appearance.
>
> One of his best character studies is that of a coffee-stall attendant on the Thames Embankment. His is not a profitable occupation, for he makes no money, but he does see life. Murderers, woe-begone women, exhilarated 'swells', and Apaches who dance with abandon, all flit across his view, but he receives this glorious half-hour of life with an unperturbed complacency.

This seems to be confirmed by the memories of Sid Field's widow Connie Field in John Fisher's biography:

> *Spotlights* lasted for a good many months and changed its name, Connie thinks, to *Spotlights Re-Illuminated* or something of that kind.
>
> In fact, whenever the takings showed signs of flagging the show was re-jigged, given a new name and some new ideas and launched once more. Moving from place to place every week, it ran about two-and-a-half years during the 'twenties.

Sid Field was juvenile lead in the show in addition to being Jack's feed; Connie remembers singing several songs with him onstage and the *Scotsman* review, above, goes on to single out 'an exceedingly clever light comedy number' sung by Field and Billy Shaw.

Despite the three-year association with Jack in the Coverdale shows, however, there is no description of Jack's act, nor estimate of his ability or his influence on the younger comic, in the Sid Field biography. In fact, there is only one passing reference to him, in the context of an anecdote about how Sid met his future wife – but it's an intriguing detail nevertheless.

Connie joined the cast of *Spotlights* in Newcastle, along with her friend Ella Barker, and John Fisher (an historian, by the way, not the TV producer) writes of a 'magnetic conjunction' between Jack and Ella which had the effect of thrusting the unwanted Connie towards Sid.

Whether there was something more than friendship between Jack and Ella is not spelt out, although that phrase does seem a pretty strong hint. John comments: 'I don't remember Jack and Ella Barker, but recall that at one time when Jack had taken his sister Rene under his wing (but wouldn't let her "show her legs" in the chorus) there was talk of Sid and her. But she was such a timid, withdrawn soul, it would never have lasted.'

John, who knew him as Bert (Jack's real name was George Herbert Butler), adds that this would have been around the time Jack got married. John says:

> He was married to Babs (Barbara), a beautiful girl whom he met in the chorus in one of his shows. She was only 16 or so, while he would be around 30. Mother, for what reason I know not, would not entertain her and she had to stay with friends until he went. She was very much like Twiggy. She left Bert to go with a man in Jack Hylton's band, maybe even Jack Hylton himself. She died in Bradford Infirmary, in the war years. Bert never got over it – he loved her very much but I think his occasional bouts of drunkenness didn't help.

'Babs' was Vivienne Marsh, niece of the comedian Neville Kennard. I'm not sure exactly when she and Jack got married, or how long the marriage lasted, although an In Memoriam notice for Clara Coverdale in June 1928 is attributed to 'Mr and Mrs Jack Herbert' so it must have been some time before then. As 'Vivienne Marsh' she can be found in *The Stage* in revues in the mid 'thirties, often supporting the Scots comic Sandy Daw.

Whatever the illness was, it seems to have been a protracted one, as there is a gap of about two and half years between a request in *The Stage* for letters while convalescing and the eventual announcement of her death in 1943. Although she is referred to formally as 'Mrs Jack Herbert' Jack's name is conspicuous by its absence from the list of mourners, and by the time of a 1949 In Memoriam notice placed by her family she is simply: 'Vivienne Marsh (Babs)'.

Hoping to find out more I was put in touch with Jack Hylton's son, who didn't think the other man was his father but added: 'I suspect one would need a large cadre of researchers to trace the "liaisons" of the band members, especially as I don't know of any still living from that time.'

So – unless anything emerges as a result of this book being published – that may be that. Whatever the faults or failings on either side – I'll say more about Jack's drinking later – the truth of the matter can now only be guessed at.

I think there's no doubt, however, that Jack later found some kind of happiness with Ruth. She is first mentioned in *The Stage* as early as 1910, described as a comedienne and dancer; she was a singer, too, as a regular feature in *The Stage* offering a blatant plug for the music publishers Feldman's praises any instance of her selecting one of their songs for a show, as in this note from April 1923:

> 'Feldmanism keeps me right,' writes Ruth Beaumont. She goes on to say that *Cute Little Love*

> *Nest* and *All Over Nothing At All* are regular features of her programme, in addition to which she works a Feldman medley. Good!

Ruth was soon appearing in a string of revues, so was undoubtedly part of the same world as Jack, although I can't actually find them on the same bill until 1932, in a revue entitled *Made for Pleasure*.

Spotlights was succeeded in 1928 by *Antics* for Coverdale Productions, again with Sid Field as feed, so this may have been a case of *Spotlights Re-illuminated* yet again. Two shows follow for other producers, *Mermaids* and *Side-Lines*, then a slightly curious announcement appears in *The Stage* in October 1929. Jack says he has terminated his engagement with the *Side-Lines* company at his own request and although 'taking a well-earned rest owing to indisposition' is pleased to consider 'anything first class.' He thanks James Brennan for releasing him and Jimmy James 'for kindness.'

What that indisposition might have been – drink? marital problems? – is not clear, and two weeks later he is already advertising that he is disengaged – 'Refer anyone or anywhere of importance.' A show which follows seems to have been shortlived – on 20th February 1930 he announces he is 'unexpectedly vacant Monday through termination of tour.'

More revues and pantos follow over the next few years, and Jack often seems to have been teamed with another comic: a review of a variety bill on July 9th 1931 notes that 'Jack Herbert and Jack Ford have some good topical patter as the Hikers.' But from 1934 onwards Jack starts to be mentioned as part of a double act with his brother Cyril. Their first *Stage* review may be a bit formally phrased but it seems to be a rave: 'There are two capital double acts in which laughter is actively promoted. One is that of Jack Herbert and Cyril Hatton, whose mirth-provoking notions cause general hilarity.' There is more sniffiness, however, in a later note:

> Jack Herbert and Cyril Hatton might with advantage use the blue pencil on some of their lines, but here is a comedian with a definite and individual comic style in association with a valuable 'feed,' and the act is so good that the gags to which exception might be taken would not be missed.

But Herbert and Hatton didn't let such qualified praise go to their heads and for the next four years worked together with considerable success.

So why didn't they break through to something bigger? One possible answer has been hinted at already with regard to his marriage: Jack's drinking. But that seems to have been part and parcel of his character. John says:

> He was always very amiable, good natured and kind. If anything he was too laid back and lacked the drive to make a success of his talents.
>
> He was very versatile and wrote scripts and songs for well known artistes of that day. I remember Gracie Fields, saying to him one day 'I like your work Herbert, write me some songs.'
>
> As an instance of Bert's lack-a-daisical attitude, he was always buying new cars, then leaving them in a garage and forgetting where he had left them. He once had a car with the bodywork of highly polished mahogany. Another was a little, white, two-seater Samson with a dickie seat.
>
> Cyril and Bert (Herbert and Hatton) were

> regulars on *BBC Radio Music-Hall*. They also were regulars at Holborn Empire. I saw them there in 1938. Ramon Novarro, a silent screen idol, was top of the bill. Supporters were Murray and Mooney and Freddie Bamberger and Pam.
>
> George Black, the great impressario of that time, thought Herbert and Hatton were the best 'front cloth' act in the business and had plans for them. He contracted them to play the London Palladium but when Jack (Bert) failed to turn up he lost interest in them.

I've spoken to old pros who knew Jack very well who said his biggest problem was he liked a drink. He wasn't an alcoholic; he liked a drink. I think he used to drink between first and second house, as a lot of acts did: used to go in the pub next door and have two or three beers. It was said that if he hadn't have liked a drink so much he would have probably done a lot better.

That's the story I got, anyway, which I have to admit surprised me, even though it's reinforced by what John says. Personally, I wasn't aware that his drinking had been a problem – I knew he liked a drink, but I only ever saw him drink halves, never thinking that was detrimental to what he was doing. It was only through hearsay that I learned about the 'drink problem', I was not aware of it first hand. John adds:

> Cyril was over the moon when they were booked for the Palladium. He thought this was the break they were waiting for. He was furious when Jack didn't turn up – 'indisposed.' I don't think he was drunk! He was really ill! But that was it as far as George Black was concerned.

Could that have been related to the mysterious 'indisposition' which caused him to leave a revue in 1929? Even if drink wasn't responsible in the specific case of the Palladium booking, John does say: 'There's no denying the part that drink played in his downfall. He was always in a pub – quite happy with his beer – too contented, you might say.'

The last prewar mention of Herbert and Hatton in *The Stage* is in February 1938. Although Cyril later joined the RAF, he appears to have split with Jack around then, as he advertises his availability in early March:

VACANT FOR REVUE OR CONCERT PARTY,
SING AND DANCE, Smart Appearance

And by June he is in a new double act with Fred E Taylor, praised for their 'clever back-chat' and for 'delivering much laughable material in an entertaining manner.'

The new double act only lasted a few months, however – the review above does seem to be damning with faint praise – and by 1939 he is a solo act, performing in panto and singing 'light comedy numbers' in a couple of revues. But as though to rub salt into the wound the name of the final show in which he appears before enlisting is: *Jack's the Lad*.

John sums up the reason for fraternal tension: 'I know they had many quarrels. Cyril, who was ambitious but hadn't the talent against Jack, who had the talent and no ambition!'

Jack continued the double act with Ruth, using the same material, as described earlier. So all that 'A telegram's a wire!' stuff was an argument between a husband and a shrewish wife when I first saw him in 1941 rather than the original silliness between a comic and his straight man – but it worked equally well either way.

The first mention I can find of Jack and Ruth doing the double act is in February 1940, when they are billed as 'Jack Herbert and Blonde', but more usually they were 'Jack Herbert and Partner'. When Cyril was demobbed in 1944 there wasn't an immediate professional reunion, although Cyril certainly saw the publicity value of his former association with Jack when seeking to revive his career, as this announcement from September demonstrates:

VACANT FOR PRODUCTION
CYRIL HATTON
LATE HERBERT and HATTON
Comedian or Feed
Just discharged from the RAF after 4 years Comic-King in the RAF Shows
OFFERS INVITED

During the war, Jack was principal comedian in a longrunning revue called *Soir de Paris,* but by 1942 he is in a show called *Joys and Girls* – one of four similar-sounding productions put on by Jack Gillam where the emphasis is on glamour.

He appears in more revues over the next few years, including some with Ruth, but it looks as though she may have given up the double act by the end of 1946. By mid August 1947 he is occasionally working again with Cyril and getting good – if, again, rather sniffy – reviews:

> Comedy, controlled and pointed in its broadness, is the basis of the success of Jack Herbert and Cyril Hatton, a couple who are able to project their personalities easily and immediately gain the confidence and good feelings of the audience.

I said earlier that by 1947, when I stayed with Jack and Ruth in London, I had the sense his career was on the way down. There was to be no forward momentum of the sort enjoyed by Sid Field. Did he consider, with the Palladium no-show, that his big chance had come and gone? Did he care? John told me: 'He never spoke seriously about his career. He was doing a job he liked and could have had greater success but lacked the "whoosh!" If he had someone to push him (although I'm sure Ruth tried) he would have risen to it but as long as he had his drink he was happy.'

Drinking was certainly an occupational hazard for variety and revue performers, as my army pal Don Auty writes. Just before his National Service, Don was stage manager of one of the last of the Number 3 touring revues in 1955, so he had a chance to observe the lifestyle at first hand:

> The life of a variety artiste could be very solitary. Although they appeared in front of hundreds of people every night they usually had few friends in the towns they visited and even in the forties and fifties it was not considered to be a respectable life by most people. There usually was a pub across the road from the theatre where they retired to each evening after the show. They got to know the landlord over the years of visiting the town and it became a second home with lock ins every night after closing time. Pubs such as Ma Edgerton's across the road from the stage door of the Liverpool Empire became famous for the hospitality to variety artistes. There was one room in this pub that you were not allowed to enter unless you were a pro. Many of them, especially comics, took to the bottle and ended their lives in alcoholic misery.

I said earlier that I was never aware of drink affecting Jack's act – and after that first life-changing show at the Salford Hippodrome in 1941 I saw him many times over the next ten years or so. But I have to concede that I don't have the perspective of John, able to compare the Jack of 1926 with the performer of later decades:

> I saw him many times. I think the first time was *Spotlights*. I never remember laughing so much at any show since. Their variety act didn't change much and through the years I saw the sparkle, the dynamism, fade until he was just going through the act like a robot. Over the years I watched the slide. The act was nearly always the same but he was not. Luckily, he always had the audience with him – he had the indefinable stage presence which all artistes wanted but alas, few had! Cyril hadn't, for one.

He certainly continued to work over the years, so long as the variety halls remained viable. But if we're judging success by the simple yardstick of the length of a show's run then *Soir de Paris,* as long ago as 1940, may have been something of a milestone. It's the last long-running revue in which Jack appeared as principal comedian; after that, shows would run for a few months at best.

Then again, that could have been as much a reflection of the times as of his drawing power: there were economic reasons why fewer theatres were willing to take touring revues. But whatever the truth of the matter – and I don't really want to subscribe to John's image of a performer going through the motions – there is undoubtedly a sad inevitability about the end of Jack's career. After the first world war, he had been present at the birth of variety; now, steeped as he was in that world and not knowing any other, maybe he knew there was no choice but to stick around for its long, dying fall.

Declaring himself to be 'unexpectedly vacant' in July 1941, he describes *Soir de Paris* as 'the record-breaking comedy revue I have been with for the past 14 months'. But it looks like that is the last record he will break.

He quickly gets more work, including a show with the Crazy Gang which promises patrons 'ladies disrobing by electricity' and a show entitled *Forbidden Fruit* – not, I think, a reference to rationing. But the writing seems on the wall with *Joys and Girls*. It's one of four similar-sounding shows put on by Jack Gillam Productions (another is *Shoulder Arms & Legs*, which gives an idea of their focus). Although Jack is first on the bill in the ad, the size of the lettering for all acts is identical, and common to all four shows is an emphasis on the number of lovelies included, in the case of Jack's show:

6 Marilyn Girls
6 Broadway Beauties

The *Stage* reviewer notes that: 'Jack Herbert is a comedian with limited chances who could be given more to do.'

Jack continued to work in variety, and occasionally revues, with Ruth until she retired; he appeared in a panto produced by Hylda Baker and in such revues as *Scandals Parisienne* (bill matter: 'The Northern Star'). In a sign of more drastic changes to come he also appeared on some variety bills booked by the Paul Raymond Agency.

The last revue in which I can find him listed is *Nudes in the News* at the West Bromwich Plaza in June 1953. But static nudes topping the bill were not enough to save Jack's sort of show, in its death throes by then. Family audiences were staying away and soon even the more specialist clientele would be getting their jollies elsewhere, courtesy of the aforementioned Paul Raymond. He ploughed his profits from some cutprice revues into a private members' club to get around the Lord Chamberlain's restrictions on girls moving, and that's how the Raymond Revuebar and an empire of soft porn began.

The name of Jack's last revue was obviously seen as its main selling point, as cast members are not listed in adverts again until September – by which time he has gone.

Eventually the business just gave him up: the variety theatres had all stopped and there was nowhere for him to work anymore. His act had become dated: music hall and variety in general was seen as dated then.

The very last appearance by Jack noted in *The Stage* is on an August 1953 variety bill topped by Robb Wilton at Douglas, Derby Castle on the Isle of Man. At least he seems to have ended in good company, as John says: 'He always admired the comics that could "time it" like Robb Wilton and his great friend Jimmy James.'

Jack played a couple of the new clubs on the burgeoning Manchester scene around the mid 'fifties, but for a performer used, over decades, to that theatre set-up – a spotlight on you and audiences facing you in serried rows without the clink of beer glasses – it can't have been an easy transition to make. At any rate, it didn't lead to a new career.

When I said earlier in the book that Jack, like many of the old pros, didn't get on with clubs it wasn't just supposition on my part: I have a vague recollection of going with him to a club once – just staying backstage with him, in the dressing room, as I was about fifteen and wouldn't have been allowed in the club itself. It wasn't his scene: he made that very clear. But there was no choice.

RUTH died in 1959 – as I said, I think she was a bit older than him – and Jack finished up in a dreadful flat in Levenshulme, south of Manchester. I used to go and see him on a fairly regular basis. He accepted his lot, as far as I could tell. He didn't seem to have any regrets; he felt it was natural. Maybe after forty years' slogging around the country part of him was glad to give it up.

You know, I have difficulty remembering whether Jack actually ever saw me work. I'm bloody sure he did, but I can't remember where, though it must have been at some point between *Opportunity Knocks* in 1964 and when he died. He must have seen me, because I do retain the impression that he was pleased for me, but didn't quite understand what I was doing.

Whether this might have been because he came from a different tradition, I don't know. And while it was true I had been forced to learn my trade in the clubs, I have always seen myself as a theatre comic: my real training began the moment Jack first took me backstage.

My memories of those later years are of meeting up with him and having a drink. Could it be that he thought I might not want him to see my act, that his opinion might perhaps matter too much? I don't know. And it's not a conversation I can have now. But I do think he was proud of what I'd achieved. John agrees – although again he offers a different perspective about Jack's attitude to how he had ended up: 'I'm sure Jack was proud but saw how unlucky he was and was rather jealous. He must have had some sombre thoughts as he lived in poverty and grime in that flat. It was heartbreaking but he never complained. He tried to make out all was well. It was, as long as he could have that drink.'

Cyril, who had left the business and was working in

Birmingham, came to see me there in panto a few times. He used to come and sit in the dressing room. He was a bit aloof and seemed quite cynical, both about the business and my success. I got the impression he didn't quite approve of my act, for some unknown reason. I never felt any warmth from Cyril: I got the feeling that there was a little jealousy there, a bit of the 'young upstart' about it – I never felt that from Jack.

Cyril did have quite a long career without Jack, both solo and with the occasional partner, working mostly in revue and panto. He also worked with Hylda Baker and was her first 'Cynthia' ('She knows, y'know!'). His last mention in *The Stage* before his 1983 obituary seems to bring both his and Jack's career full circle, as it's a review of Gordon Henson's Rambla Concert Party at the pier head, Clacton, in August 1959: 'Is there anywhere else in Britain which provides a pierrot-type show and a deckchair in the sun for sixpence a head?'

After two daytime shows in the open air the 'hardworking group', including Cyril, by then in his fifties, gave an evening performance in the Jolly Roger Theatre including a spot entitled *Gordon's Old Time Music Hall* where...

> The audience joins in with some of those wonderful songs which never seem to lose their freshness.

In latter years, just before he died, I didn't see Jack as much as I ought to have done. We were living in Blackpool and unless I was going to Manchester or nearby and had the time, I didn't make a point of it. All very well saying this in retrospect, of course, but his death was unexpected.

In 1969 I was about to go to Australia for a month, and just before I left I got a call from his landlady to say that Jack was in hospital. So I rang the doctor and asked, 'How ill is he?' He said, 'Oh, he's just an old man – he'll be here when you get back, don't worry, he'll be fine.'

When I came back, I read the In Memoriam notice in *The Stage*.

TWO years later, his landlady turned up at the stage door with Jack's bits of memorabilia, posters and stuff – and sold them to me. There was a sob story, of course: 'I haven't got your sort of money and I need money ...' She kept bringing it in bits and bobs and I had to keep giving her more.

I bought it all, of course. What choice was there?

At least I have them around me now, hanging in the study as I write: Jack in *Spotlights*, with Sid Field's name lower down the bill, Jack topping in *They're Off* at the Theatre Royal, Oldham in 1949.

Not long before Jack died he appeared in a documentary about Sid Field, filmed in the derelict Argyle, Birkenhead. He seems to brush aside the allegations about Sid pinching his mannerisms, although as his comments quickly dissolve into chuckles it's hard to be certain. 'If he did – if he didn't – so what?' may be the general sense. But while he's talking his demonstration of those gestures and that effete little cough tells its own story, and others are on hand to testify to the central importance of Jack to Sid's act.

Not a jot of this rates a mention in the sole biography to date of Sid Field, published seven years later.

I only recently had the chance to see this programme for the first time. It was very moving to have him unexpectedly given back to me again, and I shed a tear at seeing him just as I last remembered him; he had a face that I just loved to look at. But it was a bittersweet experience. The camerawork in the documentary is quite arty, and in the final sequence, as Jack's about to leave the theatre, there's a shot of his elongated shadow passing along a wall, mysterious and elusive as that of Harry Lime.

And for me it's a reminder that I'm watching a ghost – in two senses. Because earlier in the film when Jack does his hand movements, that's the memory of a performance, not the thing itself. Which gives an added poignancy to this jokey advertisement he once placed in *The Stage*:

> **Did you breathe on the vacant space that appears on page 8?**
> You found it a waste of breath.
> I have wasted mine telling you that I am a
> **COMEDIAN**
> *See for yourself. This week,*
> *EMPIRE, WOOLWICH.*
> Many Thanks,
> **JACK HERBERT.**

Jack's stage act was never filmed. No recordings have survived of the radio shows in which Herbert and Hatton appeared. I was fifteen when he last performed in front of an audience, so it's a pretty safe bet that almost every last scrap of those legions who once surrendered helplessly to laughter at 'an orgy of face-slapping and gagging', as *The Performer* put it, have themselves left the building.

Apart from the memories which John and I share, and a few scraps of Jack's own writing, these souvenirs, these relics, on the wall are almost all that remains of a life in comedy.

ACTUALLY, make that two lives, intimately intertwined.

My grandad – I like to think of him as my grandad – and the little boy standing on a chair in the back room of a pub, reciting his act.

Epilogue

JOHN Butler, my last direct link with Jack, passed away during the writing of this book. I was lucky enough to see him shortly before he died, and had the great privilege of giving the eulogy at his funeral. But what I will most remember is a magical day I spent with him in Harrogate in 2012. He was almost ninety-three then but still very alert, full of reminiscences about his older brother and the family. He greeted me with tears in his eyes, no doubt whatsoever in his mind that I was indeed a Butler.

I am seventy-seven now, four years older than Jack when he died, and the fortunate survivor of a heart attack – which would be enough to prompt a bit of reflection about my life even without this book to finish.

IT hasn't been quite the straight path I imagined when I was starting out – to put it mildly. It was Adrian Noble who first told me I'd had an amazing career, when he was auditioning me for *The Secret Garden*, and I remember being taken aback: I hadn't really thought about it like that before. Yes, I'd gone through ups and downs, but my choices always seemed to be the best ones available at the time – and I have always tried to recognise a good opportunity when it came knocking.

You often hear of gut feelings influencing decisions, which is fine if the feeling proves to be right. At several key moments in my life my gut has been wrong, or I've chosen to ignore my doubts, as when I agreed to do that second pantomime for Weston-Webb, or went on that wild goose chase for the job in Orlando ... not to mention any number of auditions undertaken in a spirit of wild, not to say lunatic, optimism.

But I've come to the conclusion that you have to get through the life that happens to you whatever. My heart problem made me think hard about my future in show business: was I fit enough to continue? Well, I've done several stand-up shows since it happened and felt fine, so for now I'm happy to say that the answer seems to be a resounding 'yes'. My wonderful GP, John Crompton, who looks after hundreds of patients, always appears to care just for me and with the arterial stents I now have fitted I should be better than ever, so why not carry on? I don't know how to do anything else, after all. Old Farts Agency here I come ...

One of my better decisions has been to engage with writer Anthony Teague, who has helped me put this tome together in a coherent way. I came across him some three years ago when he wrote a very kind blog post about me, and after several chats I had the correct gut feeling he was the one to help me along this autobiographical journey.

And now that I'm coming to the end (of the book, I mean) I find that I'm just as I was at the beginning. I still enjoy telling jokes; I am a gagster at heart. It is becoming a dying art but I love telling stories; I seem to have been doing it all my life and will continue as long as I have an audience – however small.

That urge to keep performing is perfectly summed up in a poem or song by Jack which was recently passed on to me by John's friend Margaret. Written in 1940, it describes a lost world of variety artists clustering together in the West End, hoping against hope for a booking.

It's a world of dreams which makes no sense to passers by, but Jack isn't making fun of the dreamers because he knows he's in that number – and even if I make my enquiries via the internet these days I am too.

Round Charing Cross Road

The comics were talking in groups here and there
As though in this old world they hadn't a care,
And amidst the loud laughter the gags quickly flowed –
You can bet it was somewhere round Charing Cross Road.

There were dozens of pros, some young and some old,
And I wonder what kind of stories were told:
Were they tales of approval the audience showed?
Cos you hear lots of stories, round Charing Cross Road.

There were one or two vet'rans, grey headed and pale,
Who once did an act, boy, that never could fail
But things are real duff now, the letty they've owed ...
I've heard this a few times, round Charing Cross Road.

The man in the street is at times apt to stare:
'Who are these groups standing here, standing there?
They talk a strange language, they do, I'll be blowed!'
He can't get the *polari* round Charing Cross Road.

At times they're excited – gesticulate, too;
They're about every day, and sometimes quite a few,
And how some struggle on would perplex Mr Joad ...
That's one of the secrets round Charing Cross Road.

There's acrobats, jugglers, ventriloquists – who
Are waiting for dates to come out of the blue:
It's quite a few weeks now, the last time they showed –
Hence their daily routine, round Charing Cross Road.

There's a story behind this, a tear and a sigh!
Tho' they still carry on and keep having a try:
When they fix the odd week how their faces have glowed
To get far away from round Charing Cross Road.

So keep the stout heart, pals, whatever the snub –
There's always that off-chance to fiddle a club:
You're still pulling through, though be heavy the load –
It's all in the game, boy, round Charing Cross Road.

And that's the game I plan to stay in – so long as my heart holds out.

I still fervently believe that laughter is the best medicine: to laugh out loud makes you feel so good. It's all in the telling, the delivery, the confidence and, of course, the personality. All the great comedians throughout history have that charisma, that indefinable magic drawing you into their world, just as Jack had. They take you in, then they hit you with the gag: magic.

I love it all, whether it's being part of the happy, rocking crowd surrendering to the comic or being onstage myself: to see an audience falling about and crying with laughter is just the greatest feeling in the world.

Comedy has always been king, and never more so than now. It's what music hall and variety have become. Theatres have melted into comedy clubs and television is the greatest supporter of comedy in every sense of the word, with more sketch shows and panel games than ever. Today's comedians are, in the main, anecdotal, not gagtellers, but some are very funny and I wholeheartedly endorse their approach.

Regrets, I've had a few, as the song says. Causing Jackie and my son, Kent, so much pain and sorrow when I left them is something I will always regret.

I am grateful for every minute I spend with Vanessa. We have had an eventful time together this past twenty-nine years. We have travelled the world with our cruising experiences, and that dreadful pub ownership period which would have finished most couples off eventually came to be our combined strength. I have come to cherish her friendship, love and understanding.

And finally, thanks to you for ploughing through this. I hope it has brought you some insight into my crazy world of show business. I often get stopped in the street, or get emails from people telling me how I have brought pleasure into their lives, and for that I am eternally grateful: that was, indeed, the object of the exercise.

Curtain

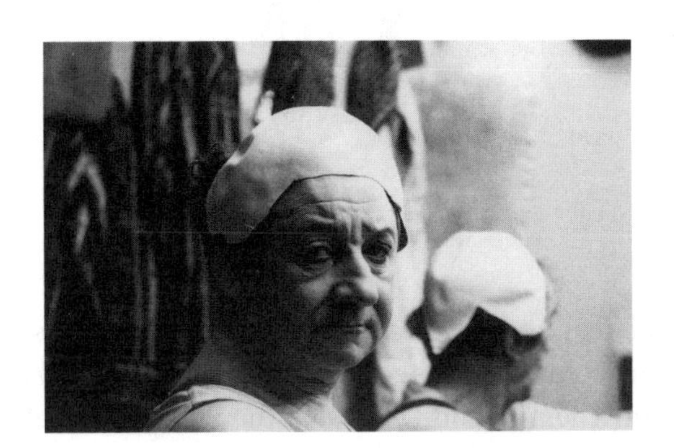

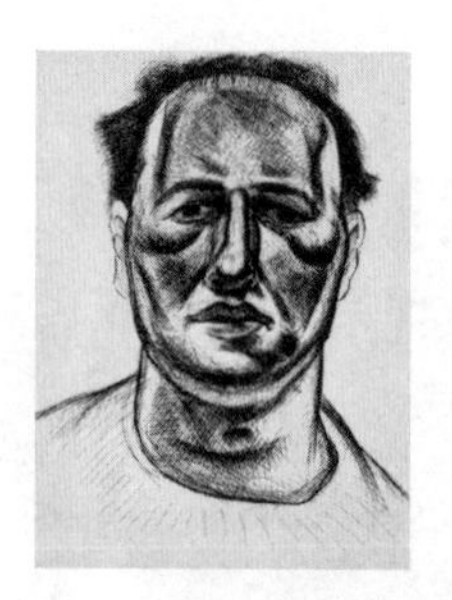

Anthony Teague (*above, as seen by Peter Howson*) has written for television and the stage. His plays include *Hello Pizza,* at Soho Theatre, and *Guards,* at the Etcetera Theatre. This is his first book.

Acknowledgement

Thanks to *The Stage* Archive and Colindale Newspaper Library.

Index of Names